HOMELAND

DAWN AT THE
WORLD TRADE
CENTER RUINS,
NEW YORK CITY,
SEPTEMBER 13, 2001

STATE ROUTE 98
NEAR CALEXICO,
CALIFORNIA

WEATHER DELAY
ON THE
RED LINE TRAIN,
SILVER SPRING,
MARYLAND

KATIE SIERRA
AFTER HER PARTIAL
VICTORY IN COURT,
CHARLESTON,
WEST VIRGINIA

PARKING LOT OF THE WAR, WEST VIRGINIA, POLICE DEPARTMENT

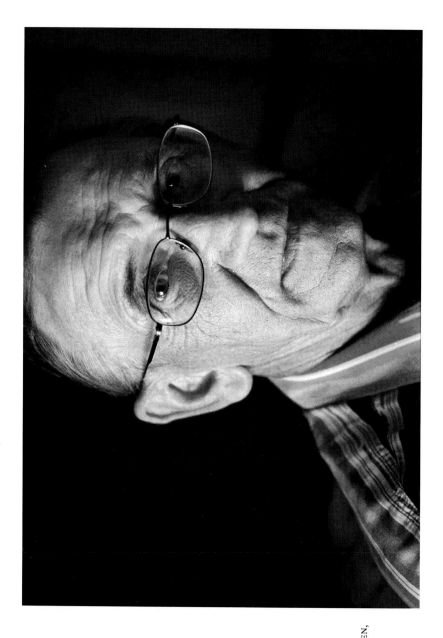

DEAN KOLDENHOVEN,
FORMER MAYOR OF
PALOS HEIGHTS,
ILLINOIS

SOUTH SIDE STREET
SCENE, CHICAGO,
ILLINOIS

JOE MARSHALL, JR.,
FORMER
YOUNGSTOWN, OHIO,
STEELWORKER
TURNED
SECURITY GUARD

THE SHELL OF
THE ABANDONED
HOMESTEAD
STEEL WORKS,
RANKIN,
PENNSYLVANIA

RANDY WEAVER AT
THE RUINS OF HIS
CHILDHOOD HOME,
JEFFERSON, IOWA

RALLY POSTERS, WASHINGTON, DC

AMRIK CHAWLA
AT THE WALL
OF THE MISSING,
NEW YORK CITY,
SEPTEMBER 2001

DECAL ON CAR IN FRONT OF A CONVENIENCE STORE,
BALTIMORE, MARYLAND

FARMER'S TRUCK,
WINCHESTER,
VIRGINIA;
HIS NEIGHBOR'S SON
WAS KILLED IN THE
IRAQ WAR

TRUCK
WITH SIGNS,
WASHINGTON, DC

MOTEL NEAR
NASHVILLE,
TENNESSEE

BONNEVILLE
SALT FLATS,
TOOELE COUNTY,
UTAH

BUS STOP,
WASHINGTON, DC

TOY FOR SALE,
TIMES SQUARE,
NEW YORK CITY

SUPPORT THE WAR
IN IRAQ RALLY
ON THE MALL,
WASHINGTON, DC

PROTEST AGAINST
THE WAR IN IRAQ,
WASHINGTON, DC

FLAG DAY PARADE, SAN FRANCISCO, CALIFORNIA

AUTO SALES LOT, SPRING HILL, FLORIDA

CATCH BIN LADEN BOMB,
HUDSON, FLORIDA

COUNTRY STORE,
DAMASCUS, MARYLAND

THE FOURTH
OF JULY ON THE
AMERICAN RIVER,
SACRAMENTO,
CALIFORNIA

BUMPER STICKER ON TRUCK,
PHOENIX, ARIZONA

ABANDONED
ELEMENTARY SCHOOL,
GASCOYNE,
NORTH DAKOTA

VICINITY SIMS,
NORTH DAKOTA

POLLING PLACE,
SUTTLE, ALABAMA

RUINS ON
BRADDOCK AVENUE,
BRADDOCK,
PENNSYLVANIA

SQUIRREL HUNTER,
ODD, WEST VIRGINIA

SOUP KITCHEN,
NASHVILLE, TENNESSEE

CHESHIRE, OHIO,

ACROSS THE

OHIO RIVER FROM

WEST VIRGINIA

STAND UP FOR AMERICA
RALLY IN THE DEPRESSED
COAL MINE REGION OF
CENTRAL KENTUCKY

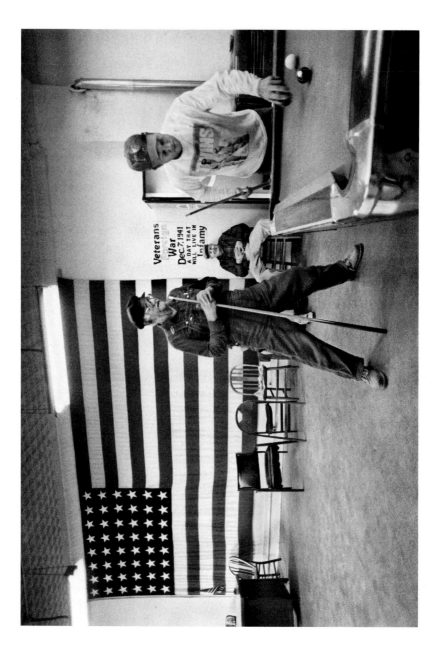

VFW HALL,
HARTSVILLE,
TENNESSEE

SERVICES AT ARLINGTON
NATIONAL CEMETERY
FOR STAFF SERGEANT
SCOTT SATHER, KILLED
IN THE WAR IN IRAQ

THE DC BELTWAY,
APRIL 2003

PRELUDE

TWO DAYS before Christmas 2001, I drove west over the George Washington Bridge, into Homeland America. Fifteen weeks had passed since I'd stood on my uptown rooftop and watched the second tower fall, the black cloud billowing over lower Manhattan. That day my gaze was drawn beyond the New Jersey Palisades; I wondered about the middle of the country. I knew that a genie had been uncorked. I of course had no idea what the genie would do—but clearly we were about to see new evidence of what novelist Philip Roth calls the "indigenous American berserk."

At a Pennsylvania truck stop, I sat over bad coffee with my notebook. "Weird leaving New York," I wrote. "Depressed. Separation anxiety."

Flags were everywhere—on vehicles, poles, in windows. The business marquees all read GOD BLESS AMERICA, or GOD BLESS THE USA. That first night, at a Motel 6 in Youngstown, Ohio, a flag poster thanked me for traveling.

The following morning, Christmas Eve, I drove on to Cleveland. This was my personal homeland—the region where I grew up. First I visited the suburb of Parma, where a white man had driven a Ford Mustang at high speed into the front door of a mosque right after 9/11. I stood looking at the boarded-up entrance.

That afternoon I stood on the edge of the Cuyahoga Valley, where both my grandfathers had worked. One had a job on the B & O, the other at Otis Steel. The railroad is long gone. What remains of the steel mill (in its latest incarnation, LTV Steel) was silent and smokeless. The works were on "hot idle." LTV was in bankruptcy. If a buyer didn't come forth, the plant would close for good.

As I moved west out of Cleveland, usually sticking to back roads, I spoke with and listened to people in towns small and large. My travels encompassed thousands of miles and hundreds of interviews over the next two years. At first subconsciously, but later with deliberation, I acted as if I were a foreign reporter working in the United States. It wasn't difficult, for the changes were so great that it seemed I was witnessing the dawn of a new nation.

I found two distinct Americas, one in the exclusive preserves of California's Silicon Valley and Manhattan's Upper West Side, the other in the country's middle—in unheralded and wounded towns with names like Celina, Girard, and Lusk. The first country was living as if the 1990s boom would never cease. The second country was languishing, as if locked in a 1930s Great Depression time warp.

On one trip Michael Williamson, my longtime photographic collaborator, and I drove from Chicago to Johnstown, Pennsylvania. In places like this, the abandoned shells of factories, all broken windows and rust, make this country look like it was bombed in a war. In other places it's as if an economic neutron bomb hit—with trees and houses intact but lives decimated, gone with the good jobs.

In April 2003, during the war in Iraq, Michael and I were on Forbes Avenue in Pittsburgh on the campus of Carnegie Mellon University, passing the Delta Upsilon fraternity house. There was construction in front. Spray painted on raw plywood were the words,

GOD BLESS AMERICA

SUPPORT OUR TROOPS

I DRIVE AN SUV

As I approached the door, lying against the house was a sign that, I learned from the occupants, had hung during the first days of "shock and awe":

BOMB IRAQ

WE WANT THEIR OIL

"Since the war started, the stock market went up and the price of oil dropped," a man inside told me with enthusiasm.

I typically heard this kind of approval in the most economically depressed areas, from people who stood to gain exactly nothing from a surge in the markets, just as they had gained little from tax cuts aimed at the rich.

MY LAST journey across America was the third winter after the attacks, the winter of 2003–04. It was my fastest trip—I was making time from the East Coast on my way back to the other side. The road came at me as I passed from the so-called blue states, solidly Democratic, into the red Republican strongholds. I dodged bad weather. An ice storm in Missouri just ahead of me left semi trucks flipped on their sides like cast-off Tonka playthings. Then Kansas and a break in the cold fronts—a waning moon illuminating the snowbound prairie—and distant farmhouses, their lights like those of ships on the ocean.

I thought of the anonymous lives in the scattered houses, the millions of Americans whose voices are not heard in the media. This is a country that is afraid, a new terror attack just one of many specters. What happened on 9/11 was not a genesis, but an amplifier of unease that had long been building. Before that day we were already a nation in which executives burned shareholders' money on $2 million toga birthday parties, while men and women who worked Wal-Mart jobs pinched pennies and still ended up begging for charity food for their children at month's end. The economic well-being of so many Americans was as brittle as the frigid air rushing over my windshield.

Americans are waiting. For what? We have no idea. We wonder what we are becoming and we don't even understand what we are.

HOMELAND

Dale Maharidge

photographs by

Michael Williamson

SEVEN STORIES PRESS

New York · London · Toronto · Melbourne

SEVEN STORIES PRESS
140 WATTS STREET
NEW YORK, NY 10013
www.sevenstories.com

In Canada
Publishers Group Canada, 250A Carlton Street, Toronto, ON M5A 2L1

In the UK
Turnaround Publisher Services Ltd., Unit 3, Olympia Trading Estate,
Coburg Road, Wood Green, London N22 6TZ

In Australia
Palgrave Macmillan, 627 Chapel Street, South Yarra VIC 3141

Library of Congress Cataloging-in-Publication Data
Maharidge, Dale.
Homeland / Dale Maharidge ;
with photographs by Michael Williamson.— A Seven Stories Press 1st ed.
p. cm.
ISBN 1-58322-627-3 (hardcover : alk. paper)
1. Social conflict—United States.
2. Intergroup relations—United States.
3. Nationalism—Social aspects—United States.
4. September 11 Terrorist Attacks, 2001—Social aspects.
5. War on Terrorism, 2001—Social aspects.
6. United States—Social conditions—21st century.
I. Title.
HN59.2.M34 2003
303.6'0973—DC22
2004003572

College professors may order examination copies of
Seven Stories Press titles for a free six-month trial period.
To order, visit www.sevenstories.com/textbook/,
or fax on school letterhead to 212.226.1411.

BOOK DESIGN BY POLLEN/STEWART CAULEY & INDIA AMOS
PRINTED IN THE USA

1 3 5 7 9 8 6 4 2

To the U.S. Constitution and the Bill of Rights,
and the working men and women of America,
who have allowed me to tell their stories.

CONTENTS

BOOK ONE

American life storms about us daily
and is slow to find a tongue.
—Emerson, *Letters and Social Aims*

West Virginia's Manufacturing Jobs Hit Lowest-Ever Mark
—Associated Press headline, June 6, 2001

1

IT's A PERFECT replica of a Shaker house, lost deep in a West Virginia hollow where a creek named Eden's Fork runs. The house is at the back of the hollow, at the cessation of a narrow mountain road lined with modest dwellings and one church. For Mr. Kale,[1] this home and the land around it is something of an Eden. The three-bedroom, three-bath clapboard structure is square and tall, surrounded by a vast, untreed lawn. The forested hills wrap around the lawn like a cove.

Mr. Kale built the house by hand, carefully following original Shaker plans, and then he furnished it entirely with Shaker-style furniture that he crafted in his shop—beds, end tables, the kitchen table, sofa, and chairs—all made of solid cherry and walnut and oak, perfectly fitted with wooden pegs instead of nails. The furniture, each piece a work of art, makes the home a museum to a prim past.

The thirty or so wooded acres around the Shaker house were all that remained of what had once been a much larger piece of Kale property. The Kale deed to this land dates to 1783, when Patrick Henry, the governor of Virginia, granted the area to settlers. John Kale was a ranger at Fort Lee on the Kanawha River. The town is called Sissonville, named for another ranger, James Sisson. This was not desirable country. The fertile flat country of Ohio to the north drew the most settlers, and only the hardiest or hardest-up came to buy the cheap, steep hardshale land. The Native Americans called these hills the "land of plenty fat doe." Yet much of West Virginia had been shunned by the pre-Columbian peoples. They considered it a territory of bad spirits, to be used as hunting grounds.

Many Sissonville families are like the Kales—they trace their roots to pioneer times. Few newcomers ever show up, though Sissonville is not far from the present-day capital city of Charleston, just a few miles to the south down Interstate 77, or old US Route 21.

That June before the attacks on the World Trade Center and the Pentagon, neighbors took notice when Mr. Kale brought an outside woman with two children to the Shaker house, where he had dwelled alone for so long. Mr. Kale, a white-collar worker with a salt-and-pepper beard and imposing manner, was in his mid-fifties, and for weekend sport he rode a Harley-Davidson motorcycle. He was quite taken by Amy Sierra, a blond and attractive woman in her mid-thirties. Amy had been a single mother for thirteen years, and had known Mr. Kale for a year and a half. A nurse who worked long hours, Amy wanted some stability for her children—Katie, fifteen, and Levi, eight. Katie immediately raised some eyebrows. It was hard not to notice her; she had spiked hair that she dyed bright blue or green.

Not long after the Sierra family moved in, a neighbor invited Amy into her home, where the woman announced, "I don't approve of your living arrangements." Amy was befuddled.

"Living in sin," the neighbor explained.

The neighbor chastised Amy for being with an older man, unmarried, and did everything but call her a jezebel. Amy and Mr. Kale were later married in the state capitol—not because of this neighbor, for the wedding had been their long-standing intention. But the meeting caused Amy to have doubts about the community.

Sissonville was also difficult for Katie, given her punk-bohemian ways. In addition to her colorful hair, she had a habit of writing poetry on her shirts with a black magic marker. Usually, these were odes to boys. She wore these shirts to a school where one out of four students is enrolled in the junior Reserve Office Training Corps (ROTC), and kids fly the Confederate flag at home and sport them on their trucks. Military buzz cuts are the norm for boys. The girls dress conservatively, and many already have the dowdy manner of the housewives they wish to become. Katie instantly doubled the minority demographics at the school. She is half Latina, as her father is Panamanian. One other student was half black, the daughter of a white teacher. All the rest of the seven hundred students were white.

This was not at all like Sebring, Florida, where the Sierra family had previously lived. Sebring, halfway between Orlando and Lake Okeechobee, wasn't exactly cosmopolitan. But it was more accepting than Sissonville.

Katie was used to moving. She'd lived in Kentucky and Florida with her mother, as well as in Ohio with her father, Raul. Raul was a computer programmer, and had come to the United States at age sixteen to enroll in East-ern Kentucky University. When Amy entered the school as a freshman, she was taken with the Panamanian who was her age, but two years ahead of her academically. After Katie was born, Amy and Raul were together for a few years, but then separated.

Katie had attended fifteen schools in her fifteen years. Despite this, her grades were good and she was never a discipline problem. In fact, Katie had something one often finds in the children of military families stationed in various locales: the ability to adapt to fresh environments. Katie knew how to deal with new kids, even in a place as mossback as Sissonville, where her classmates were descended from pioneer stock. Katie never yelled at any-one who made fun of her looks. She always spoke quietly. But most kids simply dismissed her as being weird, not worth bothering over.

That August when school started, there were a few other outcasts at Sis-sonville High School, but none as worldly as Katie. She was friends with them by default, though they were not enough to fill her needs. So Katie turned to the Internet. Earlier she had discovered an anarchy website. She began chatting online with kids in distant places. Katie found a community in which she felt comfortable. She fell in love with a boy in Lake Arrowhead, California, and had friends in other states.

Anarchy conjures images of bomb-throwers to most Americans, but to Katie, it symbolized a community of kids who didn't fit in with button-down suburban America. After the World Trade Center / Pentagon attacks, it also symbolized peace. Katie abhorred the attacks. But she also didn't like the bombing of Afghanistan.

"I don't know or have an answer for the war, but I do know that killing people is not right," she wrote at the time.

Katie wanted to do something, so she crafted fliers with a manifesto, to start an anarchy club at Sissonville High School. In part, the manifesto said:

> This Anarchist Club will not tolerate hate or violence. While we believe in freedom of speech, we do not want to be associated with any group that promotes destructive behavior. We dis-courage violence and will do our best to help others see the neg-ative effects of hate and how pacifism could cause greater change and will be better understood by non-anarchists. Not only will we discuss and teach anarchist views, but we will also talk about the negative effects of an anarchist society, and of the strengths and weaknesses of anarchist theory . . . We hope to

give students and teachers an opportunity to see beyond commonly held beliefs to discover the basic freedoms that anarchy
presents to the world.
—Katie Sierra

The constitution of her proposed club went on to say,

One of the club's purposes is to teach others the importance of
peace, equality and respect for other humans as well as animals.
The club is anti-militaristic, and will circulate pro-peace literature.

None of this sat well with Amy. Katie had once tried bringing home a
boy who wore a spiked collar, and Amy had forbidden it. Amy came from
a military family. Her father served in Vietnam, and now works in a steel
mill in Ashland, Kentucky, where Amy was raised in a tiny house. Her two
brothers are also in the military; one served in Desert Storm, and the other
is a first lieutenant in the army.

Upstairs in a bedroom closet of the Shaker house, Amy kept a big box
filled with hundreds of family photos. She'd often go to this box and rem-
inisce, looking at pictures of her daughter before age twelve—when she had
turned so weird-looking—a cute girl with bows in her hair, always smiling
for the camera.

Undaunted by her mother's protestations, on October 22, 2001, Katie
went to Principal Forest Mann, an administrator with a narrow black mustache and drooping black hair across his forehead that made him look sus-
piciously like Adolf Hitler—a resemblance not lost on the students at
Sissonville High School. Katie stood before Mann, citing the West Virginia
State Department of Education's student handbook, policy number 4372,
which allowed afterschool clubs. (There was, for example, a Christian Fel-
lowship Club and a Civics Club.) She began to ask Mann about starting the
anarchy club, but he cut her off.

"You will not be able to form an anarchy club."

Katie grew frustrated, almost tearful. She didn't know what to say. He
prohibited her from distributing any fliers for the club.

"Go back to class," Mann told her.

🦥

THAT NIGHT, Katie sat in the Shaker house, watching CNN. Images of children accidentally killed by American bombing in Afghanistan came across
the screen.

Katie was horrified. She rushed to a computer and banged off an e-mail to a boy in the anarchist group. She thought: *What can I do? I feel helpless and saddened. I don't like what happened in New York. Everyone who kills is wrong. But this, too, is wrong. I have to do something!*

Katie went to her dresser drawer. She pulled out a red T-shirt and scribbled furiously with a black magic marker, writing across the back shoulders,

WHEN I SAW THE DEAD AND DYING AFGHANI CHILDREN ON TV,
I FELT A NEWLY RECOVERED SENSE OF NATIONAL SECURITY.
GOD BLESS AMERICA.

She wrote other things on the shirt, against racism and for peace, but this stood out.

The next morning she donned the shirt. It was cold, so she pulled on a "hoodie," a sweatshirt with a hood. She boarded the bus that parked at the back end of the hollow in the predawn darkness. The bus went down the hollow five miles to Sissonville High School. Inside, she removed the hoodie.

Students muttered in the halls when they saw the shirt. As usual, Katie never raised her voice, nor was she impolite. She invited students to talk about the war. But in Jean McCutcheon's third-block English class, the situation came to a head. Sophomore Jacob Reed, seated behind her, was upset by the shirt.

"If you don't love this country, then fucking leave!" Jacob screamed.

Jacob was sent to the office. He either told or somehow related to Principal Mann that Katie had written on her shirt, "America should burn," and "I hope Afghanistan wins."

His punishment for yelling: a lunchtime detention. Mann ordered him to write down what happened. Jacob wrote,

> I was in 3rd Block and Katie Siera was in that class her shirt said Stuff about how she thinks America is the dumbest country and how it should burn and she also told the class how She hopes the war against Afganistan we will loose it So I got mad and told her if she doesnt like this country get the <u>Fuck</u> out . . .

People whow herd it was—
Jamie Myers
Daneil Kersey
Todd Shamblin

Jacob Reed
10-23-01

Katie was hauled into Mann's office. Now chilly, she'd pulled the hoodie back on over the T-shirt. Mann confronted her with what Jacob said, and the fact that she had anarchy fliers. (Katie had the fliers in a folder atop her desk.) Katie told Mann she hadn't distributed any fliers, that they were with her personal belongings. Then she offered to remove the hoodie and show the T-shirt—insisting that it said nothing like what Jacob described—but Mann said he'd heard enough. She again asked him to look at the shirt.

"Do not take off your sweatshirt, Ms. Sierra."

Mann then said she'd disobeyed him, and disturbed the other students. Her punishment? Three days of suspension. Written on the official form: "disrupted educational process."

Mann confiscated the anarchy fliers. Katie was sent to a counselor's office. The counselor scolded Katie, and said her parents had to fight to come to America.

"Why don't you love this country?" the counselor asked.

"I love this country. I love this world," Katie said. "If I didn't, then why would I want to change it?"

The counselor didn't comprehend this. Amy was called. She angrily drove to the school. When she saw Katie seated in the counselor's office, she said, "I knew this anarchy shit would get you in trouble!"

Amy put Katie in her SUV, which sported three American flags on the dashboard, and sped home to the house that had an American flag on a porch pole, near a brass plaque announcing the house's pedigree. School officials would ask that Katie see a psychologist before being readmitted.

❧

BEFORE KATIE returned to school after the suspension, David Reaser, an assistant principal in charge of discipline, called her into his office. Reaser said she was not to discuss her political beliefs in school. He then turned the conversation in a surprising direction.

"Don't you believe in God?" he asked.

"I don't see, like, how that has anything to do with anything."

Reaser spoke about a castle made of sand. If she were walking down the beach, would she think it just materialized, or that someone had made it? Did she believe there was a creator?

Katie cried. Katie knew the God talk was out of line. She knew about the Bill of Rights and the U.S. Constitution from her government classes. She assumed these documents meant something. She stewed, and thought: *I am being ordered to come back to school as someone else. It's America, isn't it? I have a right to free speech. If I can just explain myself, the adults in charge will understand.*

The school parliamentarian, Amy Leithead, suggested that Katie attend the meeting of the Kanawha County School Board. The board was holding a special visiting session in Sissonville that Monday after her suspension. Katie thought it was a good idea. That Monday night when Katie and Amy entered the school auditorium, the place was packed. They took chairs at the back of the room near the wife of the ROTC instructor, sitting through two hours of talk about school roofs and mold. In the public comments period, the parliamentarian introduced Katie.

Katie had spoken barely a word when murmurs and hisses erupted. The mood of dozens of parents was nasty. Before she could get to her shirt or say much of anything about her anarchist club, she was shouted down.

"What in the hell is wrong with a kid like that?" asked board president Bill Raglin, according to a story written by *Charleston Gazette* reporter Eric Eyre.

"That's a treasonous act against the government of the United States!" said board member John Luoni.

Board member Pete Thaw said it was as if she were waving the Japanese flag right after Pearl Harbor. "This country is facing one of its darkest hours," he said. "You must not have enough to do."

Katie cried. Amy was dumbfounded.

Eyre interviewed principal Mann after the meeting. Mann repeated what he would later claim Jacob told or wrote him, that Katie's shirt said "America should burn," and, "I hope Afghanistan wins." Eyre put this in his story.

The next morning, the community read these mistruths.

The city of Charleston erupted. Katie was the talk of the town—on the radio, on the street, at the nursing home where her mother worked. She became "that anarchy girl."

Charleston may be the capital of West Virginia, but in many ways it's a small town. With few exceptions, an entire city had overnight come to despise the anarchy girl.

It was bad. But things were about to turn worse for Katie.

2

NO ONE saw Sean Miller leave the party. It was a Saturday night that July after he graduated from Sissonville High School. Sean had been drinking. A lot. He jumped into a white 2002 Chevrolet S-10 ZR2, a graduation gift from his parents. He didn't fasten his seat belt.[1]

He had been popular at Sissonville High in the way jocks are favored, in a pecking order that prizes what boys do with a ball on Friday nights. It's the theater of high school sports in a small town, and a lot of big towns, too. Up to graduation, Sean played his star role well. He was five feet ten inches, a hundred-and-seventy muscular pounds. He liked showing off those muscles, wearing a Dale Earnhardt T-shirt with the sleeves cut out. Sean's brown hair was cut military-style, for he was a member of the ROTC program. In that way he didn't stand out. Often, he wore a Confederate bandanna. His friends called him a "rebel"—no matter that he had no distinct cause.

These Confederate flags were curious. Some explanation perhaps comes from the very birth of West Virginia, which drew together unlikely cohabitants. The state, a group of counties that broke away from Virginia and the Confederacy, was signed into the union by Abraham Lincoln in 1863. The new state sent 36,000 soldiers to fight with the Union, and 12,000 into the Confederate Army. Families were split.

Yet this only partly explains the Confederate flags of Sissonville, and the Confederate bandanna sometimes worn by Sean Miller. It wasn't that the Civil War had been lost and the townspeople pined for the Old South that West Virginia never was. Rather, Sissonville was a community that relished

being redneck in a way even the rough downstate coal-mining towns did-
n't. I've walked into public places in those terribly remote coal towns, or
what's left of the coal camps, and never have been treated with anything
other than friendly openness. Yet in Sissonville, so near to Charleston, any
time I walked into a store or restaurant, the place stopped—forks midair,
coffee pouring halted—all eyes icily on me, like in one of those cheap B-
movie Westerns when The Stranger Comes to Town.

Why? I came to believe that the explanation was economic, peculiar to
the town's pioneer origins. Even in boom times, Sissonville has never
shaken the memory of its hardscrabble roots, of the pioneer founders who
tried to wrest a living from these hard shale hills. Even when Sissonville residents were able to purchase motor homes and boats for weekend pleasure,
they seemed to nurse a deep inferiority complex beside their Charleston
neighbors. The Confederate flags were a manifestation of unity in defiance
of a hostile world.

And now jobs in the area were shrinking. Some measure of the job hem-
orrhage comes from the state Bureau of Employment Programs, which
began keeping data in 1939. That year, the state had 95,500 manufacturing
jobs, not including those in coal mining. In 1970, there were 126,500. Today,
there are 78,500. In 1940, there were 81,700 trade and service jobs; today,
392,400. That's nearly a fivefold increase in service jobs across the state, to
be sure, but many of these are "junk jobs" that pay vastly less than those in
manufacturing.

The employment situation in Sissonville mirrors what has happened in
greater America over the past three decades: well-paid jobs have been
replaced with the kind provided by Wal-Mart. For years, Charleston, situ-
ated on the banks of the Kanawha River, was a manufacturing dynamo. Its
nickname is "Chemical Valley," though perhaps "was" is more apt. The
chemical industry has been reeling from back-to-back shutdowns, consol-
idations, and mergers, leaving Charleston and its environs with a great
sense of economic unease, and anger. Union Carbide was the biggest company, with 3,900 workers at its peak. Employment shrunk to 2,600 by the
millennium. After the company was bought by Dow Chemical, there was
downsizing. In 2003, the company had 1,222 workers in the Kanawha Valley. The 2,700 jobs that were lost in the preceding twenty-five years were
high-end. While an average manufacturing job pays $38,000, a chemical
industry job pays $53,000.

I found no one in Sissonville who put it as succinctly as did a man I met in
Welch, a hundred-and-fifty-year-old redbrick downstate coal town. Deep
mines were being closed in favor of "mountaintop removal" by corporations

with distant headquarters. Huge shovels leveled whole mountains. These hard flattened mountains increase runoff, and floods like never before blow down the hollows, walls of water and shale mud that destroy towns. Welch had just been through such a flood. The despondent man stood on the main drag amid the mudstains, talking to me about how they were always taken advantage of, by the coal companies and now by the federal government, which on a minor technicality did not give him disaster assistance.

"We always get fucked," he said. And by "we" he meant just about everyone in West Virginia.

In Sissonville that attitude finds its expression in the Confederate flag, which has morphed into a talismanic symbol that guards the town and announces: no minorities. No gays. No pinkos. No "other" of any kind. Nothing that ever changes the way we are or the way we think, and that's always to obey God, our commander in chief, to go to work, perhaps in the chemical factories, and never to question anything that goes on there, either. It's a brittle little world, stressed by outside social forces and outside industrial forces.

Sissonville is one of countless thousands of small-town worlds across America, self-protecting and self-reliant.

This was the town Katie Sierra came to, where her life intersected with that of Sean Miller. It would have been bad enough if 9/11 had never happened, if Katie had kept absolutely quiet, had worn black and skulked with the four or five outcast kids who during the lunch hour hung out at the north end of the high school, quarantined at a picnic table while jocks like Sean held court near the crowded main entrance. Sean could have hated her just for being different, and not felt compelled to act.

But when Katie wore her shirt to school and questioned the war on terrorism, to Sean it was as if Katie were a turban-headed disciple of Osama bin Laden. He couldn't hit Osama. So he hit Katie, from behind, on the upper left shoulder, a hard and painful strike that left a large bruise. This happened in the hallway, and no one saw it. That was the school's official line. The hallway was crowded.

Then Sean bragged.

"I hit the anarchy girl!" Sean exclaimed. The act elevated him to hero status, above all the other jocks at Sissonville High School.

Thus Sean came riding off that senior high school year, a champion of a school united (save for a few exceptions) in hating Katie Sierra, and it was with all this behind him that he left that Saturday night party and was driving south on the Cicerone Star Route in Sissonville near the Jackson County line.

In his drunken state he lost control, went over a hill. The truck flipped, and he was thrown from it. He was discovered at 5:30 AM by a driver who saw lights on the roadside. Sean Miller was declared dead at the scene.

Sean had a huge wake in the gymnasium at Sissonville High School. Hundreds came, according to the account by reporter Jacob Messer of the *Charleston Daily Mail*. Ten of Sean's friends flew Confederate flags from their trucks, the story related, and outside the school students raised a Confederate flag and an American flag half-mast on the pole. But they were made to take down the rebel flag.

Inside, Sean lay in a silver coffin. Garth Brooks played on the speakers as eulogies rang out. Sean's friends dedicated a Confederate flag and gave it to his parents, Ralph and Jill. When it was time to go to the cemetery, engines revved and rubber burned as Sean's friends pulled out to join the procession, led by a Sissonville police cruiser and two fire engines. The back of the hearse was covered by a Confederate flag.

Students had admired Sean for punching Katie, but with his death they elevated his outburst of rage into an act of greater meaning; he was a rebel now with a cause, a tragic idol to these students who felt their high school year had been ruined by Katie Sierra.

🖎

IT HAD BEEN difficult when Katie went back to school after serving the three-day suspension. In addition to being struck by Sean, she was pushed hard into a locker.

"We're gonna take her behind the school and give her some West Virginia justice," kids, usually girls, repeated.

Two days after Katie's return, Principal Mann asked students to write down their thoughts about Katie. Student Lynnett McClanahan wrote,

> The statements and actions of Katie Serra offend me grately. I am a member of the ROTC, my dad was in the Army for twenty years and my brother is enlisted in the National Guard. The fact that there is someone walking around the school with anarchy statements on their clothing are very offensive to me. In my eyes to be an Anarchy beliver it means to over throw the government and for there not to be one. In that case she is Antigovernment. Our government is what makes America. She is against American ways. Therefore she is anti-American. I don't think it is right, and I think it is very imoral and rude for her to do these things especially at such a sensitive time in America. I

don't think she should be able to attend schools while having
actions such as these.

—Lynnett McClanahan

Student Meggan Stutler wrote, in part,

> I watched as a young lady was permitted to walk down the hall-
> ways of Sissonville High School wearing a T-shirt that spoke
> against American patriotism, and being told by that young lady
> that we never cared about our country until the September 11th
> attacks. That is totally untrue. We have always shown that we
> cared, we're now just coming closer together.
>
> Maybe if this young lady were to travel to Afghanistan, for
> example, and be beaten to death, or maybe in another case be
> shot or stoned for showing any skin on her body, she would
> come to appreciate our country.
>
> I was very offended by this girl having the audacity to write
> things on her shirt that is purposely offending my country, my
> family, my friends, my flag, and my God. This country was
> founded on a belief in God, and the American flag is a symbol
> of it. By wearing and promoting all of these things, she is dis-
> respecting this country and its founders. I'm sure that if I were
> sitting in a class that she was in, and she had on this type of
> clothing, as upset as I am, I would not be able to concentrate on
> my education while my country and everything else that I love
> is being verbally torn apart.
>
> —Meggan Stutler, 10-30-01

Did Mann have these students write down their thoughts as protection
in the event of a lawsuit?

Katie had called the American Civil Liberties Union. She had reached
Roger D. Forman, a local attorney who specialized in cases that didn't make
him a lot of money—he sued rural police departments that were harassing
citizens, and took on a lot of black lung cases, the affliction from breathing
coal dust in underground mines. He especially liked the old miners.

Roger had represented one downstate miner who suffered from black
lung in the time of apartheid, when Nelson Mandela was jailed in South
Africa. The old miner told Roger: "We have to help Mandela and those
folks over there. That's not right!" The old man was white. As Roger
explained it, working deep in the earth, skin color didn't matter as much.

Men who worked with danger on a daily basis were often a lot more community-minded and concerned for those who were oppressed in the world.

But the old miners were dying off. There were fewer of those cases. When Katie came to Forman, it was exactly the kind of case the middle-aged attorney gravitated to: lots of hard work and no pay. He didn't like the rollback of civil rights in post-9/11 America, and he saw Katie as exemplifying what America could not tolerate—speech and ideas that differed from the mainstream.

Forman called Jim Withrow, the attorney for the Kanawha County Board of Education. They talked. Forman believed he had an understanding with Withrow, who asked him to fax a copy of what it would take to avoid a lawsuit. In part, Forman's fax read,

> Dear Jim:
>
> Pursuant to our discussions of today, I believe we have reached an agreement which no longer requires litigation. The agreement is as follows:
>
> 1.) Ms. Sierra is to be admitted to Sissonville High School on Monday, October 29, 2001, without being required to produce a medical authorization or to submit herself to a psychologist . . .
> 2.) Mr. Mann will return Ms. Sierra's leaflets to her.
> 3.) It is your understanding which was conveyed to me that all school clubs require adult sponsors. If this is the case and Ms. Sierra can find a sponsor that she can have her anarchist club . . .
> 4.) Ms. Sierra may wear her anarchist shirt and freely express her opinion in a manner which does not cause disruption in the classroom . . .

Withrow never responded. So the deal was off. Forman moved forward to sue.

But his client was having huge troubles at school. The kids were harassing Katie without mercy. Amy Sierra worried about her daughter's safety; she stopped letting her ride on the bus. Amy now drove Katie to school.

One day, when Amy pulled her vehicle sporting the three American flags into the school lot, it was surrounded by teenagers. They spat on

Amy's car. Amy drove home. She took the flags out of the SUV, took the flag off the house.

"If this is what the flag means, I don't need their fucking flag," she said. The flags would not go back up.

But there was great tension at home. Amy's husband, Mr. Kale, didn't at all like what was going on. It was as if he'd brought a pox to the community. There were not-so-veiled threats from some in town to burn down his Shaker house. Katie didn't like Mr. Kale, eating her dinners away from the handmade Shaker kitchen table and spending a lot of time in her room on the second floor of the house, or on the Internet with her anarchy friends.

Increasingly, Katie hung out in downtown Charleston, where she made friends with Holly, a twenty-two-year-old woman who wasn't homeless, but who ate at the Sojourner's Shelter for Homeless Women and Families. Katie soon preferred to eat at the shelter with Holly.

Suddenly, going to school seemed intolerable. At first Katie transferred to a distant school. But she was now a public figure in Charleston, and eyes of hate were always on her. One day in April, 2002, she sold her belongings— a television and stereo, including some videotapes and other things she took from Mr. Kale—at the Trading Post, a Charleston pawnshop. Then Katie vanished with her new friend.

"This is a freaking nightmare," Amy told reporter Eric Eyre. "She's severely depressed. Katie's running and wants to get out of here. She hates Charleston, West Virginia, for everything that's happened. Her friends have turned their backs on her."

The pressure of being pilloried by an entire community had gotten to Katie. She had a list of anarchists throughout the country, and she hoped to disappear into the anarchist underground.

Amy was worried sick. Police searched for Katie. Amy also hired a private investigator.

Katie's running away only emphasized to Roger Forman the importance of helping her win her rights. Through it all, he continued to work on the case along with his partner, thirty-one-year-old attorney Jason Huber.

If Katie returned, she would face a jury representing a community that seethed with resentment. To Forman and Huber, Katie stood for everything wrong in post-9/11 America. In their view, it was easy to defend free speech in times of peace, but now more than ever, it was vital to stand up for unpopular views.

No one, even Forman in secret, expected to win with a jury selected from a place where many hated the girl who simply wanted to wear her shirt. It would be a jury of people like so many Americans, who are afraid of terrorism, unsure of what is right in this new America.

Forman and Huber began what would turn into one thousand hours of legal work in the sleepless weeks leading up to the trial they hoped would start that summer. They needed their client to enter the courtroom. To them, it would not only be a fight for Katie, or against the small minds of Sissonville and Charleston, but for America and the freedom it is supposed to represent.

If only Katie would come home.

3

DAYS AFTER Katie ran away with her friend Holly, Amy Sierra heard that her daughter had gone to a concert at the Lincoln Theater in Raleigh, North Carolina. Performing was Tanya Donnelly, a bassist/songwriter once with the group Throwing Muses and now touring as Belly. The next day, Donnelly wrote on her website,

> We gave them our food, and I spent a half-hour trying to gently encourage them to bus home . . . I think she should go home and finish her fight.

Katie and Holly hitched rides from truckers. One night they slept beside a creek. Katie's run ended at a phone booth in Greenville, South Carolina, where she was found by the private investigator hired by Amy. The investigator cost Amy $10,000. But Katie was safe, and came home.

The troubles between mother and daughter were far from settled, but Katie would remain home. The date for her civil suit against the Kanawha County Board of Education was set for July. It would be a jury trial, and the common feeling was that she wouldn't win a thing. No jury member would uphold Katie's First Amendment rights, given the mood of the community.

✌

DURING THE Vietnam era, you heard "my country, right or wrong"— a distorted echo of nineteenth-century statesman Carl Schurz. Schurz, a German immigrant, Civil War hero, and former U.S. Senator, is perhaps the most misquoted man in American history; the complete quote, spoken on October 17, 1899, at a Chicago conference opposing the imperialism resulting from war with Spain, runs: "Our country, right or wrong. When right, to be kept right; when wrong, to be put right."

It's essentially what Katie Sierra had told that uncomprehending counselor the day she was suspended, though Katie didn't know of Schurz at the time.

A few days after the World Trade Center was attacked, I was out near my building on the Upper West Side, not far from a statue in Morningside Park honoring Schurz, when a pickup truck slowly rolled by. A huge flag billowed from the driver's window, and other flags adorned the back of the truck.[1]

"Salute the flag!" the driver snarled, before he sped off in a rage when I did not honor his wish.

With Schurz's quote in my head I'd begun to work on this book, trying to understand what was happening in America. It was difficult to gauge the mood of the country from the wounded city of New York, but through the Internet, some weeks later, I learned about Katie. Aside from the Charleston papers, the mainstream press wasn't covering her or anyone else caught up in what some were already terming neo-McCarthyism.

It was suddenly as if the American press, as Molly Ivins later noted in a talk to journalism students at Columbia University, were taking a page from King Louis XIV's sycophantic court. In the year following 9/11, Katie received only two brief mentions, buried deep in stories, in the national print press. It was the bloggers and anarchists and librarian websites—the Internet underground—that spread the word about what was going on in America. At one point, for example, a Google search netted 3,300 hits on Katie Sierra, despite the mainstream blackout. (She later appeared for ten seconds in Michael Moore's film *Bowling for Columbine*.)

⟆

THERE WERE other Katie-like situations, I learned. Many of them. One began on February 25, 2002, Stephen Kent Jones's first day of student-teaching at Old Town High School in Maine's Penobscot River basin.

Jones's professors in his master's degree teaching program at the University of Maine had approved his lesson plan—"Islam and Islamic Civilization, 600–1800." Stephen figured the children needed to learn about a religion that was in the news. The lesson plan won him an A. The biggest criticism: the plan was so in-depth that it was college level. It was approved by his mentor teacher, whose tenth grade Social Studies class Stephen would be teaching.

Stephen, thirty-four, is white and was raised Catholic but now doesn't follow any faith. He graduated magna cum laude from the University of Richmond. He'd arrived in Maine with a passion for teaching, using words such as "mission" when I visited him.

On day one of the planned seven-week teaching stint at Old Town High School, Jones asked the class about Islam. Most students thought it was a country. "Who's the president?" one asked. Jones had a lot of ground to cover.

So for the next few days, he gave a primer on Islam. On March 4, a parent called school officials and said Stephen "is trying to convert the students to Islam." His mentor teacher laughed off the complaint, according to newspaper accounts. Another complaint came in. Jones grew worried. He asked to talk with the parents, but they declined. That Friday, Jones met with the principal, who made light of the calls. "You should hear the complaints about sex ed!" he said, as Stephen recalled.

On Monday, Jones was called in by his student-teaching supervisor. "You're in deep doo-doo," the supervisor said, according to published accounts. Suddenly, the Old Town school didn't want him teaching. He was fired.

Stephen recounted to me that he was told he wouldn't be allowed to student-teach again, and that he was ejected from the program for which he'd paid $12,000. He wouldn't be getting a teaching certificate. He was transferred to a lesser master's in education program. Stephen was stunned.

"I can't believe this is happening to me," he said weeks later over breakfast. "This is like McCarthyism in the 1950s. There is no due process. When a Pakistani restaurant in Bangor [Maine] was threatened and had to close for a while, the city council held its meeting there and some in the community rallied behind it. But this kind of bureaucratic action is not condemned. Open racism is condemned. This is much more insidious."

He said the parents didn't really believe he was trying to convert their children.

"When they said, 'You are trying to convert my kid,' that was their clumsy way of saying, 'You are asking my kid to think about things that are beyond discussion.' The perspective is not to challenge their worldviews."

Stephen was now jobless. He considered his options. There were three places he could teach without credentials, places so hard up they would take anyone: New York City, the Mississippi Delta, and the Indian reservations of the Southwest. Stephen really, really wanted to teach. He told me he was about to begin sending out résumés.

As I drove to New York after our meeting, I realized that for Stephen, and for Katie and the others, the problem wasn't just the Ashcroft in Washington—

there were a thousand mini-Ashcrofts scattered around the country. On school boards, in newspaper publishers' offices, among some college administrators, on local police departments. It wasn't simply a top-down repression. A significant portion of America wanted to partake in some repressing of its own, as another anarchist learned in still another case of neo-McCarthyism that caught my attention while spending time with Katie and Amy.

❧

IAN HARVEY was an English and mass media teacher in Naples, Florida, and like Katie he was deeply bothered by the bombing in Afghanistan. On December 9, 2001, Ian held a peace vigil at the corner of U.S. 41 and Golden Gate Parkway in Naples. Ten teachers and adults and ten students participated in the vigil. They represented perhaps the entire liberal community of Naples, which is called the "Platinum Coast" (across the state from Miami) because it attracts wealthy, conservative whites. Naples is where Thomas White, then the Army chief of staff in the George W. Bush administration and a former Enron executive, was using his Enron money to build a 15,145 square-foot palace on the white sands at the edge of the Gulf of Mexico.

As Ian and the others stood holding peace signs on a corner up the road from Jungle Larry's Zoological Park—a tourist attraction featuring wild African game in "natural" settings—a hundred and fifty counter-protesters appeared, many wearing muscle shirts and riding Harleys. It was ugly. A few bikers talked about pummeling Ian and the others. But wiser heads among the white collar members of the group prevailed.

They had a different kind of pummeling in mind. Suddenly, a week later, the school board was investigating Ian's teaching methods. A sixty-page report was hastily commissioned, and an investigator concluded after interviewing fifteen of Ian's 172 students that he was poisoning the minds of youth. Akin to the charges against Katie, Ian suddenly "affected the efficiency of school operations . . ." The report said he had anti-corporate and pro-labor posters on the walls. Ian countered that the school was filled with pro-corporate information, and that he presented course materials in a manner that allowed college-level academic exploration.

After this report became public, student Amanda Woodward collected 278 student signatures supporting Ian, who she said encouraged students to think for themselves.

No matter. The Collier County School Board demoted Ian, sending him to teach English as a second language to adults in Imokolee, the Florida equivalent of Siberia. Meantime, his case was sent to the state board of education for possible revocation of his teaching credentials, and some of those arrayed against Ian were telephoning Governor Jeb Bush.

When I visited Naples not long after Katie came home, I found that people against Ian were a far different breed from what I'd seen in Sissonville. Residents of Sissonville weren't standing on street corners to protest Katie, nor were they calling the West Virginia governor.

There was no one I met in West Virginia quite like Richard Somerby, a retired IBM executive and Korean War veteran who lives half the year in Westchester County north of New York City, and the other half in Naples. He led the anti-Harvey contingent. He termed Ian "a danger to our country."

I had lunch with Richard on a restaurant patio surrounded by a subtropical paradise of mimosa trees and coconut palms. It became clear that Ian represented payback time for Richard after a long tour in what he saw as a liberal desert.

"Now I don't have to hide my patriotism under the covers, because it wasn't politically correct, which I'd had to do for thirty years."

Richard showed me his belt buckle—embossed upon it was a ring of tiny American flags.

Of Ian he said, "It's a serious case. Not like raping a student on the front lawn. But it's bad. He's sort of a 2002 Jane Fonda. If he had a similar peace protest during, say, Panama or Desert Storm, my guess is there would have been very little reaction. But something happened to our country on September 11. You don't do that anymore. That's not allowed."

His dream in this new America? That Fonda would now get punished for visiting North Vietnam during the Vietnam War.

"It may be that her case comes back," Richard said. "She's the perfect candidate for a treason charge. It was politically incorrect to do it to her in the 1960s."

I met Ian, who is in his mid-forties, the next day. His spiked hair was thinning, a bit gray. He wore two earrings, a T-shirt with UNION written on it, and a peace symbol ring. One couldn't go to central casting to get a more perfect—at least by appearance—enemy for Somerby. We had a long breakfast and then we went on a tour of Naples. After a few hours with Ian, I realized that if he was a little strident at times, he nevertheless came across as a nice guy who really cares about teaching. In a place like Berkeley, he'd be a dime a dozen. He simply had the misfortune of being a Berkeley person in Naples.

Those arrayed against Ian (I met a few others who were keenly right-wing) generally came from the ranks of the one-third of America that is megaconservative. They were unabashed nationalists who wanted America to march. In contrast, those against Katie, though comprising some conservative types, were largely from the middle third, a zone equally far from the extreme right as from the left.

The question isn't whether those against Ian could be convinced to just let him be. That would be the extreme-right third trying to get along with the left third. That wouldn't happen.

That was why Katie's dilemma was so much more intriguing. What would occur if those in the middle third could hear where Katie was coming from? Could they learn anything and grow to understand her position? Could Katie learn from them?

In our society, especially in this age of invective on talk radio or Fox Television, dialogue rarely occurs. No national publication did a full story on Ian, just as there was none on Katie, though the Japanese media was all over her. Ian did end up on *The O'Reilly Factor*, where host Bill O'Reilly called him a "nut" at one point. That didn't do much to broaden understanding.

Long before O'Reilly, Ian sought judicial relief against the school board. He went to the American Civil Liberties Union. He said he was told the ACLU couldn't do anything until he was fired. The teacher's union to which he belonged was of little help. Ian couldn't sue on his own. He earns $44,808 a year and has children. He is not a man of means. So he twisted in the Gulf Coast winds, waiting to hear what would happen to his job.

"I might be out doing landscaping next time you come here, for six dollars an hour," he said.

Ian, unlike Katie, seemed to have little recourse. As the summer came on, I wondered what the jury would do with her case. It would be her way of sitting down with the people of Sissonville and Charleston.

≈

IN THE PERIOD leading up to and following her trial, Katie spent a lot of her days and evenings wandering the alleys of downtown Charleston, amid brick buildings that were last important when Coolidge and Hoover were presidents.

She usually walked alone. On those nights when Michael and I searched for Katie to give her a ride home or to Amy's work, we'd run into the cast of characters of the world she inhabited. There was a wheelchair-bound black man, a war veteran-turned-panhandler; a brooding goth, hair black as the clothes on her back, rushing in or out of her single-room-occupancy

hotel; and there were always a few Greyhound wannabes, smoking ciga-
rettes and wearing sunglasses, just out of the reach of the streetlamp.

All of them knew Katie. When we walked with her, their night eyes were
the only kindness she received. In the afternoon, the harsh glare of the city's
day eyes was an entirely different matter. She came up in conversations;
there were mutterings.

—Who does she think she is?

—Get a load of that hair.

—What kind of mother does she have?

Katie saw these people and their eyes.

—*ohmygodohmygod. They all hate me. No one understands—not just me—
everything.*

One midnight we gave her a lift. She didn't want to go home to Sissonville. So we took her to the nursing home where Amy was on night shift,
seven-to-seven, giving meds, watching beds. The road led past dark shale
cliffs, into a forest, then to the old folks' home, a fortress-like sealed building. The electronic door swooshed open, and we were hit with a blast of
too-warm air, carrying the smell of nearing death.

—Mommy, I'll sleep on the backseat.

—I ain't lettin' you do that. The backseat is full of stuff.

—Then I'll sleep up front.

—I'll get you a room at the hotel when I get my break.

—It's okay, Mommy. Just let me sleep on the seat again.

—A hotel. And you can take a bath.

—Mommy, I smell human.

—How long's it been since you took a bath!

—Two weeks.

—Oh my God, Katie, what am I gonna do with you . . .

Mother and daughter argued like usual, Amy in her white nurse's uniform, the girl with green hair, the two of them so intent on their discussion
in the television room that they didn't notice the ancient woman in an electric wheelchair creeping nearer and nearer. The woman's hair was
absolutely white, her head hung sideways, crooked to the right, drool pouring from the corner of her mouth. Her eyes seemed closed, but she piloted
her wheelchair precisely. Both mother and daughter looked up.

Katie knew the woman from nights waiting for Amy to go on break.
Words came from the old woman's barely moving mouth.

—Nobody loves me.

—I love you.

Katie took the old woman's hand, wizened, bony, and liver-spotted. She stroked it gently.

—I'm going to paint your nails again. Just like I did last time. You're beautiful.

—I don't think I'm beautiful.

—No, no, you're beautiful. You have the most wavy hair in the whole nursing home.

The old woman cried, locked in the solitude of old age, like so many others in the home. Katie knew many of them, including another woman asleep down the hall who happened to be a McCoy, from the family of McCoys who fought with the Hatfields in the infamous feud that filled the tabloid papers in the 1880s and 1890s.

It was a war that began as do most, over slights not discussed but dealt with violently. The Hatfields lived on the West Virginia side of Tug Fork of the Big Sandy River, the McCoys on the Kentucky side of the same river. The McCoys were West Bank, the Hatfields East. During the Civil War, Confederate Captain Anderson "Devil Anse" Hatfield killed Harmon McCoy, who was with the Union. That didn't put things over the edge, for after all it was a war. It was long after the Civil War when Randall McCoy, Harmon's kinfolk, got into an argument with Devil Anse over a stolen pig. Things escalated when a Hatfield began living with Randall's daughter. Open war followed, with killings (once four at a time), ambushes, and house burnings. The last killing was in 1896. Stories about the Hatfields and McCoys over the decades portrayed them as solitary and inward clans, still living with the bitterness of the war on the Tug Fork. Randall spent his last days wandering the streets of Pikeville, muttering and devastated by the loss of six of his children. Devil Anse tried to find peace in baptism near the end of his life.

The McCoy woman slept. This woman whose hand Katie was stroking could not sleep, for she wanted love. The old woman's tears now flowed more freely. Katie was overcome with sadness.

—I love you. I love you.

—You're the only person that talked to me all day. I miss my mother.

—She still loves you. I love you.

A black male orderly who seethed with dislike for Katie spotted her and glared.

—*Whydotheyhatemeldon'tknowaboutthiscountryohmygod.*

As we left, Katie sought refuge from the angry eyes in the darkness of the front seat of her mother's car, waiting for Amy's shift break, and the hotel. She tried sleeping, but could not.

4

FOG HANGS thick in the Appalachian mountain hollows south of Charleston, rising in blue plumes from the valley of the Kanawha River. It's going to be a hot July day. But not yet. The morning air still holds the chill of night. Local television vans set up outside the courthouse on a downtown street, devoid of the office workers who have yet to begin their commutes.

A crowd has already gathered in the hall outside Division 4, Courtroom 6E, the honorable James C. Stucky presiding. Sissonville residents mill in pods, apart from a smaller collection of local punk-rock kids, one of whom is wearing leather and a shiny spiked collar. There are local journalists, as well as one from Japan, and a *Court TV* crew. In dark suits are the attorneys for the Kanawha County Board of Education, Eric Engle and Gary Pullin. Engle is a tall, youthful man with a head as boxy and firm as a ceramic jug and an easy smile. Pullin is a small gray-haired man, a U.S. Marine reservist, with facelines that rarely reveal a smile. In light suits are Roger Forman and Jason Huber, Katie Sierra's ACLU defenders. Roger has a Fuller Brush mustache. Jason has happy eyes that dart around the hallway, a reddish ponytail and beard. All four attorneys pace nervously.

Roger doesn't live in a big house, at least by the standards of a defense attorney with a two-decades-old practice in a city located in the mid-South. The house is in need of repair. It's reflective of the kinds of cases Roger has taken on over the years—low or no pay, with other rewards instead.

Jason's house sits atop the valley rim west of downtown, in a middle class neighborhood—but it's the "ghetto" house, an ancient and rotting log cabin with a falling-down porch, evocative of a Walker Evans photograph.

Dinner guests are greeted by barking dogs and Jason, who is cutting up pieces of a deer he'd shot the previous season.

—Dig some 'taters. Shovel and bucket's over yonder.

Jason embraces country, is proud that he hunts and fishes, and freely refers to himself as a redneck. But he's whipsmart, an intellectual redneck in a world that doesn't understand such a creature. When he visits New York City for conferences of liberal lawyers, he senses discrimination based on his West Virginia accent, which brands him in their minds as stupid.

Roger, who hails from New York City, fears a different kind of discrimination. When a well-wisher slaps him on the back outside Judge Stucky's courtroom, talking about their synagogue, Roger hushes the man. It's not wise to let it around that a Jew is defending the anarchy girl.

All heads turn when Katie and Amy emerge from the elevator. Katie's hair is spiked and green, with blue tips. She wears faded bell-bottom blue jeans, a tie-dye shirt, sandals with no socks. On her left wrist are a dozen bracelets. Roger and Jason had pleaded for her to dress up, change her hair, but Katie refused.

—I am who I am. I'm not going to be a fake.

Amy wears a black leather vest that contrasts with her blond hair. Katie is surrounded by the punk kids. When Amy speaks, her Kentucky accent is out of place.

—They want to run me out. I came up here because I married a man from Sissonville. He was born there. Run me out? Where do you think the name "Kanawha" comes from? The Indians were here first. We're all from somewhere else here.

Katie is nervous, bounding around the hall. Everyone waits. A juror's car won't start. Katie has talked so much about what happened, she worries her testimony today will come out sounding wrong.

—You know, it sounds . . . you know.

Katie recently had her nose pierced. After it became infected, she had the spike removed.

—When they took it out, it hurt so much, I puked. I'm sure you wanted to hear that.

The doors open and everyone files in. The Sissonville people take the right side of the spectator area. Across the bar, in front of the Sissonville crowd, Principal Forest Mann sits with Engle and Pullin; Katie and Amy with Roger and Jason are to the left.

While awaiting the jurors, the attorneys argue over the admissibility of the newspaper article in which Forest Mann misrepresented what was on

Katie's shirt. Roger argues that Mann's reckless statements to the press were what inflamed the student body, not Katie.

The school's attorneys argue that the statement is hearsay. Judge Stucky agrees and says the article will not be admissible.

—But you can ask him what he said all day long. I don't think we want to try this case based on newspaper, radio, and TV accounts. We'll hear from the horses' mouths.

The juror with the ailing car cannot get it started. A bailiff is dispatched to the trailer park to pick her up. While waiting out in the hall, Roger is stoked, rubbing his hands like a fighter about to do battle.

—This is the American system at work! In the best way!

Yet one senses that Roger doesn't expect much from the jury. Roger faced a critical choice when he filed the suit on behalf of Katie's First Amendment rights—to file in county superior court, or federal court. If he'd gone the federal route and wanted to appeal, the case would go to the U.S. 4th Circuit Court of Appeals, the most conservative circuit. The 4th had two appointees made by former President Bill Clinton, but that might not be enough, and Roger feared an adverse ruling. Then the case would go to the U.S. Supreme Court. There Roger foresaw a 5–4 decision against Katie. Not an option.

If the superior court jury gave Katie nothing, as was expected, the appeal would go to the West Virginia State Supreme Court, which Roger felt was progressive enough to uphold the First Amendment. The schools could still appeal to the U.S. Supreme Court, but that would be unlikely. So he chose this route.

The jury member finally makes it and seven women and one man wearing suspenders file into the box. Two jurors are alternates. The man, a Korean War veteran and quite religious, was empaneled by Roger and Jason in selection, because they believed he'd be open enough to be convinced that he fought for the right for Katie to have her beliefs.

The jurors' eyes go over Katie. Juror "X" looks the anarchy girl up and down, and she thinks: *I do not like that girl.* Juror X's eyes turn to Forest Mann. She doesn't necessarily like the looks of him, either.

Roger opens. His voice is loud, booming, confident.[1]

—This case is about free speech in the United States of America. It's an inalienable right. It's one of the reasons we are all Americans. You do not have to speak popular opinions in America. In the schoolrooms of America, you do not leave your right to free speech at the door. If you do, we have lost our freedoms to those who destroyed the World Trade Center.

—On October 22, Katie went and informed Principal Forest Mann that she wanted to form an anarchy club. She had some kids who wanted to study it with her. And they had an absolute right to do that, because they weren't bothering or disrupting anything. Forest Mann just said absolutely no. And he was wrong. You need to tell him that. That decision was unconstitutional. That decision violates the fundamental laws we live by in America.

—The next day, Katie goes to school. She wears this shirt to school.

(The jury's eyes go over the shirt that Roger holds.)

—Sitting behind her in class was a kid . . . Jacob Reed screamed at her. He said "If you don't fucking like it here, you can fucking leave." That clearly was inappropriate. All he got for that was a lunchtime detention. Forest Mann said Katie disrupted that class. Katie did absolutely nothing to disrupt that class. She was wearing this shirt and she's guaranteed the right to wear that shirt. And what happened? She gets called to the principal's office and she gets suspended.

—Amy Leithead, the parliamentarian, decides to go with Katie to the school board. At the school board meeting, pandemonium occurs when Katie speaks. Our school board members, who ought to be more educated than the student body . . . they start screaming at her. John Luoni gets up there and grandstands and accuses her of treason. It's treason to promote peace in America? I don't think so. Pete Thaw says she is like waving a Japanese flag on Pearl Harbor Day. Bill Raglin says, "What's the matter with this girl?"

—There's nothing the matter with this girl. It's American to be different. She's very American and very patriotic. That's what America is all about.

Eric Engle opens for the school board.

—You're going to hear from teachers who didn't have Katie Sierra in their class tell you how their classes were disrupted . . . all classes, for weeks. You're going to hear witnesses tell you [about] the cause of these arguments, of these disruptions. They're not going to say it was Mr. Mann. They're going to say it was the idea of there being an anarchy club at Sissonville High School and the things that were put on those T-shirts. They upset students.

—Now, you've heard about absolute rights. And you know we don't have absolute rights in the United States. You can't yell fire in a crowded theater. You can't carry a gun up and down the street unless you go and get a license.

—If actions and if ideas and if speech cause disruptions at the school, then the principals have the right to limit that. If you start having those types of disruptions, like were going on at Sissonville High School, then education stops. You'll have students tell you . . . that their grades dropped because of all this . . . that teachers would have to stop and try to get everybody reigned back in to talk about math. Because instead they wanted to argue about whether or not there should be an anarchy club.

Katie takes the stand. She is nervous, looks at the jury often. Roger examines her, asks about the school board meeting.

—What did it feel like being there?

—I was nervous. I was kind of hurt that no one would, like, let me say anything. They just prejudged everything I was talking about. I was upset.

—Was there an atmosphere in the school that was causing you trouble?

—Yes. People called me names for reasons I don't know. People called me a terrorist. A nigger queer faggot lover.

Eric cross-examines, quoting from a deposition he took of Katie. Katie bites her thumb a lot.

—You don't call other people names? You don't make fun of people?

—No.

—Isn't it true that you've testified earlier that you don't think the kids at Sissonville High School can read?

—I didn't mean it like that. They've got the lowest reading comprehension scores in the state or something. There's a girl in class . . . she didn't know how to read the word "anarchist." She thought it meant anti-Christ. She's like, "You're an anti-Christ. Jesus loves me."

—Okay. You've said even here earlier today that people in Sissonville, the majority of them, are known for being racist.

—Uh, yeah.

—You love the country, and you love the world?

—Yes.

—In that website interview, did you not indicate this . . .

—Objection!

—. . . country was full of crap?

—Overruled.

—You stated that you learned this country is crap. And you've indicated that the school system was crap.

—At that time I probably used a poor choice of words. But I've been through a lot.

—And you have said that this place sucks and that the people are narrow-minded . . . you said these people are backward and racist and sexist.

—Everyone I have been in contact with, besides my friends, have been extremely narrow-minded, extremely racist and sexist, or at least in Sissonville. That's just how I feel.

—Some of the groups you like are Anti-Flag, the Queers, the Dead Presidents, Dead Kennedys. This is kind of an anti-establishment or anti-authoritarian type of message. Is that right?

—I guess. It's not really about that. It's real inspiring and it tells you to, like, stand up for who you are and [what you] believe in.

—Now as an anarchist . . . your idea of an anarchy society, it's one with government but without leaders. There would be no president or no George W. Bush running the country?

—Definitely not.

—No U.S. Senate. No West Virginia legislature. In fact there wouldn't even be schools, would there?

—You're making it sound bad. There would be education. But it wouldn't be like now. It wouldn't be like prisons. If you weren't forced to learn, you probably would want to.

—You have testified that you think a Ku Klux Klan club would be okay?

—I wouldn't agree with it, but if that's what someone wants to do, I guess.

—And a neo Nazi club would be okay?

—I guess so.

—And a Satan worshiping club would be okay?

—I'm not like Satanic or anything. I'm completely atheist. But if you are going to worship God, why can't you worship Satan?

—I don't have any other questions.

DAY TWO

JUNIOR AMANDA Bowles, with a 3.75 grade point average, is on the stand being questioned by Roger Forman, talking about the third-block English class in which Jacob Reed yelled at Katie. That class didn't have a regular teacher, just a rotation of substitutes. Amanda was exasperated with the boys in that class, as well as with Katie.

—Our class had several teachers that semester. That class was kind of out of control. The teachers couldn't really control a lot of the students.

—And Katie was not one of those students that couldn't be controlled, was she?

—No. Once the bell would ring, Casey Cain and Jacob would begin throwing stuff at the teachers. Daniel Cobb and them, they would always be noisy, would never do their work, backtalk constantly.

—You didn't agree with what Katie was doing, did you?

—No. Katie, she had fliers lying on her desk to join a club to get followers. She handed me one, because I asked her to, and then I gave it back. It bothers me to see what I call idiocy after what I saw on September 11.

—What role did Katie play, if any, in comparison to the other kids in causing turmoil in that class?

—She didn't start anything. But whenever someone said something to her, it would usually end up as an argument.

—But she didn't initiate any of those kinds of arguments?

—Not that I know of.

—So she wasn't yelling like they were yelling, was she?

—She did at some points. But she'd always try to keep her voice down.

—Did you ever see her misbehave?

—No.

—What would Katie do when people confronted her?

—She would just tell them to leave her alone.

Amy is on the stand, being cross-examined by Gary Pullin about her daughter.

—I believe on some of those shirts, the American flag was turned upside down with the anarchy symbol drawn through it.

—Yes.

—And that did not cause you any concern?

—I personally would not do it myself, but . . .

—In fact, didn't you see that as an indication by Katie of her disrespect for the American government and American flag? When you testified before lunch, [you said] Katie was very patriotic.

—Yes, I think she's very patriotic.

—You think wearing an American flag upside down with an anarchy symbol drawn through it is a display of patriotism?

—Absolutely.

After a battle with the school board's attorneys and several bench conferences with Judge Stucky, Roger is allowed to mention Principal Forest Mann's comments in the newspaper, in which he was quoted as saying her shirt said, "America should burn," and, "I hope Afghanistan wins." It comes up that Mann went on the public intercom at the school and talked about the article.

Now student Kippie Harman is on the stand via a deposition that is read—Roger examines her about the mood of the student body after the article appeared.

—Evil looks. Toward her, or anybody who was with her. Someone hit her in the hall. I walked her to classes . . . because somebody hit her in the hallway.

—She's an outcast the same as I am.

Jason Huber is examining Gordon James Simmons, a librarian in a nearby county and also an adjunct professor of philosophy at West Virginia State College and Marshall University. Simmons had studied anarchy since high school in the 1960s, which led to deeper study of the subject as he got older.

—To give a short definition, anarchism is the point of view in which human liberty or freedom has the highest possible value . . . those things that enhance or expand freedom would be good, and those things that diminish it or detract from it or suppress it would be evil. Historically, the government has been pretty consistent in being an enemy of freedom. And so, it would be the corollary of the anarchist belief that government ought to be done away with or abolished . . . Any form of inequality, whether it's economic or class-based or racial or sexual . . . would be in opposition to anarchism.

—Is there, in your studies and your understanding of anarchism, anything inherently treasonous about anarchism?

—I guess if improving the lot of humankind, to be less sexist, is treasonous. But otherwise, no.

—Is there anything inherently violent about anarchism?

—No. It is for whatever enhances freedom, and violence takes away from that. Violence is not part of anarchy. Some people also assume chaos is anarchy. That is a misunderstanding.

—Is there any historical basis for this misunderstanding?

—If you were to go back to the seventeenth century and look at, say, the philosophy of someone like Thomas Hobbes, who was at great pains to justify and legitimize absolute authority of government. He paints a picture of humanity without government as being one of chaos and destruction and disturbance. It's a polemical sort of point.

(Simmons notes that there are many forms of anarchy that do not at first appear to be such: the Kibbutz system in Israel, or the social structure of indigenous South American cultures.)

—Well, Mr. Simmons, Israel and South America are a far cry from West Virginia.

—The early settlers in this region got along for long periods of time without any kind of institution or outside authority coming and basically telling them what to do, right on up until the industrialized period when railroads were built and timbering and coal mining began.

—Anarchist organizations were very prominent in the campaign for the eight hour day, in a period when people worked six and seven days a week, ten and twelve hours a day, had child labor. It was a very brutal period of industrial capitalism.

—So, if you're making minimum wage and working an eight hour day, at least in part you can thank . . .

—The anarchists. Yeah. Definitely.

—Were there any examples of anarchists, individuals, who were unfairly targeted because of the content of their political belief?

—In 1886, there was a large rally in the Haymarket Square in Chicago on behalf of the eight hour day, and a bomb had gone off and that ended the demonstration. The police attacked them, the marchers, the unionists. They arrested the anarchist speakers . . . tried and convicted them . . . and some were executed. Later on, the governor of Illinois exonerated them and pointed out that their conviction had been based solely upon the fact that they were anarchists.

—There was Sacco and Vanzetti who were two Italian immigrants who were also anarchists, and they were arrested and convicted for armed robbery.

—Were those two individuals executed as well?

—Yes.

—And exonerated?

—Later, after their death.

—A lot of the early campaigns for equal rights, equal pay, this came from them. The anarchists were saying it first.

Eric Engle cross-examines, and he holds that school officials acted properly by not allowing Katie her anarchy club, because it was inherently dangerous.

—There are other people who have anarchist beliefs that are different than yours, aren't there?

—Absolutely.

—And some of those relate to the promotion of their beliefs through the use of violence? Isn't that right?

—I think that would be a marked minority.

—Isn't it true that the Russian Czar Alexander II was assassinated by an anarchist.

—Some have claimed that he was, yes.

—President McKinley was assassinated by an anarchist, isn't that right?

—Actually, there's some historical debate about the sincerity of that man's beliefs. He didn't actually seem to belong to any organizations, or have any association with other anarchists. He may have just been a lone guy who was a nut.

—Do you understand that Theodore Kaczynski, the Unabomber, has been characterized as an anarchist? And Timothy McVeigh has been characterized as an anarchist because of his views to the contrary of the government?

—I don't even think that's close to being accurate.

—Your goal is to get freedom at whatever cost.

—No sir, I never said at any cost . . . that's loading the question. I think it's clear that if you look at the historical literature . . . if you took some time to talk to people who are actually involved in anarchist groups, the vast majority do not condone violence.

—But some of them do.

—Some Roman Catholics also bomb abortion clinics. But not all do.

DAY THREE

GARY PULLIN examines Principal Forest Mann.

—How did the events of September 11 affect your school?

—I noted a change of climate on September 11. As soon as we learned what happened, I turned the intercom on, told the students and teachers what happened. I wanted students to be informed. That day at lunchtime, we had a ceremony outside the school, at their request. The events at that time served to bring the student body together. It broke down barriers that are always there between teachers and students. As I walked through the halls, I could feel that there was, oh, just a seriousness that came over the students that I had never witnessed in my thirty-nine years of experience. And at the same time, it was difficult for me to comprehend, and for all the other adults there . . . the way we handled those events about patriotic assemblies, I think that the events themselves served to polarize my students.

—Katie identified herself as dressing in an alternative style. I have other students who dress differently, to set themselves apart from other students. From day one from September 11, with those students, there was a polarization. It served to break down barriers with a vast majority of my students, but it served to put up barriers between the administration and . . . the alternative students.

—Katie expressed a belief about the lack of trust for government. At the same time, the vast majority of students had terrific trust in government and support for President Bush, and for America. The tension I could feel in the school was unreal.

—On October 22, Katie was dressed like any student was dressed. There wasn't anything that called attention. Katie came to ask me if she could form an anarchy club. She said would I look at the documents she had given me. And I looked at them very briefly, and responded that, "You will not be able to form an anarchy club at Sissonville High School."

—Katie was very frustrated at that point. I saw different kinds of emotions. She became very argumentative. She told me . . . her right to form that [club] was supported by the ACLU, that I couldn't deny that. It went from attempting to persuade; it came to demanding.

—What was the basis for your decision?

—Mr. Pullin, I remember the flier more than anything else. The flier, "Please join the anarchy club." The kind of climate that was in our school . . . If Katie was able to form an anarchy club, I think by definition that wishes to abolish the government and the leadership, and on the other hand I have a school full of students that have become very pro-government because of the events of 9/11. Those things were the basis for my decision, because in my opinion, it would have been extremely disruptive to the educational process. I had a real fear that it could turn into an unsafe environment for Katie, for all of my students.

—When did you look at the dictionary in the high school library with regard to the definition of anarchy? . . . Did you see the word "peace" in there anywhere?

—No, sir. My feeling is this: as a social studies teacher, I would fight for Katie's right to stand on a street corner and pass out her literature. In the classroom, it's different. There's a captive audience there. On a street corner, people could walk around her, say, "No, I don't want that."

—If that shirt had been worn prior to 9/11, I don't think we would have the kind of disruption we experienced.

—No one understands the kind of pressure, the stress, the concern I had for maintaining a positive school climate. I saw that deteriorating. No one has any idea.

—The counselors and administration and my staff, we had to deal with damage control. It did distract from teaching and learning.

—It all goes back to what Katie had on her shirt, and her attempts to form an anarchy club and express her views. . . . It was nothing short of a crisis situation.

Roger Forman cross-examines Forest Mann in the afternoon session.

—Did Katie offer to show you that shirt when she came to your office?

—I think she did.

—And you refused?

—I did not ask her to take her sweatshirt off that she had covering up her T-shirt.

—But she wanted to show it to you, didn't she?

—I don't know if it was a big issue. You know, as I said before, I did not ask her to do that.

—You were asked on direct examination regarding statements attributed to you. And the specific statement attributed to you that was discussed was that on Katie Sierra's shirt, it said, "I hope Afghanistan wins" and "I hope America burns." You saw that, didn't you?

—Saw what?

—You saw those statements attributed to you by reporter Eric Eyre in the newspaper, didn't you?

—I saw the newspaper.

—Did you see those statements attributed to you?

—I very quickly just glanced at it. I did not read that article until much later. I mean a number of days later I read that article.

—Do you deny telling the reporter . . .

—I did not make that statement to the reporter. I told the reporter that that was what was reported to me was on her shirt. He quoted it wrong.

—It concerned me enough to get on the intercom and announce to my students that I did not say that . . . I did that within a matter of a few days.

—In the meantime, prior to that time, you ran into Eric Eyre, didn't you?

—Yes.

—You congratulated him. You told Eric you liked that story.

—I ran into Eric Eyre and did tell him that I thought that was a good article. But as I said before . . . I glanced at it. I did not see the part where Eric had attributed any statements to me.

—You didn't even look at her shirt. Even if you didn't say her shirt said that, you didn't look it at. You put that out not knowing whether that was true or not.

—I said that a student had reported to me.

—Now that student would be Jacob Reed, correct?

—Yes.

—I would like to go to Exhibit 17. [Shows Mann.] Mr. Mann, that statement. Is that the statement you relied upon?

    I was in 3rd Block and Katie Siera was in that class her shirt
    said Stuff about how she thinks America is the dumbest coun-

try and how it should burn and she also told the class how She
hopes the war against Afganistan we will loose it So I got mad
and told her if she doesnt like this country get the <u>Fuck</u> out . . .

People whow herd it was—
Jamie Myers
Daneil Kersey
Todd Shamblin

Jacob Reed

10-23-01

—Yes.

—That statement was taken at your request, wasn't it?

—Yes.

—And in fact, it doesn't say both those statements were on her shirt . . .
saying that Jacob said that wouldn't be accurate, would it?

—Not as it is here.

—And that's . . .

—Partially accurate.

—And that's what you relied upon?

—Yes.

—You told Eric Eyre that the student said both of them were on her shirt,
didn't you?

—Yes.

—You're telling this jury that Katie's shirts and Katie's club were the
problems that were causing trouble at Sissonville, when in part, you were
causing trouble at Sissonville High School by putting that statement out,
weren't you?

—Objection!

—Overruled.

—I admit that that was . . . part of the problem that we were dealing
with . . .

—Would you agree that some of the things the Board of Education said
were of major concern, saying she was committing treason and waving the
Japanese flag? This body we are so supposed to respect, were saying these
things about Katie Sierra?

—That's asking for an interpretation on my part.

—You admit your statement was part of the problem. I want to know if
the board's statement was part of it, too?

—I know after the board meeting there was an escalation of the kinds of disturbances and Katie's role in that. Certainly the board admonished Katie. I am sure that had an effect on how people felt.

—Did you know after thirty-nine years you could get away with that kind of reckless statement and the board would back you? That you had a role in the disturbances?

—I don't feel I have a role in the kinds of disturbances at all. I attribute the kinds of disruptions in the school [to] the reaction to Katie wearing her shirt and her attempts to form an anarchy club, more than anything else.

—The morning after the board meeting, my students were angry. I don't think my students before they come to school in the morning read the *Charleston Gazette*.

Jacob Reed was out of town and not available to testify, and so Roger Forman and Jason Huber convinced Judge Stucky to play a videotape of Reed's deposition, over the objections of Eric Engle and Gary Pullin. In the video Jacob, who wears a military buzz cut, is tense and hostile. Roger holds up the shirt and asks Jacob to find the words that Forest Mann said.

—I don't see it on here.

—Nothing on here [is] talking about how America should burn.

—She said that. I didn't write that 100 percent correct.

—She never told you it should burn?

—Yes she did. During third block class when this occurred.

—Was any of that on this shirt?

—No.

—But you put that in the statement.

—Yes.

—You don't like Katie very much, do you?

—I don't like what she believes in.

—Do you like her?

—I have nothing again—I'm against her having an anarchy club. But I don't hate her.

—But it got you angry . . .

—She wants attention. It's the only reason she is doing this. The clothes, hair color. It gets attention. She created tension, sir. She wore clothes inside out, things that would bring attention to her. To me that shows all she's wanting is for people to look at her and say "humph," and notice her.

—But she didn't start arguments, did she?

—No.

—Do you believe there is another side to anarchy?

—Do you believe there's another side to the rebel flag, besides racism?

DAY FOUR

FOR THE FIRST time in the trial, Roger Forman and Jason Huber are wearing dark suits, and Eric Engle and Gary Pullin are wearing lighter-colored suits.

Katie wears a hoodie on which she has sewn a new patch. It reads, FUCK NAZI BASTARDS.

First to testify is Robert Delmar Settle, senior instructor for the ROTC unit, who spent twenty-eight years, eleven months, and sixteen days in the U.S. Marine Corps. He tells the court that ROTC membership is up, that 185 out of 700 students have signed on for the coming school year.

—The purpose of the program is not to recruit people into the armed forces. Leadership is the primary focus, but it's designed to make people all-around good citizens and help them know right from wrong. Discipline is a big thing. Whether you are a young person or adult, you have to do what you are supposed to do when you're told to do it, and we teach discipline.

—Well, my concern was when the students threatened violence toward Miss Sierra. They wanted to take her out back and give her West Virginia justice. I went to talk to Mr. Mann . . . My concern was for Miss Sierra's safety . . . I could see the hostility in their eyes. They wanted to hurt her.

—It required me to sit down and tell the young cadets that hostility was not the way to solve the problem. They would quiz me and tell me that's the way Marines always handle it. And I told them, "No sir, that's not the way Marines always handle it. Hostility is a last resort and certainly should not be used in a civilian environment." They would stomp off and kick and it required myself, or Master Sergeant Meade, to take them aside and say, "Now hold it, bud." And this was male and female. In fact, the females were more hostile than the males.

Jean McCutcheon testifies. She was the teacher in third-block English class the morning Katie wore the T-shirt. Gary Pullin examines her.

—Was the Pledge of Allegiance recited?

—Yes.

—The first day that you were there when Katie was also there and the Pledge of Allegiance was recited, did Katie stand?

—Objection!

—Let me see you at the bench.

(At the bench, the judge asks where Gary Pullin is going. The attorney replies that Roger has made a big deal out of Katie being a patriot, and that her refusal to stand showed she was not patriotic.)

—Sustained.

Roger Forman cross-examined Jean McCutcheon.

—Do you question Katie's patriotism?

—The only thing I have to judge on, other than her desire to start an anarchy club . . . is her refusal to stand for the Pledge of Allegiance. That would lead me to think she might not be patriotic in the sense that I understand it.

After lunch, David Richard Daniel testifies. He is a special education teacher. Eric Engle examines him.

—I've had kids in my class who had to remove a Confederate flag or KKK shirt. There were a lot of kids talking about, well, if Katie can wear this particular shirt, then why can't we?

—Were these thought-provoking kinds of discussions?

—No, I'd consider them more angry-type discussions, off the cuff, rather than what you would [call] the intellectual-type [of] discussion.

DAY FIVE

ROGER WALKS the hall outside Judge Stucky's courtroom, stoked. Isaac, Roger's teenage son, watches his father and whispers that Roger hasn't slept all week. Roger opened the case, and so Jason is making closing arguments.

Katie's hair is wet-spiked, and she wears the same blue hoodie with the FUCK NAZI BASTARDS patch. Jason strides into the courtroom. Through the week Roger has been appealing to the intellect of the jurors. Jason, with his West Virginia accent and downhome manner, will appeal to their souls. He will be stentorian; he will be a good old boy; he will have fire in his eyes.

Eric Engle and Gary Pullin watch Jason warily as the judge is seated and the jury files in. No matter how well the two lawyers have prepared, they cannot match his passion.

Jason rises, faces the jury.

—This case is about the fundamental right that we as Americans all possess. The right to dissent. The right to present those views in a nonviolent and nondestructive fashion. The founders knew how important the right to dissent is to our Constitution. Popular speech does not need protection. Speech like Katie Sierra's needs protection.

—Students don't shed that right at the schoolhouse door. Jacob Reed and Forest Mann are the ones who caused the disruption at school that day.

—Let's take the first issue. The suspension. Forest Mann took against Katie Sierra one of the harshest actions he could take against a student. What caused the disruption? You know the answer. Jacob Reed caused the disruption. All the witnesses have testified that Katie Sierra did nothing to cause the disruption.

—What did Katie Sierra do? Did she cuss back? Act in an immature way? Absolutely not. Can you blame Katie Sierra for Jacob Reed's reaction?

—Insubordination. Forest Mann did what he did, didn't even read the documents. He alleges she distributed the documents. Amanda Bowles testified she asked for a flier. Katie gave it to her, [Amanda] returned it. There was no disruption. [Katie] was suspended solely for the content of her speech.

—Third block was a zoo. Remember all the testimony that all the boys in that class threw things at the teachers, talked back to the teachers. Everybody agreed to that. What happened to any of those individuals? Well, eight to ten boys threatened to give Katie Sierra some West Virginia justice. That was reported to Forest Mann. Was there even an investigation to even try to figure out who those eight to ten boys were? What happened? Threatening the safety of a student is punishable by expulsion. Nothing happened.

—Two. The anarchy club. How could Forest Mann know what it was if he didn't read the materials? Who demonstrated maturity throughout this case? Katie Sierra. This is the kind of student we want. We want students who dissent and challenge the government. To be critical. That is what people fought for. The right to be critical. Forest Mann predicted there would be disruption. It was a self-fulfilling prophecy. Because Forest Mann created the disturbance.

—Three. This is the shirt she wore on the 29th when she returned. What does she try to do on the back of it? What she has been trying to do all along. Explain her beliefs. The testimony was that on that day when she returned there was no problem. That was October 29. What changed between October 29 and October 30 when things started happening at the school? The school board meeting. And the statements that were attributed to Forest Mann in the papers.

—Who demonstrated reasonableness and maturity? Who did the right things? A fifteen-year-old anarchist. Who did the immature thing? The school board. They shouted her down. They wouldn't even give her the right to free speech in the meeting. They called her treasonous. They said it was like waving a Japanese flag on Pearl Harbor day.

—Forest Mann was acutely aware of the tension. He was aware of this and then he made these statements in the press? That goes to one of two things. He wasn't aware of it. Or, number two, he didn't like her and the content of her speech. He admitted he congratulated the reporter. "Good story, Eric." Would you congratulate someone who quoted you in error?

—Forest Mann . . . blew a tremendous educational opportunity. Instead of teaching students at Sissonville High School about the Constitution, he taught them about intolerance. Even as an anarchist at this time, you have the right to your unpopular beliefs. Tell the school board, tell Forest Mann that they as educators and administrators, that they have violated her right to dissent.

Gary Pullin closes for the defense.

—This case is about much more than Katie Sierra. It is also about Sissonville High School. More importantly, it is about all the students at Sissonville High School.

—Mr. Forman stood up here in his opening statement and said that Katie Sierra has an absolute right to wear her shirt to school. He told you Katie Sierra has an absolute right to form an anarchy club at Sissonville High School. After the testimony you heard, you will conclude this is not true. There are limitations. They don't apply just to Katie Sierra. They apply to all of the students.

—In looking at this case, you have to go back to 9/11 and start there. Forest Mann, his school changed. There arose on one hand a resurgence and renewal of patriotism. On the other hand there was a small group of students who opposed that. And who openly expressed their views against that rising tide of patriotism? Forest Mann told you there was increasing polarization in the school. And a rising level of tension.

—Up to October 23, there was no attempt to suppress either view. From 9/11 to October 23, it did not substantially interfere with the orderly conduct of the school. It changes on October the 22nd. Katie comes up to Mr. Mann, requests to form an anarchy club. He could not grant it, because it would be a substantial disruption. He acted appropriately.

—He told her not to distribute anarchy literature. What happened the next day? Katie goes to class with the literature prominently on her desk, so that every student coming by can see it. Four students picked it up and read it. Katie Sierra and her attorneys want to play word games with you that because she didn't get up in class and pass them around, she didn't distribute them. Ladies and gentlemen, when she made them freely available, that was in direct violation of Mr. Mann's order.

—What changed on October 23 is that Amanda Bowles walked out of third-block English class. She didn't complain about Jacob Reed or the boys throwing spitballs at the back of the room. She complained about her T-shirts and the fliers. [Katie's] real goal was to form an anarchy club and to promote the elimination of government and its leaders as we know it.

—Katie will simply not accept that trying to force her anarchy club on Sissonville High School and the principal not allowing her to wear her shirts and that calling people in Sissonville racists, bigots, homophobes, is wrong.

—Jacob Reed and the F word. And yet Katie comes into this courtroom and sits here today and wears a shirt that says, "Fuck Nazi Bastards."

—If you do what Katie Sierra wants you to do, you will in effect turn the school over to Katie Sierra and the other students. And school officials will have no say-so.

Next, Roger Forman, redirecting:

—Ladies and gentlemen, Katie Sierra is not asking you to take the school over. You allow that club, this is the policy you give back. It has to be monitored, and controlled. We're not playing word games as Mr. Pullin says. It's your Constitution, my Constitution, everyone's Constitution.

—When Katie Sierra went to Mr. Mann, she said, "Look at my shirt." He would not. She is an extremely bright and open-minded person dealing with a very narrow and rigid administrator.

—"Treason" says John Luoni. What bull! And to think that man is in charge of the education of our children. You must tell them for the sanctity of the Kanawha County Schools, the sanctity of our process, for America, you must say no, that he doesn't have the right to violate that club.

The jury files out to deliberate. Roger and Jason take off their jackets. Beneath, unseen by the jury and pinned to their shirts, each wears a button. Jason's says ABSOLUTELY NO GOVERNMENT. Roger's simply says ANARCHY.

They face Forest Mann, seated with his attorneys. Mann is wearing an American flag pin.

5

THE SIX JURORS go to lunch. They come back at one o'clock and vanish into the deliberation room. Two o'clock passes. Then three. Still no verdict. The jury is hung on some point.

Sissonville residents, visiting anarchy youths, and the attorneys mill about the courtroom. Some speculate that the lone man is the holdout. Jason Huber talks about favorite trout streams. One anarchist speaks sadly in a low voice about Katie, saying that many anarchists wish she were more hard-core. Katie had been blasted in an Internet chat room earlier that day, he says, for agreeing to talk with *Court TV*. That was "mainstream media." The enemy. But Katie liked the woman. The anarchy youths wanted a Joan of Arc. Katie was in an uncomfortable position, unable really to fit in with those in her camp, and even less able to fit in with Charleston and its environs.

At 4 PM, the bailiff announces the jury has reached a verdict. The five women and one man file in. Judge Stucky asks the forewoman to read the judgment on the three points.

On the T-shirt question, Katie loses. Forest Mann did not act improperly in forbidding it.

With regard to her suspension, Katie also loses. Mann was justified in suspending her for three days for causing a disturbance.

On the third point—the violation of her First Amendment rights when Mann denied her the anarchy club—Katie wins. She is awarded a symbolic one dollar in damages.

45

"I have the right for an anarchy club in Kanawha schools!" Roger Forman exclaims. "That's Kanawha County speaking for anarchy!"

"She's gonna have her anarchy club!" Amy Sierra says.

The Sissonville side of the spectator area is stunned. There are whispers and grimaces as the jury files out. Mann's attorneys look like they've eaten bad raw oysters.

Was not winning on the shirts a huge loss? Perhaps so. But because everyone thought Katie would win nothing, partial success was indeed victory. Roger and Jason are elated. It didn't seem like spin. Roger says he wasn't worried about the shirts. He'd appeal that decision to the West Virginia State Supreme Court.

Out in the hall, reporters crowd around Katie.

"No, I'm not scared about going back to school in the fall," Katie says. She affirms she'll start the anarchy club. A reporter asks what she'll do with the token dollar.

"I'll have to ask my mother first," Katie said, looking at Amy, then at Roger about a dozen feet away. "I'm probably going to cut it in half and give half to Roger."

Katie and Amy and several of the staff from Roger's office walk to dinner. Then the group heads to a karaoke bar on the Kanawha River. A waitress seats them. Katie has been to the club numerous times with Amy, despite the fact that liquor is served and Katie is underage. The rules have never been enforced. Katie orders a cola.

But tonight, with news of the anarchy victory on television, the atmosphere is tense. Another waitress storms over.

"Get the fuck out of here!" the waitress shouts.

Katie leaves, waits in the parking lot. Before joining her daughter, Amy strides through the crowd to the microphone. Amy is nervous. She looks steely-eyed into the crowd.

"This is a tribute to West Virginia justice," Amy announced. And then she sings, "Rocky Top."

People get up and dance. Then Amy leaves.

In the parking lot, Amy hugs her daughter, and cries.

"You've changed me so much," Amy says.

✍

IT WAS NOW months after the verdict, in the small central Missouri town of Fayette. The old Daly School, three stories and brick, located just south of the courthouse square, stood out in the neighborhood of early-twentieth-century homes and the usual Midwest collection of dead storefronts and struggling businesses in century-old buildings.

There had been a debate whether to demolish the elementary school when it no longer met modern standards, or sell it to a private party to retain it for posterity. Some residents rue the day that the decision was made not to raze the school.

Its eighteen-thousand-square feet was now home to a man, John Tinker, and hundreds of black-capped chickadees living on the grounds. What upset the social order of the community is what it took to attract the chickadees: the man was returning the schoolgrounds to nature. He'd planted tulip trees and hazelnut bushes, and allowed natives to take over the gardens: black-eyed Susans, purple flox, bachelor buttons, mullein, sunflowers. Tinker allowed them to seed out, in violation of the town code forbidding weeds to surpass twelve inches in height.

But one man's weed is another's birdseed, and the chickadees feasted on the dried flower heads while some neighbors stewed over the wilderness growing on the venerable school grounds. The only native the occupant would not tolerate was thistle, for it denied him the pleasure of walking barefoot on the grounds.

Inside, the school was a fantasy world that might be conjured by a twelve-year-old boy with a wide range of interests. On the first floor were a host of specialized rooms. In the Print Shop were several ancient and massive iron letter presses. In the Photo Room, dozens of cameras spanning a century in vintage. In the Nature Room were birds' nests, beehives, charts, and books. There was also the Library Room, the Computer Room, and, well, a kitchen. Upstairs in the auditorium was the electronics storeroom— hundreds of computers, tubes, transistors, boards.

It was in the downstairs computer room in November 2001, right after Katie Sierra's trouble began, that an e-mail had flashed across the screen from a member of the organization Vietnam Veterans for Peace. That e-mail told about what was happening to Katie. To the man, a computer systems analyst who called the school building home, her story aroused keen interest.

John Tinker had also been fifteen years old when he had found himself in a position similar to Katie's back in 1965.

⁊₂

JOHN WAS born in 1950 to Lorena Jeanne Tinker and Leonard Tinker, who was a Methodist preacher. The family lived in the western Iowa town of Atlantic.

Leonard and Lorena were upset that blacks were excluded from swimming in the public pool, so they began working in 1955 to integrate it. For one month, this was the topic of Leonard's sermons, as he and Lorena battled to overturn a state regulation that permitted this segregation. They won, and six black children were allowed to enroll in a swim class. This didn't sit well with the community of Atlantic. It was the McCarthy era, and Leonard was called a "pinko" in a pamphlet distributed throughout that part of Iowa. He was drummed out of the congregation. The Tinker family moved to Des Moines.

Lorena, for her part, was driven to help others because of what had happened to her father, a chiropractor, in 1928. The American Medical Association of Pennsylvania had been able to ban chiropractors in the state, and her father was jailed. The family had fled to Texas so her father could work, and that injustice had set her on a lifetime of activism.[1]

In Des Moines, the couple didn't rest. Lorena went to Quaker meetings. Leonard was not affiliated with any church, but was paid a salary by the American Friends Service Committee. The Vietnam War was heating up. On December 11, 1965, Lorena and Leonard and their children met at the home of William and Margaret Eckhardt to talk about how they might express their feelings against the war, and to show support for a Christmas truce called for by Robert F. Kennedy.

Everyone, including the children in the room, decided to wear black armbands, and to fast. They'd begin on December 16. School officials heard of the plan, and on December 14, the board of education adopted a policy banning armbands. The penalty was suspension. One must remember that in 1965, the majority of Americans supported the war. Students in some Des Moines high schools were chanting "beat the Vietcong."

On December 16, Mary Beth Tinker, thirteen, and Christopher Eckhardt, sixteen, wore armbands to class. The next day, John went into the boy's room and donned one. The first two were suspended, and John was asked to leave the building. They didn't return until the first of the year, when they had intended to stop wearing the armbands.

The parents sued on behalf of their children. In 1966, a federal judge agreed with the contention of school officials that the armbands would disrupt the educational process. In 1967, a full panel of the 8th U.S. Circuit Court of Appeals was split in its opinion, which meant the federal district court's ruling remained intact. That left the U.S. Supreme Court. The case, *Tinker v. Des Moines Independent Comm. Sch. Dist.*, was heard in 1968, and a landmark 7–2 1969 ruling overturned the lower court.

Abe Fortas wrote the majority opinion. "That they are educating the young for citizenship is reason for scrupulous protection of Constitutional freedoms of the individual, if we are not to strangle the free mind at its source and teach youth to discount important principles of our government as mere platitudes," he wrote in part.

Fortas noted that "only a few of the 18,000 students in the school system wore the black armbands," and that there was "no indication that the work of the schools or any class was disrupted."

Fortas said that the lower court had cited disruption as the reason for ruling against the students. "But in our system," Fortas wrote,

> undifferentiated fear or apprehension of disturbance is not enough to overcome the right to freedom of expression. Any departure from absolute regimentation may cause trouble. Any variation from the majority's opinion may inspire fear. Any word spoken, in class, in the lunchroom, or on the campus, that deviates from the views of another person may start an argument or cause a disturbance. But our constitution says we must take that risk.

The main point of the minority opinion signed by Justice Hugo Black was that the ruling would open up a wave of permissiveness in the nation's schools. He cited the growing protests against U.S. involvement in Vietnam.

The court in the ensuing years would chip away at *Tinker*, weakening the ruling. There were fewer justices who had the opinion of Fortas, when he further wrote "It is this sort of hazardous freedom—the kind of openness— that is . . . the basis of our national strength and of the independence and vigor of Americans who grow up and live in this relatively permissive, often disputatious, society."

What would the vastly more conservative court do today? Especially in the face of the wave of fear that swept the country after 9/11? It was disturbance, as opposed to raw fear inspired by an act of terror, that concerned the 1969 court. The North Vietnamese were not attacking American targets. It was "pure" speech that motivated Fortas and the majority to rule in favor of Tinker. Can free speech be tolerated in times of trouble?

The jury in Katie's case sent a mixed message. If the West Virginia Supreme Court ruled in favor of Katie on the other points, and the school board, however difficult the burden, was able to appeal it to the U.S. Supreme Court, the outlook was grim.

℘

IN THE YEARS following 1969, the Tinker decision was embedded in the arguments of numerous court cases involving schools and students. And here it was again. In October 2001, nine months before Katie's big court date, Roger Forman first argued her case in a Charleston court, seeking an injunction. He took the position that *Tinker* protected her speech.

The attorney for the school board called Katie's shirts "walking billboards" that were a "far cry" from Tinker's simple armbands. The circuit judge agreed. Katie lost that round.

To Katie, the word "Tinker" was just a name in the argument that day. She then went online and looked up the case. The next day she tore apart black cloth and wore a makeshift armband to Sissonville High School. A week later, unsolicited by her, John Tinker sent an e-mail after he'd heard of her case from the veteran's group. He urged her to stand up for her rights, and not to lose faith.

The correspondence that grew between them prompted the West Virginia American Civil Liberties Union to bring John to the state to speak in public with Katie. The first event was called "Passing the Torch," scheduled for Huntington High School on February 22, 2002. The school had the only ACLU chapter in the state. John and Katie would then speak at several universities, culminating in a talk on February 28 at the Sissonville Public Library.

The tour got off to a rocky start. Huntington High Principal Leo "Jerry" Lake forbade the event. He told reporter Eric Eyre through a spokesman that he wanted to keep order on his school grounds. But Katie and John spoke together at all the other venues, including the Sissonville Library.

℘

IN LATE October 2002, John sat in his cavernous kitchen in what had been the school cafeteria, with the brother of his ex-wife, ruminating on what happened with Katie and the court verdict three months earlier. His hair was short-cropped and he wore a threadbare pullover sweater, faded jeans, and white tennis shoes blackened by dirt. He resembled what folksinger Greg Brown calls a "hillbilly hippie."

"She didn't have any kind of support," he said, marveling at her ability to weather the ordeal. "We had the Des Moines peace group behind us, the Unitarian Youth Group. We had each other . . . Katie was alone."

Another difference was the tone she had taken.

"There was no humor or irony in our approach. Katie was all irony. It's just a difference in times, the way kids are now. I thought her sarcasm was to the point and well done."

We left the house, walking past several cords of wood. John had cut the wood from neighborhood trees that fell during storms. He used this wood to heat the school. He lives on a bare income. John never had much of a real job—just three years earlier he held his first office job, at a telecommunications firm in Iowa. He's a self-taught electronics engineer, who has worked freelance most of his life.

We went on foot to a downtown restaurant. It was a cold winter Missouri night, and John and his former brother-in-law ordered hot chocolates. John said when he went to West Virginia to give talks with Katie, he was not surprised by Sissonville.

"It's a very conservative community."

At the Sissonville Library talk, the ROTC instructor came in with the cadets.

"They marched in wearing camos, their pants tucked in their socks. They came in like storm troopers."

Yet this did not set John off. He sat and listened to the instructor talk about patriotism. John remained patient.

"When my turn came to talk, I talked directly to him and said I appreciate that he's serving his country, and he has patriotic feelings. But how does he think we feel to be basically called traitors because we have expressed our thoughts?"

John was respectful. He invoked the Constitution, and emphasized that students have the right to voice opinions.

"It's a very American thing to do. And for the school board to say they cannot is a very un-American thing to do. And when it was over, I shook his hand. It was a good moment to reach across a little political polarization."

We talked about the blanket of conformity that had settled over America. He agreed that it wasn't just "rednecks" in Sissonville. What happened to Katie was part of a much larger societal descent. By the winter of 2002, when we talked, I had begun to view what was going on in the country as nationalism—one could often substitute the word "nationalism" where the word "patriotism" was being used. One can define nationalism in many ways, and John saw a foundation in economic stresses.

"Basically, being the have-nots in society, they gain some sense of security out of an authoritarianism in their local culture. You know, when economic times get tough, the chain of command and the command authority in a society becomes more important for the survival of the community. I think of them as hardscrabble-type people. It's seen as permissiveness to let kids say anything at all."

John harbors no ill will toward his antagonists of 1965, nor those of Katie. He sees life as a continuum, in which people can become educated. There is nothing simplistic about people, or the country. He had read the online interview on an anarchist website in which Katie was bitter about the United States.

"She was talking about America being full of crap. I took her to task a little bit about that. I worry that I screwed up, made her feel bad. But it's got to be more than 'It's full of crap.' It's a bigger country than that, you know. There's a lot of crap going on for sure, but there is a lot of good about this country. If you've traveled to other parts of the world, you know that."

As our dinner neared an end, John said he's happy living in a small town. Aside from his battle over the weeds, he's accepted in the way small towns are more accepting than bigger places—it's hard to demonize anyone or be too greedy or too "anything" when you have to face that person the next day in the supermarket.

He had spent a lot of time looking in towns all over the Midwest for a big empty building on which he could build a purposefully self-contained and self-reliant life. It was his dream to be what amounts to a small-town anarchist homesteader.

As we walked back to the dark school building that loomed over the neighborhood of older homes, our breath was sharp against the night air. Historically, those who have spoken against nationalism end up isolated. "Many of those who defy the collective psychosis of the nation are solitary figures once the wars end," Chris Hedges wrote in his book, *War Is a Force That Gives Us Meaning*. I asked John how the case affected his life.

"Not in a dark way. Right after, I dropped out of society and lived in a truck in the woods for a few years. A Henry David Thoreau kind of life. I think I wouldn't have done it," he said, if not for the case. "The court case, somehow it vindicated me. It validated me. It gave me the courage to be independent. Perhaps the armband case gave me the strength to live out of a 1941 truck in the middle of Iowa."

What can Katie learn from John?

"[She'll be okay] as long as she can avoid the slippery slope of isolation and feeling marginalized."

〰

KATIE DECIDED to go back to Sissonville High School in that fall of 2002, despite continually getting anonymous hate-message-board postings on the Internet that usually were signed "RIP Sean Miller." When Katie was visiting her boyfriend in Los Angeles and Amy went to register her for classes, many were closed. A counselor, Amy said, told her, "'If you want my opinion, the teachers don't want her.'"

Amy later called the school and the secretary who answered the phone got to talking with Amy about a flap over their new principal—Forest Mann had suddenly retired after the trial. The secretary didn't know the identity of the caller. A story about the new principal was in the papers, and the office woman said "Those reporters lie. Just like with that student, Katie Sierra. She told the biggest lies on the students, this school," everything Katie said was a "big fat lie."

"I let her go on for a long time," Amy said. "Then I told her, you have been talking to Katie Sierra's mother."

Yet Katie was determined to return. On the eve of her first day of school, Michael and I were in Charleston having dinner at the downtown Chilis with Amy and Katie, whose hair was now purple. It was the time of year when the frantic buzzing of cicadas descends from the treetops, adding a tropical ominousness to the city.

Katie said she continued to get instant messages. One said, "You're going to get your ass kicked when you come to Sissonville." "I asked, 'By who? You?' I said, 'You are really ignorant. But I don't blame you.' She says, 'I hate you. You're so stupid.'"

By dinner's end, I sensed Katie really didn't want to go back. Perhaps she was doing so for Roger Forman and Jason Huber, a debt for their heroic battle. Part of it might have been that she wanted to put it in the face of the Sissonville crowd. I don't think she herself was certain why she was going back.

As we left Chilis, the streets seemed menacing.

Suddenly behind us, a man yelled, "You bitch!"

I spun, ready for whatever, but it was a drunk barking at a waitress standing in the restaurant door. Amy couldn't find where she'd parked her vehicle. As we walked in search of the SUV, the empty streets just seemed lonely. Mother and daughter began discussing how Katie should dress for the first day of school tomorrow.

"I'll wear the black shirt."

"You should wear that one about 9/11," Amy suggested.

"Shouldn't I wear my Bush shirt? Is that too strong for the first day?" This was a shirt that said INTERNATIONAL TERRORIST, with a picture of Bush in the center.[2] In one of the oddities of Sissonville school policy, students could wear pre-printed shirts with political messages; only handmade ones were prohibited.

We found the vehicle, and as we headed to Sissonville, Amy suggested we drive Katie to the front door of the school the next morning.

We showed up at the Kale house as the first color was coming to the day. Katie came down wearing the Bush shirt. Amy beamed as Michael snapped a photo. Katie also wore a "bumflap," with an American flag on it, the words ANTI-FLAG below, the name of a favored punk group. In her arms was a hard-bound folder that contained her school materials. On the cover were the words, CLASS WAR, with a Nike Swatch beneath. There was a picture of Osama bin Laden and Bert, the Sesame Street character. Also, U.S.

"They don't think I'm coming. They think I'm scared," Katie said. "Screw them. I'm not scared."

I drove us down Eden Fork Hollow. Katie did her makeup in the back-seat. She handed over an Anti-Flag CD, *Mobilize*, which we put in the player, blasting a song entitled, "Die for the Government." The song began,

> You've gotta die, gotta die, gotta die for your government?
> Die for your country?
> That's shit!
>
> There's a Gulf War vet, dying a slow,
> Cold death and the government says,
> "We don't know the source of his sickness."
> But don't believe what they say,
> Because your government is lying
> They've done it before . . .
>
> First World War veterans slaughtered, by General Eisenhower
> You give them your life,
> They give you a stab in the back
> radiation, agent orange,
> Tested on us souls
> Guinea pigs for western corporations
> I never have,
> I never will pledge allegiance to their flag . . .

We neared the school.

"I'm gonna puke," Katie said. Then: "I wonder if my friends are still my friends?"

Now she sounded like any kid going back to school on the first day. I pulled up to the door, amid a line of school buses.

"Oh my God, what am I doing!?" she asked, looking at the buzz-cut haircuts of dozens of boys, the girls dressed as they might have when Mamie Eisenhower defined fashion.

"These kids HATE me!"

Then Katie took a deep breath, got out, and vanished through the front door.

Katie lasted one week. It wasn't that anyone overtly threatened her. She was too high-profile. But the underlying tension was incredible.

Katie was now a high school dropout. With the help of Roger Forman, she took a job filing and copying at a lawyer's office. When I visited in October, she was working at a Taco Bell in the downtown mall. She kept herself politically active. When President Bush came to Charleston, not long after he choked on a pretzel in the White House and banged his face in a fall, Katie went to the event and handed pretzels out to passersby.

Katie and Amy were again fighting. Katie had a packed bag when I picked her up from Taco Bell, for she hadn't spent the previous night at home. I didn't need to be a shrink to sense a growing depression in Katie, the kind that John Tinker talked about. I encouraged her to talk with John not about politics but the personal side of things. Katie was about as depressed as I have ever seen a young person.

But there was a much larger funk. What I saw in Katie epitomized everything I was feeling, and the emotions of many dozens of people I was interviewing around the United States—progressives, Republicans, others. All felt impotent and depressed about the direction of the country. There had to be many millions of such people, though each one I talked with thought they were absolutely alone.

※

STEPHEN KENT JONES was typical of this collective mood. After I left him in New England, he'd spent his final days demoted in the program at the University of Maine, trying to get a job where he'd be able to teach without credentials. He was rejected by New York City. They had an overabundance of social studies teachers and needed mathematics teachers. He never heard back from the Mississippi Delta. Of the twenty-some Southwest Indian nations, he was accepted at the Jicarilla Apache Reservation, in the town of Dulce, New Mexico. Dulce is in the north, between Farmington and Taos.

Stephen packed his late-model Toyota Camry and drove 2,584 miles west. He came to a hill on U.S. 64 overlooking Dulce ("sweet" in Spanish). The view resembled those old tintype photos of Western towns—scattered dwellings, no trees, haphazard layout. Except it was mostly trailers and not grayboard shacks. He drove past the Apache House of Liquor, a Best Western Hotel, a single gas station, a tribal market—the entirety of the town—to the $200-a-month trailer he'd call home. It was here that he'd try to rebuild his life after the nightmare of Maine.

On his first day, students informed him that he wouldn't last; his position had 100 percent turnover for each of the previous ten years.

I showed up that winter. Stephen had asked me to talk to his students about Katie Sierra, because he found solace in her story, and the students might learn from it. To Stephen, Katie was making a stand in a country where few were standing up for their beliefs. I realized through Stephen and others just how much of an underground hero Katie had become in Homeland America.

Stephen's class was indeed a tough crowd. One girl slept through the entire class as I spoke, head down on the desk. It was school policy to allow this, Stephen whispered to me afterward. Also, only half of that first class showed up, which was common.

The second class was larger, perhaps thirty students, and there were a few more sleepers. But at least there were four or five lively faces who asked questions about Katie as I passed around Michael's photographs of her.

Dulce Independent Schools rank in the cellar. Just 30.8 percent of tenth-grade students passed the high school competency exam in the 2000–2001 academic year, according to the New Mexico State Department of Education. The statewide average was 64.4 percent. The district placed 88th in the state on the test, second-to-last. Stephen said that to pass the state test they had "to have a substantial ability to read eighteenth-century English—James Madison's Federalist papers."

Over dinner that night at the Best Western Hotel's restaurant, seated beneath the stuffed head of an elk, Stephen and another newbie teacher lamented the pressure to pass kids even if they didn't show up. Some kids played basketball to sellout crowds and needed good grades to participate. They wouldn't automatically pass kids, with bitter results. An hour earlier, I had witnessed a parent screaming at Stephen's colleague.

Stephen was a man of standards. No one was going to slide in his class. He vowed to hold his ground.

"This is just a prison with a sports program," he said as I left him that evening. "I guess I just jumped into another inferno."

But he was excited that I was going to arrange for Katie to give a talk for his students by speakerphone. He felt that the several students who came alive during that second class would learn from hearing Katie.

I drove away from Dulce. The Katie talk would never happen. Five days later, on November 18, 2002, Stephen e-mailed me in Chicago, the message header announcing, GUESS WHO'S BEEN FIRED!

> Yes, surprise, surprise, surprise . . . I was fired today from my social studies teaching position. Why? Apparently, several people did not like my personality and the fact that two thirds of the kids failed . . . that is, failed to turn in their work.
>
> Here's the deal: I seem to TRY to place myself into the worst fixes. I CHOSE to teach a unit on Islam to a community of yahoos in Old Town, Maine—filled with white people who believe in their hearts that it is America's RIGHT to control the world and its darker inhabitants. Then I go to Dulce Independent Schools in New Mexico, on the Jicarilla Apache Reservation—a district run by white people who are simply writing the next chapter of oppression and low expectations . . .

Coming so close on the heels of my visit, I felt my presence was certainly an added cause of Stephen's joblessness. The administrators had eyed me as if I were a heroin dealer as I walked the halls with Stephen. A lot of teachers watched me talk to that second class, and though I didn't say anything radical, even mentioning Katie Sierra's name in post-9 / 11 America seemed a supremely radical act.

※

BY THE TIME I made Chicago after Dulce, I was deeply in sync with the dark moods of Stephen and Katie. I was looking at the front end of a long and cold winter, feeling my own pinch by a few of the thousands of mini-Ashcrofts, those fearful of or in line with the new megaconservatism.

Here I was flying and driving all over the United States, having quit my day job teaching at Stanford University, spending many thousands of dollars with no income—and no one wanted to buy this book. Several publishers had said, "It's too Arab."

At that point, the seventy-page proposal contained not a single Arab character. There was a Sikh, whom the editors might erroneously have considered Arab, but otherwise the manuscript featured whites such as Stephen, a Republican mayor you will read about later, and Katie.

Some months earlier, I had been in Los Angeles, telling my dilemma to an actor friend. Unknown to me, she subsequently talked with a producer she knew, and this producer grew excited about the idea of doing a film on what was then the work in progress of this book. That producer talked with her boss, a big-name Hollywood executive producer. I was once again pulled into the Hollywood vortex, assuming something serious could be sold in that town. Michael and I worked up a treatment, which we pitched to a major studio.

"It's too Arab," the executive producer said just before we walked in to meet the studio bigwigs. The film, of course, never got beyond the pitch. We may as well have tried to sell them smallpox-infested blankets.

Then some good news. My new agent rang and said several editors were interested. One at a big house wanted to talk with me. When I called this editor, she began the conversation by saying, "I've been waiting for a book like this." Those are words a writer lives to hear. A few days later, an editor friend at a mid-sized house told me, "I want to buy this book. We'll make an offer Friday."

Friday came. Everything melted down. The bosses of both editors nixed the deal.

"It's not you," my new literary agent sputtered. "They all know your work, respect it. It's not the proposal. It's the material." Days later, trying to regroup, I called the agent, and she now said, "Uh no, no. It's the proposal. The proposal isn't, uh, working."

Click. I sent e-mails to the new agent. Silence. I never heard from her again. Everyone had scattered like cockroaches hit by light.

I was alone, working Chicago that November and December. I spent nights walking the ice-crusted sidewalks outside my suburban residence inn, despairing. The end of Stephen Jones's e-mail echoed in my head,

> I am hesitant to be called a "hero" in the story of Old Town, Maine . . . the story you tell in your book. I'm not a hero; I'm an antisocial oaf with progressive principles . . . Exhibit A for the prosecution's case of why the Left makes no headway.

It wasn't that he was an antisocial oaf. He was just feeling defeated, as was Katie, as was I. We were all white Arabs, as anyone was who questioned what was becoming of our country. A lot of bad news was to pile on. One of the few media outlets that eventually looked at Katie's story had been Phil Donahue, who came back to the air on MSNBC, and had Katie on his show in 2002. His ratings were bad, though getting better, and even so his was the network's highest-rated show. That wasn't enough. He was cancelled on the eve of war in Iraq. An NBC News study was leaked to Rick Ellis at *AllYourTV.com*:

"A tired, left-wing liberal out of touch with the current marketplace," the report said. It went on to say he presented a "difficult public face for NBC in a time of war . . . He seems to
delight in presenting guests who are antiwar, anti-Bush and
skeptical of the administration's motives . . . [the show is] a
home for the liberal antiwar agenda at the same time that our
competitors are waving the flag at every opportunity."

In place of Donahue, the network added an hour to its show, *Countdown:
Iraq*, about the coming war. That week, MSNBC hired Dick Armey as a
commentator.

Later, in 2003, Roger Forman would lose his appeal of Katie's case to the
West Virginia State Supreme Court.

But there were glimmers of hope back in that cold December. I'd sell this
book on my own to a publisher with some guts, my own personal Homeland hero. I'd also found hope in other areas, a process that began when I'd
gone back to Charleston.

≈

FOR MONTHS, I'd wondered what went on in the jury room. A few jurors
outright refused to talk. When I called one, she said I'd dialed the wrong
number. This was the woman I am calling Juror X.

In turn, Juror X was curious about me. She called Roger Forman and
talked to a friend who works at one of the Charleston papers. She'd written Roger a fan letter of sorts after the trial, telling him she'd learned a lot
from the case. In all his years of practice, Roger had never had a juror contact him after a trial. Roger and the newspaper friend encouraged her
to talk.

And so it came to pass that I was sitting across from Juror X in a downtown Charleston restaurant. She was initially reticent, but quickly relaxed.
We had a three-hour lunch. Throughout the conversation, she repeated,
"I'm not very educated." That may or may not have been true, but she certainly had the requisite tool for changing that: curiosity.

When she was called to jury duty, she said "I really, really wanted to be
on the case of the anarchy girl."

Why, I learned, is a long story.

The life that led her to the jury box seems out of a country song. Juror X
had married her high school sweetheart. They lived to the west of Charleston.
They didn't have children. But it was a traditional marriage: she did little with-

out her husband, had few friends, made few decisions. Then when Juror X hit middle age, the husband had an affair with a younger woman, and dumped X.

"I don't know how to be single," she said.

She had moved into a house across the river. Even though she grew up and lived around Charleston, she'd only come downtown a few times. She stayed home a lot. For several years after the divorce, she didn't unpack her boxes. A friend admonished her.

"'When are you going to move in and start a new life?'" she recalled the friend saying. So Juror X started unpacking.

She was unpacking many things. For instance, she worked with a Filipina woman. She never had friends of other races. When Juror X had to attend a family gathering a few states away, she invited the Filipina to go with her, to make the trip more fun. Some of her co-workers were shocked. "'People are going to say you're a lesbian!'" some told her. She was exasperated by such silly talk. Juror X and the co-worker went on the trip. They had a great time.

Then the towers fell, the Pentagon was hit. Juror X was so depressed that she couldn't read the papers or watch television for three days. She has friends at a local hospital who had always complained about immigrants.

"Before 9/11, it was, Why don't they learn better English? After," she said in a whisper, "it was, 'Those ragheads. Why don't they just kick them all out of here?' If they did that, we'd have no doctors and nurses."

Then Katie's story broke. Juror X was fascinated. She couldn't articulate exactly why, only that she felt free—she was moving beyond her ex-husband, save for one last vestige: a car they had owned together.

The day she walked into the courtroom, she wasn't impressed by either Katie or the principal. "I didn't like Forest Mann. He looked like a used car salesman." Katie looked so weird. But as the days advanced, her opinion of Katie changed.

"I found her to be very intelligent and educated for her age."

A fatal move by the school board's attorneys was an expert witness they brought in to talk about school safety, to justify Forest Mann's decision to bar the anarchy club. The witness billed the board $175 per hour. Oddly, the expert was very smug about her wealth when Gary Pullin asked her about her qualifications, as is done with all expert witnesses. "I'm pleased and grateful to say . . . that I make frequently more than $175 per hour. But I'm just a fortunate person."

Anything the expert could have offered evaporated at that moment in a cloud of populist resentment.

"I hate, and I don't use that word very often, but I hate arrogance," Juror X said. "She makes all of that money. That's my tax dollars right there, I thought."

By the time of deliberations, most jurors had made up their minds. The shirts were dealt with rapidly. None felt Katie should have worn them. The content was not the issue.

"We saw the shirts close up. It's not so much what is written on them," said Juror X. It's difficult to read handwriting on someone's shirt, and thus, she said, "It's going to take away from learning in the classroom. Everyone will be trying to read it."

She said she was fascinated by anarchy, and the trial taught her a lot. But in the end, the definition of anarchy was irrelevant.

"I'm not saying I'm for or against it. It said right there in that . . . student handbook, that she should be given a chance. There's a lot of things I don't agree with that people say, but they should be able to speak their piece. We debated if it was fair. She wasn't given a fair shot."

It wasn't the male juror who held out. He agreed with the majority. It was a woman. The five jurors in favor of awarding Katie on the point of the anarchy club worked trying to convince the sixth juror.

"'Can you tell her why?' we asked," Juror X said of how they talked to the holdout juror about Mann's intransigence. "That's like a mother telling a child, No! It shouldn't have been handled that way. Forest Mann, he did the wrong thing."

They finally swung the holdout. Then Juror X lived through hell after the verdict.

"I took a lot of, excuse me," she said, lowering her voice, "shit over this. Friends, acquaintances, said 'What are you, an anarchist? A communist!' This went on two, three, four days. Then it died down. I was secure with my decision."

Her continued fear of getting grief is why she asked that her name not be used in this book.

As we got up to leave, Juror X told me that right after the trial, she shed the last vestige of her old life with her husband: she sold the car and bought a new one, even though the car had a lot of miles left.

※

IT'S AT THIS point that I began to understand some things about the meaning of Katie's case. Her fight often seemed a quixotic exercise, given the noise of the right in America, and the marginalization felt by people like Katie, Roger, Stephen, and so many others. Yet two very important lessons came out of the case: education and vocalization. Katie educated Juror X, and likely many others in Charleston. This was the middle third, the group that will determine America's future. If they are presented with reason, they will respond with fairness. This is what John Tinker was talking about when he said that Americans are capable of change. The jury was certainly nothing like the kind of people who are against Ian Harvey in Florida.

Juror X was impressed by Jason Huber's closing argument, which really was a populist appeal to fairness. A lot of people who are religious and socially conservative, just as Juror X is, are not about to go with the crowd and give up basic American freedoms. I wished she had seen the First Amendment value of Katie's shirts. I was heartened, though, that the jury's logic for denying her right to wear them at school wasn't the content of the speech on those shirts.

Katie spoke out in the face of tremendous adversity. It's shocking that in a country as huge as America, so many who should have been speaking out were silent during the first post-9/11 years. Especially so-called Democratic leaders. But where were the Republican moderates? During Vietnam, Lyndon B. Johnson received some of the harshest criticism from his own party, and Richard Nixon in turn had Republicans pressuring him over Watergate. But in those first two years, save for the few, such as Howard Dean or Senator Robert C. Byrd or Congressman Dennis Kucinich, the Democrats were worthless. The Republican Party, for its part, had been almost completely taken over by radical extremists.

American journalism, save for rare exceptions such as the *New York Times*'s Paul Krugman, was perhaps the greatest disappointment of all.

In the midst of this, it took a very brave fifteen-year-old girl to stand up, and that should shame the alleged leaders.

That fall after Katie's trial, when I was feeling gloomy, Michael and I ended up in Bruce Springsteen's dressing room after an East Coast performance. (Springsteen had based his song, "Youngstown," on the first of our books, *Journey to Nowhere*.) In the room were the actors Tim Robbins and Susan Sarandon, who was off in a corner talking on a cellular phone about some Hollywood business. Sarandon was doing her best to ignore us as we talked with Robbins, but when she heard us discussing Katie, she ran over. She knew every turn of Katie's case. We began shouting our disgust over the silence of politicians who should be vocal in protesting curbs on liberties, and the failure of the media to inform.

It was some months later that Tim Robbins would do some leading of his own. He and Sarandon had been increasingly pilloried for their stand against the Iraq War. It culminated in the Baseball Hall of Fame cancelling the fifteenth-anniversary event honoring the 1988 baseball film *Bull Durham*, which starred both Robbins and Sarandon, along with Kevin Costner. Dale Petroskey, Hall president, stopped the event because political remarks by the actors "ultimately could put our troops in even more danger." Robbins had no intention of politicizing the event—Petroskey was talking about Robbins's public stand in general.

Unlike the wussy politicians, Robbins did not shrink from the attack. He spoke at the National Press Club in April 2003. Robbins noted he wanted to go to the event to talk about baseball—and nothing else. And have fun. It was Petroskey who was pushing a political agenda—the Republican administration's agenda of censorship.

"Susan and I have been listed as traitors, as supporters of Saddam, and various other epithets by the Aussie gossip rags masquerading as newspapers, and by their fair and balanced electronic media cousins, Nineteenth Century Fox," Robbins said, referring to Australian Rupert Murdoch, who owns the FOX cable news channel, Twentieth Century Fox, and the *New York Post*. "Two weeks ago, the United Way cancelled Susan's appearance at a conference on women's leadership. And both of us last week were told that both we and the First Amendment were not welcome at the Baseball Hall of Fame . . . Every day, the air waves are filled with warnings, veiled and unveiled threats, spewed invective and hatred directed at any voice of dissent."

He went on to note that after he spoke out, Petroskey ended up on the losing end of the public relations battle. Because Robbins stood up, even some detractors admired him as a man of principle.

"Sportswriters across the country reacted with such overwhelming fury at the Hall of Fame that the president of the Hall admitted he had made a mistake and Major League Baseball disavowed any connection to the actions of the Hall's president," Robbins said.

He added, "a bully can be stopped, and so can a mob. It takes one person with the courage and a resolute voice . . . And any instance of intimidation to free speech should be battled against. Any acquiescence to intimidation at this point will only lead to more intimidation."

Robbins had nailed it. As we will see later in this book, the worst thing that people can do is to cower. As history shows us, there is grave danger in silence.

Amid the slow but growing movement for people to speak out, Katie was moving on. Judge James Stucky signed an order approving her to take the high school equivalency test, as was needed for someone under eighteen.

Katie passed the GED, of course, and then in the summer of 2003 she went to live with her paternal grandfather in Panama, where she holds dual citizenship. She wanted to learn Spanish and something of her roots. She took a job in telemarketing, selling long distance service for Qwest Communications. She was supposed to make two sales a day. The first day, she made five sales, and continued at that rate. When I again talked with her in the winter, she was living in a dorm and attending Marshall University in West Virginia. She was happy and her only complaint was that the classes were too easy.

NEWS DIARY I

THE PICKUP TRUCK rolls into Lusk, a town at the Great Plains edge of Wyoming. A century-old building, shattered neon that will never again glow announcing SILVER CLIFF HOTEL, the registration cards from the final days scattered amid snow upon the floor, revealing that the rate had risen to three dollars per night by the end, in 1981. On the main drag, a diner open since forever, run by two near-death women, serving bacon and eggs to near-death farmers, who know loss, whose Chekhovian orchards are wheat and corn. The lettering CITY CAFE on plate glass is chipped and faded. There are eight tables and six counter stools of rust-flecked chromed metal, and the orange plastic covering the stools is cracked from years of use. Today's specials: beef salad sandwich and sour cream raisin pie for a buck sixty-five.[1]

The waitresses and customers, soon to be deceased. And then City Cafe will be shuttered. The town's people are going each day. An empty storefront is now occupied by an auctioneer, with estates listed, including that of Thelma Carlisle, who just passed on. Up for auction: Thelma's Kirby vacuum, a headboard, mattress, Crockpot, blanket. Each item is carefully listed in longhand on a sheet taped next to six other sheets. Who will wrap themselves in the dead woman's blanket when the winter prairie winds blow?

Who will farm the land?

The empty country comes at the truck's windshield. Now Nebraska, windswept, dusted with snow. Ice crusts the creeks. Nightfall in an abandoned town, loose boards snapping in the wind, people blown out. Leaning against the truck parked in the center of the two-lane road empty of cars, dreaming the night sky that is heavy with stars, jetliners above booming over the snowbound and harmed land.

New York City and Boston and Washington exist across the insane flatness, a night and its millions of lives in those frigid metropolises. Behind, in what California essayist Carey McWilliams called the "island on the land," the Golden State and its millions cling to the cold fogbound edge.

Meanwhile, the market is storming back. A recent book, *Getting Rich in America*, by Dwight R. Lee and Richard B. McKenzie, promises, "The accumulation of substantial personal wealth at retirement time will be a matter of choice open to almost all Americans at the start of the next millennium." James K. Glassman, writing about the book in the *Washington Post*, asserts, "If you are relatively young today and don't become a millionaire by the time you retire, you have few excuses." The annual sales of non-union Wal-Mart have surpassed those of unionized General Motors, which had been the largest company in America for half a century.

We're told it's a new economy, a new America.

The coasts and some who dwell there are another America apart from the rotting barns and dead Main Streets in the middle: two halves of a society, each unknown to the other—one comprised of the Visibles, the other the Invisibles.

For three decades, the Visibles were seen in disproportion to their actual numbers—on television, in the papers and magazines, billboards—so that they appeared to constitute a majority. Some of them lived on islands and hilltops and beachfronts, in trophy homes that you read about in the magazines. They were the new new thing. They were intellectual property, stock options, and bonuses. At their pinnacle stood a group of men identified by their annual salaries: Gary Winnick, Global Crossing, $512.4 million; Ken Lay, Enron, $246.7 million; Scott Sullivan, WorldCom, $49.4 million.

The Visibles were fresh as the plastic-wrapped furniture wheeled each week by truckloads into Silicon Valley start-up offices. They were triumphant, as indicated by an ad campaign launched for an investment bank by the agency Wieden & Kennedy. "Thanks, old economy," proclaimed the double-page ad in the newspapers of record on August 10, 2000. "We'll take it from here."

In 2000, the Invisibles included 13.5 million American children living in poverty—one out of every five kids. The Children's Defense Fund found that 74 percent of their parents worked. They took absolutely no welfare. Many held two or even three jobs in the service economy, but the wages weren't enough to bring their children out of poverty. In 1990, the Invisibles received 476 million pounds of food from America's Second Harvest, the nationwide food bank. Ten years later, that figure had more than doubled, to one billion pounds. Yet this charity by the ton wasn't enough—because of demand, many working families only got a single bag of food each month, enough for a few days.

Kids are going to bed hungry amid the reviving economy. One reason is the high rents their parents pay. In 2000, the National Low Income Housing Coalition said that in Nashville, $12.04 per hour was needed to afford a two bedroom unit; $13.44 in Austin; $22.44 in San Francisco, the nation's highest. The federal minimum wage was $5.15.

Wal-Mart was now the country's largest employer, with jobs that pay $7 and $8 an hour. There are over a million Wal-Mart workers, and more of these jobs to come, as the company aggressively opens superstores.

We Sell for Less. Always Lower Prices. Always.

—Our suppliers will have to conform to our pricing standards. We now control the bulk of retail trade in America.

Some 65,000 companies supply Wal-Mart, and march to its orders. Among them was Rubbermaid, a company in Wooster, Ohio, a town of tree-lined streets south of Cleveland. Its union workers made kitchen products and other things such as plastic laundry baskets. Good products.

—You must sell to us for a lower price. You must become leaner.

Under pressure from Wal-Mart, the union workers had to accept a two-tiered wage system at Rubbermaid, with new hires making far less. Resin costs were going up. And wages were still too high by Wal-Mart's standards.

—Get your costs down even more. We'll sell imports. So what if they're made poorly? They're cheaper. Lower your price or we will put you out of business.

Nowhere to give. If you don't sell to Wal-Mart, you don't survive. Rubbermaid was forced to merge with a larger company.[2]

Wal-Mart is now the world's largest private employer.

Cheaper. Got to have it cheaper. *Always.*

Bricks and mortar are dead.

—Steel? In 2003, let's rescind the protections against unfair trade. Import it from Russia. So what if they sell to us for less than it costs them to make it? They'd sell it for pennies just to get dollars. Let Russia have steel. That's good business for us. We have technology.

—Farming? Thousands of pigs in sealed factory buildings, never seeing the sun or earth, mechanically fed, mechanically impregnated. Genetically engineered corn, herbicides. One man with a computer and chemicals, farming a thousand acres. Don't need farmers anymore.

—Textiles? Hondurans and the Chinese will work for a few bucks a day.

Men and women let go by the Rubbermaids and General Motors and Levi Strausses. Hired by Wal-Marts and Home Depots and Office Depots. Men and women who made things with their hands, now selling things made by the brown hands of others in distant lands for three dollars a day, lands where children are not children, just small hands on assembly lines.

—Lots of jobs here. New jobs. Change with the times. If a man or woman wants to work, there's plenty of work. We've lost our work ethic. Welfare? Get off your ass and get to work.

In Kansas, Alabama, Arizona, and sixteen other states, when people call the welfare office to check on their benefits, cheerful operators answer the phones—from over eleven thousand miles away. The states now contract with a company in Bombay, India, where the operators are paid $200 a month. Delta Airlines, American Express, and many other American companies are also outsourcing phone work to Bombay.[3]

Get up off your ass and find work—in India.

Meanwhile, the bosses of those who are now employed in the United States make on average 419 times the lowest paid workers, according to *Business Week*—up nearly ten times from a factor of 45 in 1973. In Japan and Europe, the executives on average make no more than 40 times the lowest paid worker.

When nine Pennsylvania coal miners are trapped underground and are rescued alive in 2002, the *New Yorker*'s Hendrik Hertzberg puts it in economic perspective by pointing out that the mine is owned through a network of companies overseen by Citigroup Inc. Its chairman, Sanford Weill, made $18 million in 2001; he earned in five hours what one of the non-union miners got for an entire year of dangerous work that included lots of overtime.

You don't have to stand in a food-bank line to feel cheated. Many people who don't make 419 times the other workers are on the edge of becoming Invisible because of mounting bills, high housing costs, the impossibility of getting good and affordable health care. Everyone knows somebody who's been downsized. We are a nation of men and women frightened of losing ground.

Hundreds of cutbacks and closings—tens of thousands and then hundreds of thousands and then millions of diminished men and women. We've been taken, but we don't bring forth our wrath against the boss men, the money people, the corporate boards, the Republicans and Democrats, the aggregate collection of the Visibles who've sold us out.

We're Americans. We're proud. We endure.

Few of us are on welfare. At peak enrollment, amid the right wing thunder over it, only 5 percent of Americans were on it. By the millennium, just 2.5 percent were on the dole, and that figure was falling. Instead, the diminished took Wal-Mart jobs, became night watchmen, cobbling as many as three part-time jobs to make work that taken together paid less than the single manufacturing job we once had. When this doesn't enable us to pay our bills and our kids are hungry, some of us find the courage to stand in a food-bank line, to hell with pride.

No one should ever underestimate what happens to the soul of a man or woman who puts their child to bed hungry.

A year before September 11, 2001, the Invisibles were already desperate. In one house, a woman shielded her refrigerator from a visitor, who happened to catch a glimpse of nothing more than a head of cabbage and a few potatoes. She and her husband, a hardworking man now ailing, were having trouble feeding their eleven-year-old boy.

IT WAS A January night in the heart of the Cleveland winter in the year 2000 that one couple made a big decision. Times were tough, and Kenneth[4] and Pam sat at their dinner table, bills spread before them, their boy asleep in the next room. They were about do what Americans have always done. Rather than sit and suffer, it was better to be proactive: go down the river, hit the road, move on. Go somewhere, do something.

—I'm working two jobs now, an' you're workin' one, an' taken care of Joey. We ain't makin' it. Rent's goin' up. They's chargin' us like we's livin' on the beach in California. We's living with trash. Joey's pickin' up bad stuff at school. Rough kids. He's twelve. Don't want him in a gang.

—Our heatin' bill's three hundred since they deregulated. Just buying food puts us over the top. Can't buy health insurance, clothes, nuttin' else.

—Let's get out. Get where it's cheaper. Go where it's warm, won't have a heatin' bill.

The car loaded, everything stuffed in the trunk and backseat. Down to Texas—Dallas, Austin. Rents mutha expensive. They backtracked to Florida where it was worse. Two months on the road, money running out.

—Fella says there's work in the Smokies. Lots of hotels, tourists. Gotta be cheaper there.

The old car pulled into Pigeon Forge, Tennessee.

—Here we are, Pam, in the God almighty arms of the Smokies. Plenty of jobs. Five-fifty an hour. Rent . . . a grand a month.

—Just like Cleveland! How can that be? We got nowhere to go!

Up the road an hour, in the hollows with the hillbillies, where rent was six hundred a month for a shack or trailer.

—Let's live out of the car while we save dough. Five-fifty an hour, that looks good now.

A man and wife and twelve-year-old boy, camped on the riverbank.

—We're down to a few potatoes for dinner.

—Why'd we leave?

—I'll do sumpthin.' I'll fish. I'll dig for roots. I'll hit the food bank.

Gentle Touch Ministries, Newport, Tennessee, Pastor Thomas Cutshaw. Holy rollers with hearts of gold, running a food bank/used clothing store on two grand a month.

—Sure we'll give you some food, brother. See lots like you. Last month, a hunnerd and seventy-five families like ya'll. Hi't ain't no good. Things is worse than fifteen year ago. Hit's rough. Used to pay a man for a day's work.

—My Daddy made fifteen an hour back then. That'd be twenny-five now, if we still had them kinda jobs. I always thought things went up. Not back.

—Hit's bad. Folks steal the road signs to sell the aluminum. We see 'em from all over, New Jersey, Michigan, Pennsylvania. Folks startin' over.

—I'll do okay. I'll do it legal. I'm willin' to work. Me, my wife, my boy, we're gonna make it. I gotta work for the food you're given us.

—Ain't got no meat to give ya'll. Ain't much but some rice, pasta, a few cans of tomato sauce. You don't gotta do nothing. Take the food brother, and praise the Lord.

—It's a blessing, sure. Now, I'm gonna work for you folks. I don't take nothin' for free. Your sidewalk's gonna be like new when I'm done.

Kenneth took a broom, swept the sidewalk in front of Gentle Touch Ministries, on a side street of the forsaken mountain town. Pastor Cutshaw looked out the window at the man sweeping each pebble from the cracks, taking gasoline and a rag to the gum splotches.

—Lord almighty, they keep comin.' How we gonna keep feedin' 'em all?

THERE WAS NO eruption of anger from these people. The reality is that the Invisibles in any society, at any time in history, seldom connect their condition to the overarching forces doing them harm.

The only noticeable fury was among angry white males who occasionally made headlines, usually during election cycles, or when a young one took a gun and shot up a school. These white males were often found in the suburbs, and they theoretically were the most privileged members of the society, but in fact were just as likely to be one of the Invisibles or on the verge of joining their ranks. It was only the illusion of their position of power, to themselves and society, that gave them any voice in the media. The young ones in the outer suburbs slam danced to furious metal music, the older ones voted right-wing Republican and listened to right-wing talk radio. Commentators wondered why they were angry, but few ever got close to the real reason. After an election, these men and their anger were again forgotten.

Even if it were not always overt, theirs was the deep and volatile anger of a taken people ruined by a marching phalanx, a term that in olden times meant an army walking shoulder to shoulder, a shield in one hand and a lance in the other, but today was defined by an army of bankers, politicians, lawyers, and business titans gaming the system against ordinary working Americans. The rage of working men and women waited to be harvested in dark ways by someone, something, some event.

AFTER SEPTEMBER 11, 2001, the nation embarked on a new and different kind of repression, unlike the response in World War II when Japanese-Americans were rounded up. (Duly noting that there were as many as twelve hundred instant and secret detentions of Arab-Americans in 2001, 762 eventually acknowledged by the government.) A larger roundup, if not politically impossible, was unnecessary.

The team of advisers behind the president had other ideas. All the president's men and one woman had a package of policies they'd been waiting to roll out.

Six days after the towers fell, U.S. Attorney General John Ashcroft demanded Congress quickly pass the USA PATRIOT Act. It would extend wiretapping authority, and the government's power to detain anyone anytime, among other takebacks of civil liberties. It would also permit an FBI agent to get a search warrant for "any tangible thing," including library records, records of Internet use, and book purchases. There would be no need for probable cause. The FBI agent would only need to prove the information was needed for an investigation. It would also allow FBI agents to break into any home without a warrant, even if the resident was not present.

In addition to Ashcroft, John Poindexter was already inside the Pentagon working on advanced techniques to spy on citizens. (Poindexter, pulled out of retirement by George W. Bush, was the Navy rear admiral who had set up a secret government operation when he was Ronald Reagan's national security adviser. He sold arms to Iran in order to fund the Nicaragua rebels, and was convicted and sentenced to six months in jail for five counts of lying to Congress. The sentence was later overturned because of a technicality on appeal.) Others in or close to the administration, such as Deputy Defense Secretary Paul Wolfowitz, a neocon hawk, had a master plan for the world in which the United States' empire would expand even further.

This team well knew the psyche of a large block of the American people at that moment. Armed farmers roamed the empty Great Plains on night patrol, watching for terrorists digging in the earth for naturally-occurring anthrax spores. A mayor told a reporter her town was a terror target because of "Beanie Babies"—the ear tags said MADE IN OAK BROOK, ILLINOIS. Travelers looked at your bag on the subway or in the airport terminal as if you were the villain in a Hollywood terror epic. And that's if you were white.

The Bush administration claimed the precedent of World War II to justify secret detentions and secret military tribunals, but in that war a secret trial was convened once only, after eight Germans transported by submarine came ashore in 1942 to carry out terrorism. One group headed to New York City, where they shopped at Macy's and hired hookers with their operating funds. In this group were two men who hated Nazi Germany and intended to expose the plot—one a man named George Dasch. When Dasch called the FBI in New York, however, he was dismissed as a crank. He then took a train to Washington, went to the FBI, and was shuffled from office to office, no one taking him seriously. Frustrated, Dasch finally dumped $84,000 in cash on a desk to prove himself. J. Edgar Hoover wanted credit for the FBI's brilliant sleuthing, and desired to hide what had really happened. And so there was a secret military tribunal in which the defections were not mentioned. Franklin Roosevelt gave Hoover a medal for handling the case, and six of the spies were executed; Dasch and another man were thrown into prison. Dasch was released in 1948 and then quickly deported by Hoover.

That was the only tribunal in a war in which over 400,000 Americans died.

The secret detentions of non-citizen Arabs were not even controversial at first. Nor was the USA PATRIOT Act, passed by Congress five weeks after the attacks, just before Katie Sierra was suspended for wearing her shirt to school. One year later, a special appeals court would uphold the government's secret surveillance powers. Ashcroft said the ruling was "a victory for liberty, safety and the security of the American people."

GOVERNMENT AGENTS VISIT A HOUSTON CAR MUSEUM

. . . To FBI special agent Terrence Donahue and Steven Smith of the Secret Service, it was a routine mission to check out one of the more than 435,000 tips they have received since Sept. 11.

To Ms. Huanca, whose gallery was opening "Secret Wars," an exhibit on U.S. covert operations and government secrets, it was something else. "What's anti-American about freedom of speech?" the docent blurted out . . .

. . . A. J. Brown, a student at Durham Technical Community College in North Carolina, faced forty minutes of grilling by two Secret Service agents and a Raleigh police officer in her doorway (she wouldn't let them come in, and they had no search warrant). By her account, they said they were investigating a tip that she had "un-American material" in her apartment. From the doorway, they took particular note of a poster of George W. Bush holding a noose. It read: "We hang on your every word," referring to his unflinching support of the death penalty as governor of Texas.

Then there's San Franciscan Barry Reingold, who was awakened from his afternoon nap by a buzzing intercom on Oct. 23. He called down to the street to find out who it was. "The FBI" was the response. He buzzed the two men up, but decided to meet them in the hall. "I was a little bit shaken up," says Mr. Reingold. "I mean, why would the FBI be interested in me, a 60-year-old retired phone company worker?"

When they asked if he worked out at a certain gym, he realized the reason behind the visit. The gym is where he lifts weights—and expounds on his political views.

Since Sept. 11, the sessions have been heated. Once, he recalls, discussion turned to [Osama] bin Laden and what a horrible murderer he was. "I said, 'Yeah, he's horrible and did a horrible thing, but Bush has nothing to be proud of. He is a servant of the big oil companies, and his only interest in the Middle East is oil.'"

Some fellow weightlifters called Reingold a disloyal American. One, apparently, called the government.

So it was that two agents were standing in his hall. "They said, 'You know you are entitled to freedom of speech.' And I said, 'Thank you. That ends our conversation.'" When Reingold closed his door, he heard one of the agents say, "But we still need to do a report."

—*Christian Science Monitor*, January 2, 2002

Many Americans who thought they never would be affected were caught up in the act. Out of hundreds of incidents, one stood out in early 2003, described by Jason Halperin on the *Alternet.org* website and in the *Los Angeles Times*.

Halperin, who works at Doctors Without Borders in New York, and a friend were going to see the musical *Rent*. They stopped at a Midtown Indian restaurant. After the meal arrived on their table, police burst in, guns drawn. Doors were kicked open, restaurant staff—Mexican men, mostly—made to crawl out of the kitchen.

Halperin was patted down and then ten plainclothes officers with computers entered. One identified himself as an officer from the Immigration and Naturalization Service (INS), another as from the Homeland Security Department. Halperin's friend insisted they had no right to hold them.

"Yes, we have every right," Halperin reported one of the agents as saying. "You are being held under the Patriot Act following suspicion under an internal Homeland Security Investigation."

Halperin said that until then, he hadn't understood how invasive Ashcroft's law was—it negated the Fourth Amendment. When they suggested they were going to leave anyway, a New York City cop came over, Halperin wrote, hand on gun. He taunted: "Go ahead and leave, just go ahead."

Halperin was grilled because he had an out-of-state license, and was asked if he had something to hide. "We are at war, we are at war and this is for your safety," a woman cop said to him. Halperin and his friend were held for an hour and a half, then were allowed to leave. Nothing was found at the restaurant.

Most mainstream media didn't make news out of USA PATRIOT Act abuses involving ordinary diners, much less ordinary Indian restaurant owners, who ended up with guns pointed at their heads. The print press and television entertainment news played to the fearful mood of the country.

Ashcroft later admonished the press to be even softer on the USA PATRIOT Act, when he spoke to two dozen editors, publishers, and TV executives at a conference called, "Journalism and Homeland Security," sponsored by the Aspen Institute.

"The Patriot Act simply does not allow federal law enforcement free or unfettered access to local libraries, bookstores or other businesses," Ashcroft said, baldly lying. The attorney general reassured the media representatives that his department was misunderstood—that the powers of the USA PATRIOT Act were just a good tool for fighting terrorism.

AT THE *Daily Courier* in Grants Pass, Oregon, on September 15, 2001, columnist Dan Gutherie wrote about the heroism of the firefighters and those on Flight 93. The column ended with Gutherie's opinion about how Bush fled in Air Force One and did not appear in public.

He didn't storm back to the capital and lead us through our darkest hour . . . He skedaddled. The president's men are frantically glossing over his cowardice . . . They also say they were adhering to the military playbook for national emergencies. Such feeble excuses just make what Bush did look worse. The kid has lived a pampered life of privilege and games. His first time under real pressure, he bolted.

Hundreds of negative calls and letters and e-mails poured in, among them one from a man who wanted Gutherie fed to crabs. Gutherie's column was discontinued, and he was assigned to the copy desk. Two weeks later, publisher Dennis Mack fired Gutherie. Then managing editor Dennis Roler (who had initially approved the column) wrote a front-page apology.

The proper tone for the television media was demonstrated by Dan Rather, on CBS's *David Letterman Show*, six days after the destruction of the World Trade Center.

"George Bush is the President. He makes the decisions and . . . wherever he wants me to line up, just tell me where," the teary-eyed Rather said.

At the same time, Clear Channel Communications, a Texas-based radio corporation that has more than 110 million listeners nationwide, circulated a list of 150 songs, recommending its stations not play them. Among those on the list were:

—"What a Wonderful World," Louis Armstrong.
—"Imagine," by John Lennon.
—"Peace Train," by Cat Stevens.
—All Rage Against the Machine songs.

Billboards, often bearing a waving United States flag, appeared in many dozens of American cities, with the words:

UNITED WE STAND

This message was placed by the Outdoor Advertising Association of America, Inc. (OAAA), and given space by a host of billboard companies. Some ten thousand billboards went up in the days after 9/11, with the bulk, about six thousand, hosted by three corporations: Lamar Advertising Company, Viacom, and Clear Channel Outdoor, a division of Clear Channel Communications, Inc., according to Stephen Freitas, chief marketing officer of the OAAA.

Clear Channel became a giant after passage of the Telecommunications Act of 1996, which allowed ownership of multiple radio stations in the same market for the first time. Clear Channel went from forty-three stations to 1,214. Company Vice Chairman Tom Hicks is a longtime associate of George W. Bush. Hicks's purchase of the Texas Rangers made Bush a multimillionaire. Along with Viacom, Clear Channel sought further deregulation from the Federal Communications Commission. Colin Powell's son Michael was in charge of the FCC, which at that time was considering rule changes.

Being united meant not saying certain things. Bill Maher, on his television show *Politically Incorrect*, commented that the terrorists were bad, but that they were not cowards: it was cowardly to lob cruise missiles from hundreds of miles away. This drew the ire of White House spokesman Ari Fleischer, who said of Maher,

> It's a terrible thing to say, and it's unfortunate. There are reminders to all Americans that they need to watch what they say, watch what they do, and this is not a time for remarks like that—there never is.

Maher's show was soon cancelled by ABC.

Being united meant not talking to certain people. In early October 2001, Dave "Davey D" Cook interviewed Congresswoman Barbara Lee, a Democrat, on his show *Street Knowledge*, aired on San Francisco's KMEL-FM, 106.1. Lee was the only member of Congress to vote against a measure that gave George W. Bush unlimited military response power. After the vote, Lee had said, "As we act, let us not become the evil we deplore." Days later, Davey D was fired. The show was in its eleventh year on KMEL. It is a Clear Channel Communications station. General Manager Joe Cunningham said it was economics, not politics.

Being united meant not asking any questions, even at universities where questions are supposed to be asked. In November, a report was released by the American Council of Trustees and Alumni, an organization founded by Lynne Cheney, wife of the vice president. The report, "Defending Civilization," posted on a website, listed 117 comments by professors, naming them as "weak links" in the war on terrorism for asking too many questions and making statements such as "intolerance breeds hate," and "there needs to be an understanding of why this kind of suicidal violence could be undertaken against our country."

Any questioning drew the wrath of corporate giants and the White

House. The message spread rapidly: Don't Question. The television media was only interested in ratings and, beyond Maher, never was much of a problem in the eyes of the White House. The print media, which might have been, clammed up. There were few additional Gutheries after that fall of 2001, because either writers censored themselves, or their editors held them back. There was broad acquiescence.

When the executive editor of a major American newspaper visited to talk with my eager young journalism students at Stanford University in the spring of 2002, one student asked why the paper hadn't been at all critical of President George W. Bush. As his personal assistant snapped photos, the editor looked incredulous at what, to him, seemed a supremely stupid question.

"Of course we've been going easy on Bush since 9/11," the editor said.

BEFORE HE entered public office and then after he became auditor of Missouri in 1973, John Ashcroft spent weekends traveling through different states singing Southern gospel music.

> CARRY THE CROSS
> by John Ashcroft
>
> We wrestle not against flesh and blood
> But the darkness of this world
> Put on the whole armor of our God
> Let his banner of love be unfurled
> I want to carry the cross for the Savior
> I want to carry his cross; that's my goal

Like his father before him, Mr. Ashcroft is a Pentecostal, a follower of a branch of Christianity that believes in speaking in tongues, healing, and prophecy. He grew up in Springfield, Missouri, a center for Pentecostalism. His religion forbids him from dancing or drinking, but allows singing.

When he ran for president in 1997, he said: "There are voices in the Republican Party today who preach pragmatism, who champion conciliation, who counsel compromise. If ever there was a time to unfurl the banner of unabashed conservatism, it is now."

In 1999, while receiving an honorary degree from Bob Jones University, he said, "Unique among the nations, America recognized the source of our character as being godly and eternal, not being civic and temporal . . . We have no king but Jesus."

Mr. Ashcroft, while a U.S. Senator, sponsored seven failed constitutional amendments, among them the banning of abortion and flag burning, and one that would have made it easier to amend the constitution.

In a bid for reelection to the U.S. Senate, he was defeated by a dead man.

And then the Texan came calling. Mr. Ashcroft, U.S. Attorney General, enforcing the law of the land. Forty-two senators voted against their former colleague, the most negative votes ever cast in confirmation hearings for an attorney general.

Each time he took a new governmental position, he anointed himself with oil, as did the ancient kings of Israel, David and Saul.

One of his first acts was to erect curtains around two Art Deco statues—the Spirit of Justice and Majesty of Law—in the Great Hall of the U.S. Justice Department. The one exposed stone breast was now hidden. And he held devotional meetings in his office.

Like his boss, George W. Bush, Mr. Ashcroft says he seldom reads newspapers or magazines. Mr. Ashcroft hardly even watches television. He doesn't read many legal documents.

And then came the Pentagon and the towers.

We must have every tool to fight terrorism, the attorney general said, and if that meant the power to obtain information as to what books Americans were reading at their library, so be it. But certain lists were sacrosanct. For example, the FBI began examining records to learn if any suspected terrorists bought guns, finding some matches. Then Mr. Ashcroft stepped in and ordered records of gun purchases destroyed after twenty-four hours, a stance promoted by the National Rifle Association.

So the FBI could not discern if suspected terrorists had purchased guns.

SIGNS—spaced like those old Burma Shave roadside ads—posted in the brown winter stubble of a cornfield, near the hamlet of Funks Grove, Illinois, adjoining the northbound lane of Interstate 55 at milepost marker 146:

A log cabin
Castle
Or geodesic dome
Homeland Security
Starts at home
Gunssavelives.com

MR. ASHCROFT WRITES A NEW SONG

IN 1997, while walking in the predawn light of his 155-acre Missouri farm, John Aschcroft prayed about the spiritual condition of the United States, due to his concern about President Bill Clinton's sexual proclivities. He then spotted several flying eagles. He saw a prophetic message, and he penned a song.

> Let the eagle soar
> Like she's never soared before
> From rocky coast to golden shore
> Let the mighty eagle soar
> Soar with healing in her wings
> As the land beneath her sings
> "Only God, no other kings"
> This country's far too young to die
> We've still got a lot of climbing to do
> And we can make it if we try
> Built by toils and struggles
> God has led us through

There is a very strong feeling in the evangelical world that this hotly contested election . . . [meant that] God was working to put into the White House a man whose life had been transformed by accepting Christ. Then, when 9/11 happened, there was this sense that God had blessed us again to have in the Oval Office such a man when such a horrible thing had happened . . . God put George Bush there for a time like this.
—Gary Bauer, Christian Right leader, in an interview in
  American Prospect

The liberty we prize is not America's gift to the world, it is God's gift to humanity. [Applause.] We do not know—we do not claim to know all the ways of Providence, yet we can trust in them, placing our confidence in the loving God behind all of life, and all of history. May He guide us now. And may God continue to bless the United States of America.
—George W. Bush, State of the Union address, 2003

Why do they hate us? The answer to that is because we're a Christian nation. We are hated because we are a nation of

believers. . . . George Bush was not elected by a majority of the
voters in the United States, he was appointed by God.
—Lt. Gen. William G. "Jerry" Boykin, deputy undersecretary
   of defense for intelligence in the Bush White House, speaking from the pulpit after showing slides of Osama bin Laden
   and Saddam Hussein to an Oregon congregation

Our enemies are fighting in the name of Satan. You are fighting in the name of God.
—voiceover from the training film of the *Groupe Salafiste pour*
   Predication et Combat, an Algerian Islamic organization of
   fighters closely linked to Osama bin Laden's Al Qaeda

On February 25, 2002, Mr. Ashcroft sang the eagle song at a seminary in
Charlotte, North Carolina. No one could remember when a sitting U.S.
attorney general had sung in public. He omitted the lines: "We've still got
a lot of climbing to do / And we can make it if we try / Built by toils and
struggles / God has led us through." He added in their place,

> Though she's cried a bit for what we've put her through
> She's soared above the lifted lamp
> That guards sweet freedom's door
> In the dews, the damps, the watchfires
> Of a nation torn by war
> Oh she's far too young to die
> You can see it in her eye
> She's not yet begun to fly
> It's time to let the mighty eagle soar

Each computer in the public library in Monterey Park, California has a
warning taped to the screen, telling patrons that anything they read can be
the target of secret government examination.

"It feels like Big Brother," says librarian Linda Wilson, who adds she'd
violate the act if the feds ever show up. The Library Board, she says, voted
unanimously to resist.

In Maine, libraries began a campaign to get their patrons to read George
Orwell's *1984*. In Santa Cruz, California, the ten-branch library system daily
destroys records of patron's reading habits, distributing pamphlets that
say, "How can you tell when the FBI has been in your library? You can't."

MR. ASHCROFT toured the nation promoting the USA PATRIOT Act in invitation-only "public" meetings, usually with law officers, from which most of the press was barred, during August and September 2003. Advance notice of some of the meetings was kept secret. At one of them, just after the second anniversary of 9/11, he mocked the concerns of librarians as "baseless hysteria." The National Library Association and others had wanted to know how many times the USA PATRIOT Act was used to search libraries. But Mr. Ashcroft said that would compromise national security.

A study was done one year after 9/11 by the Library Research Center at the Graduate School of Library and Information Science at the University of Illinois at Champaign-Urbana. The center surveyed 1,505 public libraries out of the 5,094 in America. In that year, federal or local law enforcement officers requested patrons' records at 545 of the libraries surveyed; of these, 178 were visited by the FBI under various pretenses, said Leigh Estabrook, director of the center. Fifteen libraries said they did not answer the survey because they were legally prohibited by the USA PATRIOT Act.

A few days after labeling librarians hysterical, Mr. Ashcroft declassified information on library searches, and said that the USA PATRIOT Act had been used "zero" times.

Was someone lying?

"It's possible his agents aren't giving him all the information," said Estabrook.

IN 1965, the U.S. Government proposed the National Data Center, to collect information on private citizens. After an outcry by civil libertarians and some members of Congress, it was shouted down.

IN 2002, the U.S. Government proposed the Total Information Awareness (TIA) program, run by the Pentagon's Defense Advanced Research Project Agency, or DARPA. It would electronically spy on all Americans, recording e-mail, credit card purchases, travel and telephone records, ostensibly to track terrorists. Leading the TIA office was John Poindexter, a "can-do" kind of man—break the law, do anything, to get the job done.

> Contrary to some recent media reports, IAO [the Information Awareness Office] is *not* building a "supercomputer" to snoop into the private lives or track the everyday activities of American citizens.
> —from a report on the DARPA web site, italics from the agency

In early 2003, Congress forbid TIA from conducting further research into spying on Americans without first coming to Congress for consultation. "They've got some crazy people over there," said Senator John P. Murtha, D-Pennsylvania. The agency later changed its name, hoping to gain public acceptance with the dropping of the word "total." It was now Terrorism Information Awareness. Poindexter later resigned from the TIA office after it planned FutureMAP, a "futures market" that would predict terrorism by promoting investor speculation, with those correct profiting, as would the successful speculator in pork-belly futures. FutureMAP operated on the assumption that the marketplace could better predict terror acts than government agencies. The plan was met with ridicule and scorn from the public and some officials, and was killed. But the work of the TIA continued.

Scientia Est Potentia (Knowledge Is Power)
—The sign over Poindexter's Pentagon office door

Remember Ruby Ridge
—A homemade sign, held up by a stout steel pole on the south
    side of Nebraska Highway 12, just east of the town of Naper,
    to honor Randy Weaver, the white supremacist who in 1992
    endured an eleven-day siege of his home by the FBI on Ruby
    Ridge in Idaho. Agents shot dead Sam, his fourteen-year-old
    boy, and an FBI sniper assassinated Vicki, his wife, while she
    was holding their baby. After her death, agents greeted her
    body each morning over a bullhorn. Weaver had been set up
    on a gun charge by an informant—and after he missed a
    court appearance (he'd been given the wrong date), the Feds
    surrounded his house. The U.S. Justice Department found
    evidence of a cover-up. His surviving family was awarded
    $3.1 million in civil damages. Weaver moved back to Jefferson,
    Iowa, where he had once lived.

BOOK TWO

A flight to Baltimore-Washington International Airport. Babies crying. Full flight, all middles taken. The Washington Monument, bright spike in the night. Plane descends. A white man from Nevada, in seat 23C. Loudly says, "I hate immigrants! We should stop all immigration! Ruining the country!" Grudgingly, he adds, almost shouting. "I guess I can live with Latinos. But Muslims? Incinerate them!" Many eyes turn his way. No detection of any disagreement.

It's great. Now blacks and whites are getting along better.
    —a New York editor

Since 9/11, blacks and whites have been getting along better.
    —heard from three different people in Chicago

1

NEW YORK, **September 11, 2001**

THE CAB stops. The bearded passenger in a suit and tie is frustrated. He's in a hurry to catch a PATH train at the base of the World Trade Center for a business meeting in New Jersey. The cabbie speaks over his shoulder.

—I can't go anymore.

—Why not?

The cabbie throws up his hands.

—I think the World Trade Center is on fire.

Amrik Chawla, the passenger, cranes his head out the window, looking up at the towers four blocks distant. He sees smoke. Amrik opens the door, jumps up on the divider of the West Side Highway. To his right is a tire. A smoking airliner tire.

The tire had moments earlier blown through the building, shooting the four blocks to career off the back end of a police car crushed in the road. Amrik stares without comprehension at the wheel. He walks north, around the towers. He has no idea where he's going or why.

A roar. Amrik looks up at the belly of a jetliner, his widening eyes following it into the second tower.

The building has swallowed the plane, he thinks.

Screams. A rainfall of papers and metal and pieces of building. Bodies.

Is this one of those dreams, where I am running and getting nowhere?

A bloody woman crawls on hands and knees. Amrik helps her beneath the shelter of scaffolding. They pause. A break in the cascade of debris.

Amrik puts his briefcase over his head to protect himself. He bolts, becoming part of the mass of people fleeing toward City Hall.

Two white men in blue-collar work clothes across the street point to Amrik. The men break into a run. Right toward Amrik. They move against the crowd, opposite everyone. The man in front screams.

—You terrorist! You take off that fucking turban!

A third man joins in.

Amrik is a Sikh, not an Arab. But these men don't know the difference. To them, he's Osama bin Laden. It's a good thing he's only twenty-six, fast on his feet. Amrik sprints from the three men with violence in their eyes, running for his life for the second time in fifteen minutes.

Amrik is the first American to be victimized in the post-September 11 racial backlash.

I am seen as an enemy in the land of my birth, a country that I love.

CHICAGO, **September 13, 2001**

FOR THIRTY-ONE hours, Patrick Kelly has stewed with rage. He's watched the burning towers on television. Watched them fall, over and over and over and over. Now it's evening in the town of Justice, Illinois. He's fresh home from his job as a union heating and air-conditioning man, in his tidy little house with the brand-new deck he's just built. He's a strong man with reddish blond hair that stands up and flows back over his head. He looks younger than his forty-four years.

I want to enlist. But the Army won't take me. I'm too old.

So he fixates on the attack, feeling helpless.

The phone rings.

A neighbor says he's just driven up the "Gaza Strip," their name for Harlem Avenue on the southwest side of suburban Chicago, the heart of a community of 55,000 to 60,000 of the 150,000 Arab-Americans in greater Chicago. Many moved into the formerly white suburbs in the past two decades.

—Man, a bunch of people are marching toward the mosque. Let's go!

Patrick jumps into his truck and speeds east down Seventy-ninth Street, turning right onto Harlem Avenue and the city of Bridgeview. It's not Patrick's intention to do harm to anyone or anything—he just wants to fly his flag and show his patriotism.

As he nears the largest mosque in Chicago, he joins a crowd of at least a thousand whites, probably a lot more (no one is counting), carrying hundreds of American flags, converging, rage in their eyes and voices. The whites had already tried storming the building just west of Harlem Avenue, near Ninety-fifth Street. Police from ten departments hastily assembled a protective ring, joined by state troopers in riot gear, with shotguns. So the crowd has to settle with driving up and down Harlem Avenue with flags hanging from car and truck windows. Patrick unfurls his and joins in. Horns beep. Shouts fill the air.

Patrick nears a police officer directing traffic. The cop points to him.

—Put your flag down and go home.

Patrick drives south, turns around, continuing to parade with the other vehicles and their flags. On the return trip, the same officer again points. Patrick listens from the open window, the flag hanging between him and the cop.

—I thought I told you to put your flag down and go home!

—The Mexicans have their day. The Arabs have their day. They fly their flags. Now I'm an American in America and you're telling me to put my flag down?

The officer motions him to move forward. The cop will later say Patrick swerved at him. Patrick will say the cop walked on purpose into the side of his car.

The next thing Patrick knows, his face is being ground into the pavement. He's handcuffed, taken to jail, beginning an odyssey with the court system, and growing outrage that makes him sputter when he talks about it.

—*Thousands of people have died. They just blew up New York. This is unreal. What country am I in? Do I have to put a turban on my head and change my name to Mohammed and then scream racism? What does a white guy do? As far as I'm concerned, they come from terrorism. They believe in terrorism. If it comes down to it, they will stab you in the back. They've been throwing rocks since the beginning of time. I can't sit back and see this stuff happening.*

CHICAGO, December 28, 2001

ANNA MUSTAFA was born in Palestine. Her father was a naturalized American citizen who had returned home to Palestine. As a teen, in 1962, she came to the United States with her parents. They settled in Chicago, and she became a citizen. She later married, had seven children, ended up living in Tinley Park, in southwest suburban Chicago.[1]

She became active in community affairs as her children were growing up, serving on boards and volunteer groups dealing with youth issues, the elderly—the Chicago Commission on Human Relations, the Chicago Community Trust—and so on. She became known as an effective and reasonable organizer. In 1990, Chicago Mayor Richard Daley appointed Anna to the Chicago Board of Education. She was the first Arab-American to serve.

By the fall of 2001, she was fifty-three, her children were grown, and she had eight grandchildren. She was employed as an administrative assistant for Cook County Circuit Clerk Dorothy Brown.

Anna was horrified by the events of that fall. And she had a personal horror that came as winter set in—her father was ailing. He took a sudden turn for the worse and on December 27, she learned that he'd died. She booked a flight on Swissair to Zurich, with a connection to Tel Aviv, so she could make the funeral in the West Bank town of Betunia.

Her family took her to Chicago's O'Hare International Airport—fifteen of them in all, including her husband, children and grandchildren. They approached the check-in counter.

Anna was weak. She'd spent the night crying, sleepless. She was tired. The agent took Anna's ticket and passport. The agent saw the name, and place of birth. Her eyes rose.

—Would you like a Muslim meal? Or a regular meal?

Anna didn't think that an hour before the flight they could not accommodate special food needs. She was not thinking logically at all.

—Muslim meal, thank you!

Anna turned to her daughter.

—See how sensitive they are!

The agent disappeared into a back room office. A bit later, the agent reemerged.

—Come with me.

—Where are we going?

—Somewhere especially for you.

They walked and walked. Across the airport to a distant station with a big machine. The agent put the bags through slowly. At the far end, when they came out, the agent went up to the inspector.

—My second one today. I hope I don't get any more of those people.

This triggered a surge of anger in Anna. She'd been trained in race relations and discrimination as part of her work with the Chicago Commission on Human Relations. But she didn't need to be an expert to recognize this profiling.

—Ma'am. Can you tell me what that machine is?

—A bomb detection machine.

—Do you put all luggage on it? Please forgive me. The reason I am asking is that if you don't put all the luggage on it, I have been singled out, for whatever reason.

—FAA regulations.

—What FAA regulation?

—I am just doing my job. What they told me to do.

—Which regulation?

—I don't know. You can ask my manager.

The agent and Anna made the long walk back. At the counter, Anna asked to talk with the manager. A man who appeared to be another agent stood up.

—I'm the manager.

Anna was skeptical.

—Can I see your ID?

—I don't have any ID.

Anna could see the ID clearly around the man's neck, hidden by his tie.

—Sir, don't insult me. You are wearing it.

Another man suddenly appeared.

—I'm the manager.

Anna could see his ID. It said, CONTRACTOR.

—Right now I feel I am being toyed around with. Gentlemen, I am an American citizen and I am asking a question. And I think I deserve an answer. I was told the manager could answer it.

—What is it that you want? Your luggage has been screened. And everything is okay. You are going to be escorted to say goodbye to your family and escorted to the boarding gate . . .

—You don't escort ordinary people!

She was now angry again. But she realized that she was about to miss her plane. She held up her purse.

—Please, I want to catch my plane. You forgot to search this. Can you search it by hand, or put it through that bomb detection machine, or whatever . . .

An agent for a different airline, seated some distance away, heard the word "bomb," and began shouting.

—She said bomb!

The Swissair agent looked at Anna, himself dumfounded.

—She said bomb! What are you waiting for! Call security!

Two officers appeared, a man and a woman. The woman questioned Anna and realized there was no threat. Things seemed to be calming down, when two additional officers arrived, another male and female team. The male cop grabbed Anna's purse.

—Give us your purse! I hope you have something in there you shouldn't have!

—Here, be my guest. I have nothing to hide.

—We're not asking you. We're ordering you. Shut the fuck up!

—Sir, why are you talking to me like . . .

—You shut your face! You cannot say one word or you will be arrested!

—Wha . . .

The cop slapped handcuffs on Anna. Anna's son Murad, some distance away, was shocked.

—Can't you be a little sensitive! She just lost her dad! Why are you arresting her!?

The cop put his finger right up to the son's face.

—Six thousand people lost their moms and dads because of you people!

The cop was about to pull another set of cuffs and arrest the son, who was born in America, went to DePaul University, and had never been to the Middle East, when Anna's husband pulled him back. In the confusion, the cop lost interest as Anna began yelling not to arrest her son.

They placed Anna in a squad car, handcuffed.

The cop who cuffed her came over to the open window before they drove Anna off for booking at Grand Central Police Station. The cop pointed to his boots. The cop had a forced and sick smile on his face.

—See these boots? These fucking boots are going to stamp and dance on your father's and mother's graves!

Anna was placed in a holding area. The Federal Aviation Administration officer came in.

—I cannot make a statement without a lawyer.

The arson and bomb squad officer came.

—There is no arson and no bomb here. I cannot make a statement without a lawyer.

She overheard officers in a nearby room.

—She checks out with the FBI. They don't want anything to do with her. There's nothing in her background. She's as American as apple pie.

Then there was the voice of a woman officer.

—We don't care. We're going to get her. She fits a profile.

This woman officer came in.

—You are not cooperating.

—I want an attorney.

—You are not cooperating.

The woman officer cinched the handcuffs tighter, pleating Anna's skin. The pain was unbearable. Anna began praying to God to relieve the pain. The woman officer was happy but suspicious of Anna's work identification card.

—We don't know if you work for the clerk of the Circuit Courts or not, but if you do, we're going to make sure you don't work there anymore.

Anna was taken to the intake and booking area. The woman who did the fingerprinting sighed, talking while she printed Anna.

—Why don't you Arabs just give it up? Let them just do what they want to do to you at the airport. It says here you said you had a bomb in your purse. You know what? Here's what I recommend. My sister is married to an Arab, so I know. What I recommend is they get all the Arabs in one place, interview them one by one. And the ones they feel are not a threat, don't bother them. The ones they feel might be a threat? Deport them, or put them in some kind of camps.

Anna was now simply so tired, she didn't respond. The woman cop came in and was angry that Anna had been printed. That meant the cops could only keep her one night. Anna was soon to learn that the fingerprints did not "take," and that she would have to wait another day for a second fingerprinting. It was the weekend. That meant two nights in jail instead of one. She was held on three counts of "felony conduct."

Anna's husband was finally able to post bail. Anna was released. They had long since buried her father in Betunia.

She could not help but think: *I am a high-profile member of the Arab-American community. They are trying to make an example out of me, for every Arab-American in Chicago.*

Against the advice of her lawyer, Anna held a press conference at her home the following Wednesday, for her name was now being dragged through the mud in the papers and on television. Anna felt she had nothing to lose. The police were saying she had been screaming at the airport, and that she claimed to have a bomb in her purse. The media event went well. But she was inundated with hate mail and phone calls threatening her with death.

She would spend $20,000 on an attorney, plus an additional $5,000 she forfeited for the bond. Her trial was held nearly a year later, in November 2002. Judge Mary Ellen Coghlan found Anna not guilty of any crime.

But Anna was fired from her job for the clerk of the Circuit Court. Officials said they did not care about her guilt or innocence, that she had violated "standards."

Anna was free. But ruined financially. And without work.

2

IT WAS A DAY when the Muzak at the airports blared "God Bless America."
It was wall-to-wall 9/11, all the time, utterly inescapable—in the papers, on
radio, television. It was September 11, 2002, and I was on a jetliner heading
from California to the center of the Homeland.

The United Airlines aircraft was ascending when the pilot thanked us—
eighty-eight passengers in the cabin, another twenty-four in first class—for
flying. The plane was half full. It was 6:55 AM Pacific Standard Time. Exactly
one year to the minute earlier, I had stood on my Manhattan rooftop
watching the black cloud. Now I was looking down on rice paddies north
of Sacramento, soft and green, set in the graceful curves of dikes. Then I
was looking at grim-faced passengers. No one talked.

It seemed every journalist and writer and producer in America was
working on a 9/11 anniversary story that day. I was no different. But where
I was going there was no national press, no bands, no politicians working
a crowd, no emotional tales of heroism or loss.

✌

ON SEPTEMBER 11, 2001, Bob and Dan Sullivan[1] left their construction jobs
and came to stand on the corner of Southwest Highway and Ninety-fifth
Street in the town of Oak Lawn, southwest of downtown Chicago. The two
brothers began using their cellular phones to call friends. Their friends in
turn called other friends. The Sullivans came with giant American flags.
They felt they had to do something. They were the first to show up. By mid-
evening, there were hundreds of whites with flags. Some throttled around

in trucks with wall-sized American flags affixed to poles in the beds, or with flags simply stuck out of car windows. Rubber burned. Horns blared. There were shouts of "USA! USA!"

Police broke up the crowd. People moved west down Ninety-fifth Street. The destination was about a mile distant, where Patrick Kelly had headed: the Bridgeview Mosque, the largest in Chicago. At the same time, a different group of whites marched south down Harlem Avenue, the "Gaza Strip" to them, from an area where there are trailer courts.

The merged group faced police from ten departments and state troopers with shotguns and riot gear. The cops closed down Harlem Avenue between Eighty-seventh and Ninety-fifth streets, because it was packed with milling whites. Clerics credit the officers' fast action with saving the mosque from being burned down that night.

"We've got them out in riot gear!" Bob Sullivan said, pleased with the storming of the mosque that would continue for the next two nights. That first night, the crowd settled for roaring up and down the streets, flags flapping in the wind.

The Sullivan brothers, however, wanted some action. They saw a Muslim man with a Palestinian flag. They burned the flag and beat up the man, escaping as the police came. Later they chased a carload of Arab-Americans with their Camaro. The fleeing driver overcorrected, and the vehicle flipped over. The Sullivans would laugh when they talked about it later.

Others smashed the windows of Arab businesses, attacked people. There were numerous incidents. For example, motorcycle mechanic Robert J. Shereikis, thirty-nine, was charged with a hate crime for assaulting a Moroccan gas station attendant with a machete in the town of Palos Heights. He struck the attendant repeatedly with the blunt edge of the weapon. Shereikis was later convicted.

Alaa Naji, nineteen, was arrested after he drove on South Pulaski next to a white woman in an SUV with a GO USA sticker. "Fuck Americans," Naji allegedly said. "We are going to kill you and your whole country. Arabia will rule the world." He, too, was arrested and held in lieu of $60,000 bail on a hate crime charge.

What happened in Chicago didn't make national news. All attention was focused on New York and Washington. In other places, there were a handful of killings. Among them was the murder of Balbir Sodhi, a Sikh who, on September 15, 2001, was planting flowers outside a gas station he owned in suburban Phoenix. His family had purchased the station by pooling taxicab earnings. That morning, Sodhi had made a donation to the September 11th Relief Fund in a supermarket checkout line.

A man in a black pickup came by and shot Balbir three times in the chest. The killer was identified as Frank Roque.

"I'm an American," Roque told the officers who booked him for the murder. "Arrest me and let those terrorists run wild?"

✍

ON THE ONE-YEAR anniversary of 9/11, I pulled up to the Bridgeview Mosque in my rental car. The blocks around the mosque were festooned with tiny American flags freshly planted in the lawns. Large plastic tarp signs with flags upon them were affixed to poles at corners of the building:

AMERICAN MUSLIMS FOR UNITY AND PEACE

On one corner was a group of young Arab-American men. They were surprised that a white man parked and approached.

Three of them in their late teens took charge. When it was clear I presented no threat, all three spoke excitedly in unison, explaining why they were here—to protect the mosque from whites on the anniversary. The sun had not yet set, and that was when the trouble was expected.

"Hopefully, nothing goes down today," Jalal said, giving his real name. "But we're here."

His friends asked me to use the names "Wally" and "Tony." Wally had a Palestinian headscarf of the kind worn by Yasser Arafat hanging out of his pants. Tony told me his e-mail address was "PrinceofPalestine."

"We want them to come through!" said Tony. "We'll smash them!"

A carload of women in hijabs passed. The women looked nervous.

"We're here to protect them," Wally said. "We're going to fight back. We're not going to be pusses."

Jalal nodded toward Harlem Avenue a few blocks away, where there were already parading cars with American flags flying from the windows.

"No matter what we do, we're going to be looked at as the people who care very little about this country," said Jalal, who as a kid was struck by a rubber bullet in his native Lebanon. "I don't think it's right what happened on 9/11. But look what's happening to us now."

All three poured out a litany of bad experiences: white men trying to hit them in cars when they were crossing streets, cops stopping them all the time, people calling them "sand niggers."

"How many Japanese were put in camps?" Wally asked. "They want to do the same to us." He said they were Americans, too. "After us, it will be the Mexicans, and whatever. I thought we were one country!"

A white guy drove up and stopped. The white man glared hatefully. Then he sped off.

"Fuck you, too!" Wally shouted.

They began talking among themselves, sometimes in Arabic, other times in English, as I fell back to watch. I thought about what I'd been told a month earlier by Ray Hanania, a Palestinian-American stand-up comic and longtime journalist who also runs a local Arab paper.

✼

AS RAY EXPLAINED it, the Arab-American community in Chicago is complex. The first immigrant wave was Lebanese Christians, in the late nineteenth century. Later came two other large groups, the Palestinians and the Jordanians. The Palestinians on the North Side were Ramallah Christians; on the South, where I stood, were the Betunian Muslims. (Ramallah and Betunia are adjacent West Bank cities north of Jerusalem, the former once largely Christian, the latter Muslim.) Many Jordanese also live in South Chicago. The Arab-American and/or Muslim community was divided in Chicago, with four distinctions: the secular, the Muslim (which Ray said is largely led by "fanatics"), the Christian, and non-Arab Muslims.

Ray is a Lutheran married to a Jewish woman.

"If you are secular, you get the brunt of the hatred, and none of the 'salvation,'" Ray said.

Ray told me this about a week before he was scheduled to open for Jackie Mason, the Jewish comic, at Zanies Comedy Club. Michael Williamson and I had come north, the day after we drove Katie Sierra to school on her first day back in August 2002, hoping to catch Ray's act. But as Michael drove us into town, I read a front-page article in the *Chicago Sun-Times* about how Mason reportedly had Hanania cut from the billing. It said Mason wouldn't allow an Arab to open his act, though Mason publicly denied this. There was a very bitter public exchange and Ray—who served in Vietnam and whose father served in World War II—got the brunt of the hatred he'd talked about.

A lot of Arab-Americans also hate Ray. He knows the problems in the community and isn't shy about pointing them out, much to the resentment of the religious sector.

"There's this blonde-headed pig son called the Arab community in Chicago," said Ray, in the kind of utterance that angers some people. "No one can get along. We are here physically. But mentally we are living back home. When it comes to our own issues, we surrender to our demagogic roots. In the Arab world, self-criticism will only start a war. The Arab community doesn't want to learn how to get out of [its] hole."

Ray also blames the press for repeatedly contacting the same one or two religious Arab-Americans who always say crazy things, ignoring other, saner leaders.

Ray's fear is that the community is doing nothing to steel itself against the inevitable backlash when there is another terror attack. He agreed with me that Chicago is where it will be bad when that happens. While many journalists trek to Dearborn, Michigan, where the U.S. Census shows the greatest concentration of Arab-Americans, Chicago is much more unstable and racially divided.

It's a most upsetting prospect to Ray. It could mean a riot worse than the storming of the mosque. Or something even more off the charts, with many dead.

"Before September 11, I started keeping a journal. It had to do with hate, how I sensed a lot of anti-Arab hate. How I felt like a vampire. You can't feel you are part of the society until you see your reflection in the water. If you don't, you might as well be a ghost. If you can't see yourself in the mirror and by that I mean in the media, elsewhere, do you really exist? We aren't in the media, in the Hollywood movies, except as bad guys. We're not on the school board, in the mayor's office, on the councils. Suddenly on September 11, it's so much worse."

Ray said he made it a point to make a mandatory diary entry each day after 9/11. And now, a year later, many days were going by with no entries. He was having trouble expressing his emotions.

"It's been a while since someone called me a camel jockey. Perhaps my fears are greater than reality. But my fear is it is the calm before the storm. I think it's easier to keep tabs on people today than it was back during World War II. So they don't have to put you in a concentration camp—in a physical concentration camp. They can put you in a cyber or mental concentration camp. That's where they've put us."

Ray feared the DARPA agency and its all-seeing eye. He has firsthand experience of being watched. After coming home from Vietnam, he started a newspaper for Arab-Americans. Years later, he learned the FBI had begun investigating him back then. He filed a Freedom of Information Act request and obtained a forty-five page report. Most of it was blacked out. Of what wasn't, "it said I was involved with organizations that were involved with terrorism."

He hadn't been, and near the end, the report concluded so.

"The problem with forty-five pages is no one reads forty-five pages. They read the first paragraph that says, 'Oh, we think this guy's a terrorist.'"

Because of his experience, Ray believes he is again being carefully watched.

"I just assume my phones are tapped. And whenever my computer flickers, I assume they're reading my e-mail."

✍

IMAM JAMAL SAEED pulled up in a black car and spoke in Arabic to the dozen young men. Wally whispered that the imam was not pleased with the appearance of an Arab gang so near the mosque. The youths obliged, moving two blocks away, closer to Harlem Avenue.

Jalal wanted to show me the $20 bill trick—if folded in a certain manner, on one side there is the smoking Pentagon after the attack; on the other, in a much more striking semblance, the World Trade towers, with smoke billowing from the relative floor levels where they were hit. Also, on the side that says "United States" is the tower hit by the United Airlines plane. On the side of the bill that says "America" is the tower hit by the American Airlines jet.

Amy Sierra had shown me the trick just days earlier, and I had that pre-folded bill in my wallet. I pulled it. This impressed the young men. They suddenly trusted me more.

"It proves they knew about it!" Wally said, and by "they" he meant the Jews that he believes run the U.S. government. He pointed out that the bill was redesigned in 1998—thus it was a code for what was to come. "Osama didn't do it," Tony said. It was the Jews, he insisted. They repeated all the well-known crazy and untrue conspiracy theories (but which they believed) about Jews who didn't go to work at the World Trade Center that day.

I ask about work. Their parents had come to America for freedom and economic opportunity. All three erupted with worry about what work they will be able to find when they stop living at home. This was the biggest fear in their lives, more than the whites they were waiting to fight to protect their mosque that night.

"I hope I'm not going to stay at McDonald's!" Jalal said.

It was getting dark out. Soon I would make my way over to the white side, to see what was going on there. Before I left, Wally said, "My Grandpa wants us to move back to Palestine." He wondered if that was not a bad idea. "It's going to be worse here. Look over there! There's cops on every corner."

The police presence was stunning. Dozens of cop cars roamed the streets, or were parked on Harlem Avenue.

"Yeah, I can walk to the store here without worrying about being shot in the back," Wally said, referring to the risk of attack from Israeli soldiers in Palestine. He wondered aloud whether, if something else happens in the U.S., such random violence might follow, with whites targeting Arabs.

Then Wally said, "Being here is worse."

"I'd rather fight for my country than be around ignorant people," said Tony. And then, in an echo of what Patrick Kelly had told me, Tony continued, "I had a Palestinian flag hanging from my car. My dad says, 'Don't go out with that.' He was afraid I'd get hurt. The white people can wave the American flag. The Mexicans, their flag. And I want to have my flag."

I HEADED up Harlem Avenue. Hundreds of whites were gathered near the trailer court. I then went over to Oak Lawn, where a growing group of white flag wavers stood along Ninety-fifth Street. Dan Sullivan wore a biker scarf head wrap and a GOD BLESS AMERICA shirt. Bob wore a black Harley Davidson shirt. Both men waved refrigerator-sized American flags hooked to six-foot poles, which they thrust toward passing traffic.

Two women had three flag pins each in their hair, and also had white T-shirts upon which they'd written, with glue and glitter: PROUD TO BE AMERICAN.

"Flash them your tits, Jan," one of the women yelled to a buxom friend wearing a low-cut top. Instead, Jan waved her flag. The women flirted with the Sullivans, but the men weren't interested. Two men from Chicago's Polish community waved American flags, doing a dance. A kid, maybe ten, suddenly yelled, "There's a towel head!" He pointed to a lone Arab-American man driving past.

Every man I talked with was a construction worker. Most of the women, ranging in age from eighteen to twenty-one, were students at nearby Moraine Valley Community College. I asked several what their fathers did: they were factory workers, some on layoff, or employed in low-wage jobs. I thought about what one local Muslim woman, in a doctoral program at the University of Chicago, had told me earlier about these southwest suburbs: "It's basically lower-class whites and lower-class Palestinians," she said. "It's a bad mix."

Indeed. As I watched the Sullivans and others, what was most frightening was the reaction of those going past on Ninety-fifth Street, many hundreds of cars per hour, as they came out of the Chicago Ridge Mall. In an unscientific observation, I'd estimate that three-fourths of the whites reacted to the flag bearers by beeping, waving with enthusiasm, giving thumbs-up, or happily screaming. This wasn't a patriotic reaction to the flags—while what happened here after 9/11 had never become a national story, locals well knew the nature of these gatherings, that these were the people who had stormed the mosque the previous year. Rare was the driver who sneered, or sped past while looking away.

The night wore on. The women shouted till hoarse: "USA! USA! USA!" At one point, the Sullivans jumped on their Harleys with flags affixed, a throttling metal thunder, joining other flag-adorned vehicles racing up and down the avenue. They returned, and we stood talking. A black Grand Am slowed. The car contained three Arab men and a woman in a hijab.

"Fuck America!" one of the Arab men yelled. The car sped off. Dan Sullivan instantly sprang after it on foot.

"Look at him running!" one of the Poles said.

"Maybe he'll catch them at the light!"

The car stopped for a red light. Dan neared it, running in a rage.

"Go back to your fucking country!" shouted Sarah, a friend of the other college women.

"Look at him! He's still going!"

Dan was now almost to the car's door, when the light turned green and the car sped off. Dan came back, fire in his eyes, muttering about wanting to kick some ass.

"And it begins!" Dan said, to cheers of the group.

I went to Sarah, now sitting glumly in her car. The rear driver's side window was soaped with these words:

USA 9/11/01

ALL THE WAY

[A drawing of a heart]

The driver's window was down. In her lap, she held a burning candle in a jar. Sarah was sad that more people weren't out with them, that others in the group were having so much fun. She was drawn to come out on September 11, 2001, by anger. This year, she wanted to commemorate the dead.

I mentioned I'd interviewed some Muslim kids.

"Did they have 'attitude'?" she asked with sudden intensity. "Attitude" is the key descriptive word I've heard in Chicago from whites in describing Arab-Americans. Just by existing, by walking down the street, that often constituted "attitude."

I told her they feel that the whites out here waving the flags are racists.

"I'm speechless." She seemed genuinely shocked and hurt.

"Do you feel they hate you?"

"Yes."

She began explaining, but was drowned out by a blast of horns and screams from the nearby group, as a Trans Am burned rubber at the red light, smoke rising like a black funeral pyre; it peeled off on the green.

"—It's mutual," she said, when I could again hear. "There's no talking. From what happened last year, the Muslims hate us. And we hate them."

Pause.

"If you try to talk, you are one person going up to another person and saying everything is cool. How is that going to get around the world? It's just one person with one person. It won't do anything."

Pause.

"I'm very sensitive to the subject right now."

She stammered.

"When someone comes up and says, 'Fuck Americans,' uh, 'Fuck America,' how can they say this and call me a racist? I'm not a racist. My Dad . . . he supported me coming out here. He's so hateful against them. It is really sick. It makes me nauseous. I don't want to hear it. I really look past skin.

I'm not here to hate them. I feel something about the people who lost their lives."

She looked down at the flickering candle in her lap.

"Everyone should be holding a candle." She looked at the crowd. "Everyone here is laughing and having a good time."

I went over to Harlem Avenue where there were hundreds of whites, most with American flags. Two bare-chested men had flags painted, neck to navel, on their bodies. The crowd roared in unison.

"USA! USA!"

More screams and peeling rubber. Dozens of cop cars, both unmarked units and black-and-whites, aggressively stopped vehicles. Cops ordered people to go home or face arrest. It was the only thing that halted violence that night. I'd never seen anything quite like this in America. I stood, stunned, watching.

Nancy Pietrowski, who is fifty-six, was steamed. She and her thirty-five-year-old son, Jim, carried American flags and had walked here from their nearby home.

"It really bugs me!" said Nancy as a cop ordered her to move on. "Our very freedom!"

ON A SNOWY NIGHT three months later, I picked my way through a deep drift near Nancy and Jim's front door. We hadn't gotten to talk much in that first encounter, since the cops were ready to arrest them. Now I wanted to pull back the curtain on their anger. Nancy answered the door. Her greeting was neither warm nor cold, but wary. She walked with a hobble into the kitchen.

"Been better," she said to my inquiry.

Jim came into the room. He is a very large man, on the serious plus side of two hundred fifty pounds. He was not wary. He launched into what he saw on the evening of September 11, 2001, when he went out to the avenue with his American flag.

"They arrested anyone who wanted to stand up for their country," Jim said. "Yet they treated the Arabics like gold. The police were all around, with M-16s. The police were guarding them, their mosque. If you went over there, they said we'd suffer the consequences. They told us if we didn't leave, we'd be charged with hate crimes."

The cops had been stopping cars. Because he lived nearby, Jim had been able to steal around on foot. This had given him the freedom to watch from the yards of neighbors. Among those he observed were a group of Arab-Americans at an apartment complex on Harlem Avenue. When the cops weren't around, they shouted nasty things at the whites. Later that night, that group had an American flag.

"There were ten to twelve of them. And then they lit a match. They burned the flag."

He looked into my eyes and fell silent.

"How did you feel?"

"Do you really want to know?"

"Yes."

"I felt rage."

Now a longer pause.

"If I had a gun, I'd have shot them."

Another pause.

"How could you celebrate when at the time you thought more than 5,000 people were dead? Some of their own. Some eighty different nationalities were in the buildings."

Jim runs through a list of insults. The time he worked at the Shell station on Ninety-fifth Street in Oak Lawn, and he pumped gas for an Arab-American.

"Then he gives me twenty dollars, says, 'Go get me three Pepsis.' I said, 'No, I don't do that.' He says, 'You know what? You Americans are so stupid. You have all this trouble, black and white. And we're coming in and taking over your whole country!'"

More recently, Jim said, "They beat up my nephew over here in the park. Five of them. I went over. The kid said, 'Fuck you Americans. Bin Laden should have done more.' The one boy was about fourteen. The anger was deep in his face. The anger coming out of that kid was just terrible."

Jim said that the Arab immigrants get federal medical care. (In fact, most legal immigrants stopped getting health benefits under 1996 welfare reform—but legal immigrants who have refugee status are today still eligible for Medicaid for five years.)

"We're the infidels! If you actually hate this country, then why the fuck are you here! You can come and make all this money . . . They get the best medical care!"

Nancy grew animated, spoke for the first time. From both now poured an animosity based on their health problems: since April, Jim has had two heart attacks. Her knee is blown out, and the managed care health plan to which she belongs won't fund an operation. Nancy pulled back her top and showed a pain patch on her shoulder that she had begun wearing two days earlier. She was battling with the HMO to get the operation.

Jim cannot get Medicare. He's uninsured. He excused himself from the room. Upon returning, he held a shopping bag stuffed with papers. It dropped with a loud thud on the kitchen table.

"These are my bills. Two hundred of them. Ten thousand dollars, one of them. Fifteen thousand, another."

On the table: some $200,000 in medical bills that he cannot pay.

I thought about how the United States had never passed national health insurance, how it had been derailed in the 1930s and again in the 1990s. In 2000, the U.S. was ranked thirty-seventh in health care out of 191 countries—behind every other industrialized nation—in a World Health Organization study. The U.S. was behind most of Western Europe, Canada, and even some Middle Eastern nations. France was number one. A WHO spokesman said there were three Americas: the top 10 percent, the healthiest people in the world; the middle, which had mediocre care; and the bottom 10 percent or less, who "have health conditions as bad as those in sub-Saharan Africa."[2]

"Go see what kind of medical care they get!" Jim shouted of the immigrants. "The best!"

"They won't even give him a medical card to help him," Nancy said. "I called. I told the woman, 'It's because he was born here.' 'That's not true,' she said. I said, 'Bullshit.'"

One of Jim's prescriptions cost $96 for a two-week regimen. They cannot afford it. Nancy said a doctor took pity and gave them a few months supply on the sly. Jim hasn't been able to hold a job for two years. Nancy works at JC Penny's, selling window coverings. She rides a bus to that job.

As they angrily talk on, Jim brings up Timothy McVeigh. He launches into stories about his friends who served in the Gulf War, and how they have anger. He empathizes with the anger. Jim mentions the anthrax attacks.

"It was someone here. Not them," Nancy said. Both feel it was someone mad at the government. Nancy talks about the waste, how she read about a window part at the Pentagon that cost $10,000.

"A lot of people are losing jobs around here," Jim said. "It's a lot of blue-collar tradesmen. Some business people. People say business is not the way it used to be."

"I see a depression coming," Nancy said. "A big, real depression."

Nancy said she felt the worst of the economy. She first played the stock market in the 1980s.

"I got burned eighteen years ago, lost ten grand," she said.

That was it for Nancy's forays into the stock market. Then she watched the market going up at the end of the 1990s. She decided to plunge back in. "My neighbor said buy this one stock. He bought it for $4. I bought it for $72, just before 9/11."

She laughed a sick laugh.

"Now it's worth $4."

It was with all this as background that Nancy and Jim came out to Harlem Avenue with their American flags in hand in 2001 and 2002.

After spending time again with Jim and Nancy, I also visited Patrick Kelly in the last days of 2002. Patrick sat at his kitchen table reflecting on his arrest for refusing to put down his U.S. flag, and what had happened since.

His trial had been scheduled for early 2002. The prosecutor and Patrick's lawyer haggled, playing pretrial let's-make-a-deal. The first offer was pleading guilty to a misdemeanor charge of disobeying an officer. "No way," Patrick said. He countered: nothing on his record, six months supervision. The prosecution agreed, but added a $250 fine.

Patrick took the deal, and walked. But he was $1,600 poorer after paying his attorney and the fine. That didn't count missed work. As he left the courthouse, the prosecuting attorney warned him to keep clean. Patrick told him to tell the cop who had arrested him that this was still America.

He was free, but depressed. He desired to escape the cause of so much turmoil. So he and his wife sold their house and bought another in a more distant suburb, where there were few Arab-Americans. Now he sat in this new house, on the eve of a new war in Iraq.

"I kind of avoid that whole part of town," he said. "I saw what was going on. Rather than sit around and wait, see the value go down, I left. Like I tell all my friends, now is the time to get out of there. Some friends, they just had a baby. I said you're going to send your kid to school and you know where you are going to have to send her—any school around here, it's going to be 50 percent Arab."

Patrick was a mix of emotion about the state of America: he was cheering the coming war in Iraq—he saw it as vital—but at the same time he was fearful of what the White House and Justice Department were doing in the name of Homeland Security. He said the terror alerts were all part of a plot to take away Constitutional rights.

"The more fear he [Bush] puts in the American public, the faster it will go through. So they blow the little threat into a giant threat. And everyone says homeland security, yes, we don't care how much it costs, give it to him. It's going to be an open checkbook for wherever they need money. They are going to classify everything as homeland security. To the moon with the price. It's just another way the government is going to get into you. They're going to know everything. You're going to be a number in a society and they will know what you are doing. I'm not for it. That's why we have a military—the navy, the air force. If they do their job, we don't need homeland security. The whole thing is leaning toward that new world order."

He also worried about work and his retirement.

"This is the worst I've seen it in a long, long time," he said of construction work in Chicago.

"I had an annuity that went down the toilet," Patrick added, about his retirement account. He didn't say how much, but he said that someone he knows lost $300,000.

"The big boys are already out and gone. That's a slap on guys like me. It blows your mind when you hear about Enron and WorldCom. They're going to separate the rich from the poor again. They don't want a guy with the Local 73 of the Sheetmetal Workers' Union going out and buying a $300,000 house."

Everywhere I turned in Chicago, I witnessed anger. Nancy, Jim, and Patrick were among several dozens whites with similar stories. The ones I heard were depressingly repetitive. Prick the anger which on the surface may be pro-war and anti-Arab, and one hears of ruined 401Ks, health problems, lost work.

ON MY FIRST day of reporting in suburban Chicago in December 2001, I was searching at random for white people who had marched on the mosque after 9/11. I went straight to the Chicago Ridge Mall, because many of the marchers had been students who'd gathered at Oak Lawn High School just to the east on Ninety-fifth Street. I was worried they might be difficult to find.

It took me ten minutes.

"Man, that was the party," one youth said of the march. He was with six other teens who all started talking at once about that day. After hearing them out, I spotted two goths about a hundred feet away, both sixteen. Charlie wore a black sweatshirt with a fluorescent skull crowned with a clown hat on it; the skull had a red bulb nose. His hands were covered with all sorts of ink marks, crosses, the word HATE spelled out, à la James Agee's *Night of the Hunter* screenplay, across the top middle of the four digits. Kevin, a quiet, skinny kid, simply wore all black.

Charlie was a white supremacist goth. He hadn't been in the march. It was irrelevant. There had been enough action at school. In the previous three months, he'd been in and witnessed numerous fights with Arab-Americans.

"We call them sand niggers. Human bitches," Charlie said. They get trouble "when they make themselves known."

"What's being known?"

"A lot of kids with attitude problems. One of them said stuff."

"What kind of stuff?"

"Just being arrogant. A lot of them are blamed for what happened. Most of us atheists, we won't take it."

"Atheists?"

"Gothics. You can figure that out pretty easy."

Charlie rolled up his sleeve. HATE was written in huge letters on the underside of his forearm, along with an anarchist symbol. The fights have continued.

"There were two on Christmas day," Charlie said of the previous day. Anger reigned because his school cancelled the Christmas party. "They figured it would disturb the Arabs, cause racial problems. It pissed us off. They deprived us of Christmas. I think they should ban all Muslims from coming here. Get rid of them. A lot of us here feel just fuck the government. Just nuke 'em and forget it."

Kevin piped up for the first time, speaking of the campaign in Afghanistan. "We have nukes. We should just use them. Why search the caves? Just take one bomb and do it."

"If something else happened like September 11, what will happen here?"

"People will just start shooting," Charlie said, fast. "People will take it into their own hands."

Over the following week, I saw much of Charlie and his friends. I ate with them. Charlie gave me a neighborhood tour. After one meeting in the mall, Charlie and Kevin and a friend named Joe needed rides. I offered to take them. As we walked toward the Sears store, a group of Muslims wasn't far ahead.

"They were saying America sucks," said Joe, a police officer cadet, speaking loudly of Muslim kids in the high school. Loud enough for the Muslims in front of us to hear. "We're the best country on the planet! You don't like it, leave!"

The Muslims kept their heads down. Joe talked about kicking their asses. "They have been laying low," he said, "and they better lay low."

I dropped Charlie and the others off at anonymous and modest suburban houses, the kind that long signified the American dream, before it swelled to 6,000-square-foot trophy homes. The working class parents of these kids struggled to pay the mortgages on the tiny dwellings that, however modest, surpass Charlie and Kevin's prospects.

Instead of worrying about their bleak tomorrow, they focus on pleasures of today. Charlie and some of his friends have a group they call FTF, or "Friends That Fuck." It's a high school sex club. These kids wear vials around their necks to signify membership. I thought he might be blowing smoke, but a few days after he told me about it I saw girls with neck vials hanging on Charlie at the mall. Charlie had a hickey from the previous night.

Charlie and his friends are lost suburban kids who know their place in a service economy—a place far below the bottom rung on the ladder of success. Charlie might not be the brightest kid, but he knew his future. One afternoon, I asked about his job possibilities.

"Paper or plastic?" he rapidly responded, pantomiming bagging at a check-out counter. He laughed a sad laugh.

In other eras, Charlie would slink off to a menial but well-paid factory job, turning a bolt on an assembly line. He'd earn enough to stay drunk all weekend, get up again on Monday, go back and make the mortgage on a suburban Oak Lawn bungalow somewhere off Ninety-fifth Street. He'd muddle through, be too consumed with this life to bother with acting on his anger. We could forget about him, and our lives would go on. But today we cannot forget about Charlie, because in post-9/11 America, his anger is part of our lives.

The last time I saw Charlie, I watched him walking in the mall, HATE spelled out on his arm and fingers. I thought that if I were a billionaire, I'd do a public service television docu-advertisement featuring Charlie. I'd announce that this is what the de facto oligarchy has purchased over the past three decades with policies that enriched their kind at the expense of millions of members of the American working class.

Charlie's parents had hung on somehow during the three-decade onslaught waged upon them, and they raised a son who is about to begin adult life defeated. Now Charlie-without-a-future was with us—a whole army of Wal-Mart Charlies—friends that fuck, with HATE on their fists. *We Sell for Less. Always.* Charlie is a product, manufactured by those who live up in Kenilworth and Winnetka on the shore of Lake Michigan, over in Bloomfield Hills, Michigan, on Manhattan's Upper East Side, out in the Woodside hills overlooking the glittering Silicon Valley.

The morning of 9/11, I stood on my Manhattan rooftop wondering about the genie being unleashed. Now here was Charlie, eager for any excuse to stomp someone, something, anything. He was hitting Arabs that Christmas season, but Charlie later exercised his best option—about a year after we met, he joined the U.S. military.

3

I AM IN Chicago sitting across from an earnest young man with chiseled features, in a hash house on a shopping strip. The restaurant is named Phoenix. It's just three months after 9/11, and we're talking over dinner about what kind of America is emerging. I am trying to see a future of hope. The young man, whom I'll call Mark, sees the future in flames.

We have communicated until this moment via e-mail. He doesn't want his real name used. He is soft spoken and has intense eyes. His face is lean, but not hard. He is nervous. He should be. He's never talked with a writer before. Most writers don't talk with guys like him. He thinks I have come for a confrontation. I have come to listen. This surprises him.

Mark is a member of the World Church of the Creator, a major white power organization. The church is by many accounts the second most influential of these groups. The National Alliance is first—its founder wrote the Turner Diaries, inspiration for Timothy McVeigh.

I've sought Mark out because weeks earlier I spotted a flier on the World Church web site:

ARE YOU PREPARED
TO FIGHT THE ARAB HOLY WAR ON AMERICAN SOIL?

Beneath this was a picture of the burning towers.

"In a lot of ways, we agree on a lot of things," Mark announces a minute after we're seated. He's gone online and read some of my work in advance of our meeting. "I'm a socialist. And I don't mean a national socialist. I'm very pro-union. Very pro-environment."

This is more unsettling than anything else he could have said. We talk about unions, the environment. Indeed, if the racial component were out of the equation, one could term Mark liberal-progressive. I find myself forgetting Mark's views on race, and it is jarring to come back to the subject later.

I was also keen on talking with Mark because of a report by the Center for New Community (CNC), which said his group and others had been organizing successfully after 9/11. The center, a faith-based organization in Chicago, counted 338 "white nationalist" groups in ten Midwestern states. The report said these groups were using the terror attacks to organize.

The report stated that hate in the Midwest was changing and growing in the wake of the attacks. It described a "middle American nationalism" that was beginning to "move toward electoral and political arenas, and the targeting of young people." In defining middle American nationalism, the report said "Middle American nationalists regard the governing elites in the United States as 'globalists,' committed to the international free markets, cultural universalism and 'one world government . . . Middle American nationalism only developed as a distinct phenomenon in the years after 1990, as ethnic and racial nationalist movements mushroomed in every corner of the globe."

The scenario recalls *One Market Under God*, a book by Chicagoan Thomas Franks. Franks argues Americans were sold a bill of goods with free world trade, that we were hoodwinked, and that many Americans harbor deep resentment of the double-cross. Franks's book was dismissed by many leaders and journalists, but even if you disagree with Franks, the reality is that a large body of American workers are bitterly angry about globalization. This anger is being channeled by groups like those in the CNC report. I don't think it's a coincidence that the state with the most (seventy-three) white nationalist groups, according to the report, is Ohio: the state is at the heart of the crippled Rust Belt.

In the days after 9/11, Mark tells me, the World Church of the Creator had two organizers at the Bridgeview mosque when it was stormed, handing out fliers to whites on Harlem Avenue.

"Not many members have come out of that," he says of the immediate impact. "It's slow. We talk with them. They talk with us. It takes time. We even have cops. They have to stay real low key, because they could get in trouble."

He adds, "But they are coming. The worse it gets, the better it gets." I don't ask if he knows this was the old Communist Party line from the 1920s and 1930s.

"It's the best thing to happen," he says of the World Trade Center attacks. He quickly says this doesn't mean he's glad people died. In an act of horror, he sees redemption. "It's terrific. It takes something like this to get people listening. And they are listening. A lot of people are angry, toward immigrants, Middle Easterners."

He emphasizes that like Matthew Hale, the leader of the World Church, he does not wish any violence on immigrants.[1] I point out that opponents blame his church for stoking the hate of Benjamin Smith, whose 1999 shooting rampage killed two and wounded nine in Illinois and Indiana. The victims were black, Jewish, and Asian. His answer? He'd simply like to see non-whites leave the country. I ask if he considers himself part of a hate group.

"It's about love for me," he says, "of my people. I don't look at it as hate. I hate some individuals, but I don't hate groups. Some people in this [white nationalist organization] hate groups. Not me."

He tries to explain, saying just two weeks earlier he had spent an hour talking with a black bartender. "He was okay," Mark said. He tried to talk the bartender into hating Israel. "He didn't buy all what I was saying, but he listened."

He points to South Africa.

"Look, the blacks hate whites. When we become the minority, they're going to do bad things to us. There's no case in history where whites became a minority that they did not get attacked, their property taken."

I'm curious about Mark's economic status.

"All the good jobs are leaving the country, done in China for twenty cents an hour." He was laid off after 9/11 by a company impacted by a severe drop in business. "There are no jobs around here."

His new job requires travel. He dislikes it. But he says he needs at least ten dollars an hour to survive, and all the jobs in Chicago for which he qualifies pay seven dollars.

He talks about using economic issues to forge alliances with skinheads and others, and to bring in new members. What Mark and others tell me backs up the contention that the white nationalist groups are becoming more organized and political. From "bullets to ballots," as the Center for New Community terms it.

The World Church of the Creator and the National Alliance are not at all like the Ku Klux Klan, which Mark views as both irrelevant and a joke. Mark is proud that his group and some others are now strong organizers. Mark says they have squelched any disagreement, again confirming the CNC report.

A lot of National Alliance and World Church members don't much care for skinheads, for instance, but they don't speak about the differences in public.

"The left, they always fight each other," he says. "The left is stupid, just plain stupid. We'll beat them any time. Because we stick together."

⁂

I'D FIRST MET David Neesan, the Chicago area unit coordinator of the National Alliance, within days of my dinner with Mark. Eric Hanson, David's predecessor in Chicago, had been killed six months previous in a gun battle with cops, in which Hanson wounded two of them.

Our meeting was at a very Germanic suburban brew pub named Weinkeller. ("That's Vine-kellah," David had said on the phone.) I'd know him because he'd arrive wearing a Bavarian hat. Everything about that night was tense. David was distrustful. I was paranoid—it seemed half the restaurant spoke German, as I ate sauerbraten and those in nearby booths eavesdropped. David was more guarded with me than Mark had been.

Now, a year later, in late 2002, the Weinkeller is out of business, and we meet in front of my hotel.

David is wearing a black shirt with NATIONAL ALLIANCE embroidered over the left breast pocket, and a black leather porkpie hat. He's arrived by cab. He pulls a fat roll of bills he wants me to see, with which he pays the cabbie. I drive us to a much less tense place for dinner. He's more relaxed this year.

"I've read the Qur'an," David says. "It's brilliant. Goethe speaks high of it, so does Nietzsche." He says he understands this book, and the plight of Arabs.

"The Muslims have suffered under oppression. We're about the only group who has stood up for the Muslims in Israel. These are people from a great and honorable culture and the only reason they are being oppressed is because of the Jews."

What about Muslims here?

"We want them happy and free and living lives of fulfillment—in their own country."

A few months earlier, David had tried to bridge the gap. He telephoned a Muslim leader in Bridgeview, trying to get her to bring Muslims to a protest the National Alliance was holding in front of the Israeli consulate. They talked for an hour.

"We were making common ground," he says. "I told her your people have suffered under Israel."

But the following weekend, the leader of the National Alliance, Dr. William Pierce (who died not long after), made a broadcast from his West Virginia compound saying American Muslims should all be sent back to the Middle East.

"She didn't call me back after that."

I wonder out loud how odd it is for him to want to work with Muslims, whom his group classifies as being among the "mud people."

"The enemy of my enemy is my friend," David quickly replies.

In David's view, his issue is not with ordinary Jewish Americans. It's with the people who control the world's money and media.

"The enemy is international Zionists. It's not someone going to work making bagels, who goes to synagogue."

I turn talk away from race. Would he work with the left over common interests such as fighting the USA PATRIOT Act?

"Absolutely."

David goes on to explain that since 9/11, National Alliance members have come under increased scrutiny and have been hassled by police. He grows animated and worried when talking about John Ashcroft.

"I will work with the left, the gays, the lesbians and even Farrakhan," says David. "I will do anything and work with anybody to protect our freedoms."

As with Mark, I find myself forgetting David's racial views. In the middle of this discussion, I ask about Mark, whom I have unsuccessfully been trying to contact. David dials his cell phone and hands it to me, goes off to the restroom. I talk with another National Alliance member, who informs me that no one has heard from Mark in months. Mark had vanished into the underground of the Christian Identity movement.

When David returns, he says he'd been trying to recruit Mark to join the National Alliance.

"He's a smart guy, the kind we want." He laments not getting him to join. But recruiting has been going well.

"The National Alliance of Chicago, and I'm not blowing my own horn here, we have been the biggest recruiter." He told about a recent drive. Across the United States, the National Alliance handed out 136,000 fliers. His Chicago unit handed out 15,800.

"On most mailings and handouts, you get 1 to 5 percent callbacks, even when you are selling pizza. We get callbacks from a little less than 1 percent. We then meet with people, and let them know what we are."

He and two other members, all three of whom have full-time jobs, meet the potential recruits during their off hours.

"I spend about twenty hours a week working for the National Alliance. That's in a short week. My girlfriend left me. She didn't like not seeing me. But as wonderful as she was, there is a higher calling."

David says they have people in the unit with master's degrees—teachers, and so on.

"We seek an elite. A unit coordinator has the right to accept or reject any-one. I've had people escorted from our meetings. I'm not going to have a bunch of 'heil Hitler' morons, or guys talking about going out there with rifles. Not that I think that it's a bad idea. But we'd lose. We're in a fight for ideas. We want what Dr. Pierce called the two percenters. Those are the Americans who think for themselves. Dr. Pierce called the others lem-mings who follow the prevailing social views."

Since 9/11, they have had a more receptive collection of recruits, David said. "You can sit down in proper Chicago society and say these things," David said of the post-9/11 mood.

"We're not haters and we're not prejudiced either. Let them have their area, and just leave us alone. Let's do a war of words and a war of truth. The truth is our greatest weapon. We don't encourage violence. You have to get the truth out to the people."

Will things blow here, if something like 9/11 happens again?

"My sense is not if, but when. There's a lot of anger in people now. You can take notes on this—get this down. We do not encourage violent activ-ity. My battle is a battle of ideas, not threats of violence. But I can see it hap-pening. The very real possibility of a race war in America. The idea expressed on our website is that white people will be the last battalion stand-ing. White people are strong. White people survived the ice age."

It always comes to this—race war—David had spoken this way the previ-ous year. And so did Mark. The white nationalist right loves to invoke apoca-lypse. Over the years, as I drifted in and out of studying far right movements for newspaper stories and then for a book, I'd heard visions of fire and doom. I never gave them credence, even after McVeigh. Once in a while, a guy would go over the edge, but most of them were just doing what David talked about, a war of words that kept them occupied, along with an occasional fist fight with Jewish Defense League protesters at their rallies.

After witnessing the tension in the Southwest Chicago suburbs, I began to wonder whether another terror attack might actually lead to widespread violence.

※

MANY ON THE progressive left see a dark future. Among the most optimistic I spoke with in Chicago was Devin Burghart, a balding young man who is director of the Building Democracy Initiative at the Center for New Com-munity. As we drove past the Ernest Hemingway museum to eat lunch in downtown Oak Park, he said organizing can stop nativism and white nation-alism. His group first identified it as nationalism in 1997.

"We argue that what has happened since the 1990s is that American identity is again up for contestation," Devin said of his definition. "During the postwar period, until essentially the collapse of the Berlin wall, the United States defined itself in opposition to the Soviet Union. We weren't the communists. We weren't those godless totalitarians. Remove that from the equation, the issue of race again comes bubbling to the surface as there are those who want to define America as essentially a white Christian nation.

"I'm not an economic determinist. I don't think that economic downturn is in any way a cause for an increase in white nationalism. It does provide ample opportunity for white nationalists to organize. But it is not in and of itself cause. The perfect example of that is what happened in the farm belt in the eighties. You had a massive dislocation of families due to a variety of economic circumstances, leading to the collapse of family farming in the United States, which provided ample opportunity for white supremacists like the Posse Comitatus to come in and organize. And they did. It also provided an opportunity for progressive activists to go in and organize, like the Iowa Farm Unity Coalition."

Devin is correct in thinking that racism can exist alone, minus other factors, although I see a stronger causal relationship between economic strain and racism than he does. Devin does allow that the racial landscape is vastly different in a post-9/11 world.

"Certainly, another incident like 9/11 would have a serious impact on the American psyche. The National Alliance, it sees a second civil war. They live for that stuff. There are those two paths. We can either try to live out the ideals of being a multiracial, multiethnic pluralistic democracy. Or we can break down into some kind of protean Balkans conflict."

In the days after 9/11, Devin and a friend went to Bridgeview with a video camera and taped the whites with their flags marching around the mosque. He was terribly upset by what he saw.

At this point, a year later, does he see any energy coming from the left?

"No, none at all."

Does that make this era more dangerous?

Devin thinks for a long time, clinking the cubes in his glass of iced tea.

"Yeah, that's really the question."

4

Chicago.

OUT HERE, the suburbs, an amorphous mass of big box and old strip malls. From highway overpasses, the Sears Tower is visible as a faint spike on the northeastern horizon. In the course of an hour of driving, one sees a dozen brand-new Walgreens, evenly spaced like carpet bombs dropped during the London blitz. You always make your turn at the new Big Kmart. Landmarks notable not individually, but for their sequence, as if strands of DNA: the Big Kmart after the McDonalds, which is after the Blockbuster; not the Big Kmart after the Walgreens, which is after the Starbucks.

But then you notice differences. In the town of Justice, on Seventy-ninth, a trailer park as bad as anything in sorry-ass Alabama, a collection of ancient cheek-to-jowl doublewides. In front of one trailer is a pickup truck with a huge American flag on a pole as well as a Confederate flag, and a bumper sticker that reads AMERICAN BY BIRTH, SOUTHERN BY THE GRACE OF GOD. On Eighty-seventh: HOMEMADE POLISH SAUSAGE, and POLISH AMERICAN FAMILY COOKING. In Oak Lawn, on Ninety-fifth: BECAUSE OF YOU WIGS. MAL'S MEN'S SHOP. VELI'S KOFY KUP RESTAURANT. THE DANISH BAKER. Then Harlem Avenue, old strip shopping centers not claimed for chain stores, so they are claimed by Muslim businesses, with Arabic writing on the signs for the video store, the shish kebab house, ISLAMIC BOOKS & THINGS.

Worlds. White / black / white-Danish / white-Polish / Arab / Arab.

The radio, as you flip the dial, is Wayne's World. Zeppelin, Seger, AC/DC, Supertramp, the Doobie Brothers, Electric Light Orchestra. Almost nothing new. All white, frozen in time, a time when the race issue was just black and white, and simple. Then Martin Luther King caused all the trouble, blacks got their rights, moved in around you, so you moved out here with other white people, case closed. It's 1975 forever. Or so you'd hoped. But now Wayne's World meets Muslim World in the formerly very white suburb of Bridgeview, where on Friday you can hear the call to prayer broadcast from outside speakers on the mosque, a sad-soulful Arab voice drifting over the rooftops toward Harlem Avenue.

I watched 1,500 Muslims pour out of the building after I'd attended prayers. As I stood there, I fingered a business card given to me by David Neesan, whom I'd interviewed a few days earlier.

NATIONAL ALLIANCE CHICAGO
TOWARD A NEW CONSCIOUSNESS; A NEW ORDER; A NEW PEOPLE.

I flipped the card over:

> The National Alliance is the world's foremost organization working for the long term interests of people of European ancestry, wherever they live.
> We are not multi-culturalists. We do not want diversity. We are White men and women from all walks of life who are proud of our race and are dedicated to the concept that we must secure the existence of our people and a future for White children.
> Join us in making America safe, clean and White again!

I got in my car and drove to a place where no one publicly says such things, an ordinary-appearing suburb. Two miles south of the mosque is a sign announcing the city of Palos Heights. Despite the huge Arab population to the north and south, the town remains nearly all white, with few blacks, virtually no Jews, and some 450 Muslims out of 12,000 residents.

I thought of David in his Bavarian hat, and how, in a way, I respected him. David had struck me as honest, unlike many of the white people I would talk to in Palos Heights. This was a town with a history of conflict with Arab-Americans that predated 9/11, a history that smoldered on. Talking to David, even if there was only the slimmest of possibilities that he was open to changing his views, it was clear that he was really listening.

≈

IT HAD BEGUN on the night of May 16, 2000, at the meeting of the Palos Heights City Council.

Mayor Dean Koldenhoven started that meeting by explaining why he'd vetoed the transfer of $300,000 from the water and sewer fund to the road fund. Alderman Jim Murphy talked about procedures to remove members from the library board. Another alderman complained about too many hearses and limousines on a piece of property. It was the stuff of local government, mind-numbing to outsiders, absolutely riveting to some locals.

Then, in a report on planning and zoning, Alderwoman Julie Corsi read from a registered letter sent to her by Koldenhoven, regarding the pending $2.1 million sale on contingency of the Palos Heights Reformed Church to the Al Salam Mosque Foundation. The mosques to the north in Bridgeview were getting tremendously overcrowded and the foundation was seeking to expand; it saw the Christian church that had been sitting empty for five years as suitable for conversion to a mosque. In the letter, the foundation's attorney, Rouhy Shalabi, asked that before the sale was made final the city approve use of the church for both a mosque and a school.

Some days earlier, there had been a special planning and zoning committee meeting, and because Corsi chaired this committee, the acting city attorney had advised Mayor Koldenhoven to inform Corsi of the foundation's interest by sending the letter she was now reading. In that letter, the mayor outlined how Shalabi wanted in writing that the city would allow the mosque and school.

Koldenhoven had also called Corsi earlier on the day of that committee meeting. He asked that she not mention the sale of the Reformed Church that night, because that would be a violation of the open meeting law, which stated the city had to post the agenda publicly and in advance. She had responded: to wait longer would be irresponsible, and if she violated the Open Meetings Act, so be it. Corsi had brought up the sale at the meeting. Word had spread. And now, days later, some citizens were in the council audience to learn more.

Palos Heights was a city of twenty-one churches. But what the Al Salam Mosque Foundation wanted was not just another house of worship. The white residents knew that Muslims liked living near mosques, where weekly prayers are held. The mosque meant that Palos Heights would become a lot more Arab. No one publicly mentioned this fact the night of the council meeting, but if the mosque came, the "Gaza Strip" would stretch south into Palos Heights.

Corsi told the council that the city could not honor Shalabi's request to put in writing that the use be allowed.

"Let the buyer beware," she said. Further, Corsi suggested the city instead buy the church for use as a public recreation center.

Koldenhoven reminded Corsi of some history. He read the minutes of the March 10, 1998, council meeting, in which Corsi had then suggested the site be purchased for use as a recreation center. That led to a study. On April 14, 1998, the recreation department director recommended "that the City not purchase the building due to its cost and the cost to remodel."

Undaunted by this history lesson, and after much debate, Corsi put forth a motion to condemn the church and buy it for the city.

In the audience was Sandra Broadbent. Sandy, who is white and in her fifties, was attending a council meeting for the first time in her life. She felt like the only one who supported the Al Salam foundation—all other residents opposed the mosque.

"What struck me was nobody was talking about the mosque," Sandy recalled. She was witnessing in her neighbors what smart whites have learned—when it's a question of race or religion, one should never, ever, say so. "Nobody was saying a word about Muslims. Suddenly we need a recreation facility. If you have cancer you don't want to call it heart trouble. If they don't want the Muslims in the community, let's say it and let's deal with that. I was ashamed that I didn't say anything."

One reason she remained silent was the palpable mood of her neighbors. She was scared of them, afraid they'd do something like vandalize her car if she spoke up.

The council voted on Corsi's motion. Only Corsi and Alderman Murphy voted in favor.

The matter was far from over. The city's residents buzzed. Word was out that Corsi had lined up more votes from her fellow alderman, and that the mayor was going to be trouble.

⁂

DEAN KOLDENHOVEN grew up in what had been countryside southwest of Chicago, on a farm with three horses. As a boy, he'd sold chickens and other farm products to the mostly black town of Robbins. He is white but got along well with black people. That was in the early 1950s, and he'd detected no animosity when he walked the streets of Robbins.

Dean is a tall man, imposing and yet kind, with huge ears that extend beyond his preferred buzz-cut hairstyle. He'd married a woman named Ruth, embarked on a trade when he joined the Local 21 Bricklayers' Union in May 1954. Later he founded his own company. The couple had four children. In the early 1970s, they moved to Palos Heights.

Dean became involved in girl's and boy's softball, then grew active in the nuts and bolts activity of local government, becoming a member of the zoning board of appeals, and then zoning commissioner. He also was a Republican precinct captain and was a deeply religious member of the Palos Heights Christian Reformed Church.

In numerous ways, Dean was typical of the residents of Palos Heights, a large number of whom, like Koldenhoven, traced their roots to the Dutch; another dominant group was the Irish. Because Dean was Republican and he fit in and knew the community, he decided to run for mayor in 1997. He was easily elected.

By all accounts, he'd been a good mayor for those first three years. Dean had worked with the Cook County Tax Assessor to reduce tax rates charged to local business owners. And he'd garnered $9 million in grants from the county, state, and federal government, having numerous face-to-face meetings with higher officials to land them. He stood out among the dozens of mayors of the suburban cities that ring Chicago. Many residents affectionately called him "Mayor Dean." His campaign flier summed up his attitude about life. The flier's cover, quoting a sign on the wall of *Shishu Bhavan*, a children's home in Calcutta, said in part,

> People are unreasonable, illogical, and self-centered, love them anyway.
>
> If you do good, people will accuse you of selfish, ulterior motives, do good anyway.
>
> The good you do will be forgotten tomorrow, do good anyway.

※

BECAUSE OF THE expected crowd over the mosque issue, the next council meeting was held in the city's current recreation center, across from the empty church that was for sale. The center could accommodate a larger audience than city hall.

When Dean showed up that evening of June 20, 2000, a mob waited outside. People glared, stood in an intimidating manner. He saw expressions that he'd never seen worn by Palos Heights residents. He looked each resident in the eye as he walked to the door, tight-faced, hands almost forming fists. After all, he was a bricklayer, used to the rough and tumble. No one was going to intimidate Mayor Dean.

In addition to this public challenge, he and Ruth were going through a private one. Their thirty-five-year-old son, Donald, had been diagnosed with terminal cancer.

The crowd filed into the recreation center on West 127th Street. It was standing room only.

In the audience was Michael Vander Weele, an English professor at Trinity College, a small Christian university located in town. He had come because a friend opposed the mosque, and Vander Weele was appalled. How could he be a Christian and condone racism? Like Mayor Dean, Vander Weele was Dutch. There was no synagogue in town, for there were virtually no Jews. The conflict was definitely Arab-Christian, the more befuddling to Mayor Dean and Vander Weele because of the history of Dutch tolerance of other cultures.

As Mayor Dean walked in, Vander Weele raised a fist.

"*Sterkte!*" Vander Weele said, using the Dutch word for "strength."

This buoyed Mayor Dean.

Among the two hundred or so whites were a smattering of Arab-Americans. Most whites of Palos Heights were anti-mosque, and their main allies among the aldermen were Julie Corsi and Jim Murphy. Murphy had made a slip two weeks earlier, when in an interview with the local paper, the *Daily Southtown*, he said the city should have acted earlier to buy the church. He told the reporter, "If someone had intervened early on to stop Adolf Hitler, there might not have been a world war."

Murphy violated the subtlety of modern racial code. Had he kept on message, kept to the script, he would have intoned the mantra that the city needed a recreation center. When the quote hit the paper, Murphy apologized and gave the usual backpedaling remarks men give in such situations. But the whites against the mosque, who by now had gathered 1,700 signatures saying they wanted the new recreation center, stuck to the script. Print reporters noted in their stories that it was difficult to get residents to speak honestly on the record. They were smarter than Murphy. But off the record, they told reporters that they hated Muslims, and didn't want them to come. This is the kind of animosity that already existed against Muslims in some parts of America in the year 2000. It's what had made many Americans blame Muslims immediately after the 1995 bombing of the Alfred P. Murrah Building in Oklahoma City.

The Pledge of Allegiance was recited. Several Muslims stood but didn't say the words. The routine business was rapidly dealt with, and then the meeting turned to the Al Salam Mosque Foundation's desire to purchase the empty church.

Alderwoman Corsi told of a resident who said her family had spent $8,700 in fees to use recreation facilities in other nearby communities, a situation that could change if Palos Heights expanded its recreation center.

Then residents spoke, their lengthy comments filling the city council minutes for several pages of the official record, though abbreviated. Many stuck to the need for a recreation center, while others said there would be too much traffic during Friday prayer services. When a Muslim spoke, there were snickers in the crowd.

The public comments period ended, and the council attended to other business. At the very end, the mosque again came up. Corsi and Murphy had cooked up a plan. Another alderman announced an offer: the city would give the Al Salam Mosque Foundation $200,000 to "cover its expenses" and drop its bid, which would allow the city to purchase the church. Murphy seconded the motion. It was approved, 5–3.

Eyes in the room turned to Mayor Dean. Would he commit political suicide and veto the offer? The easy way out for him, one that would mirror politics in Washington, would be to hide behind the cover of the aldermen: he could go on record as being opposed, but say it was out of his hands, allowing the anti-mosque aldermen to win.

The meeting adjourned just before midnight. Mayor Dean gave no hint what he'd do. But as he walked into the June night, he knew. There wasn't a second of thought behind his decision.

⁕

EMOTIONAL WOUNDS FESTERED in Palos Heights. Behind the closed doors of the suburban homes, ugly things were said about Muslims. The speakers were people who then went on Sundays to the town's twenty-one Christian churches, where there was silence about the issue from the pulpits.

At St. Alexander's, a Catholic church just off Harlem Avenue, Father Ed Cronin had been bothered by the hatred that brewed among his parishioners. As the weeks wore on, he'd bit his lip and didn't say anything. Then came Pentecost Sunday in May, when he was listening to a reader reciting from Acts of the Apostles:

> When the day of Pentecost had come, they were all together in one place. And suddenly from heaven there came a sound like the rush of a violent wind, and it filled the entire house where they were sitting. Divided tongues, as of fire, appeared among them, and a tongue rested on each of them. All of them were

filled with the Holy Spirit and began to speak in other languages, as the Spirit gave them the ability.

Now they were devout Jews from every nation under heaven
living in Jerusalem. And at this sound, the crowd gathered and
was bewildered, because each one heard them speaking in the
native language of each. Amazed and astonished, they asked,
"Are not all these who are speaking Galileans? And how is it that
we hear, each of us, in our native languages? Parthians, Medes,
Elamites, and residents of Mesopotamia, Judea and Cappado-
cia, Pontus and Asia, Phrygia and Pamphylia, Egypt and the
parts of Libya belonging to Cyrene, and visitors from Rome,
both Jews and proselytes, Cretans and Arabs . . ."

And Arabs.

With those two words, something snapped in Father Cronin. It was like
the spirit entered him. He thought:

*And Arabs, too. We're in America! What does it mean to support the Constitu-
tion, my faith? They're alongside us voting, they are nurses and doctors at the hospital. What are we doing? If we are in the spirit of Jesus, they are our brothers and
sisters, too.*

He threw out his prepared homily and excoriated parishioners for not living the words of their faith by opposing the mosque. His voice rose, and he
knew he was pushing the congregation out of its comfort zone. The sermon
struck deep. At the end, many parishioners walked out with their heads
hung. Others glared angrily.

The sermon flew across town. No media covered it. In an age of dis-
connected community, word of mouth still functioned, and the words of
Father Cronin were a hot topic in Palos Heights in the following days. A few
other churches were suddenly embarrassed. Father Cronin began talking
to them. Thus began an ecumenical coalition to counter the hate, comprising just six out of the twenty-one churches in town.

"We can't call ourselves America if we do this," he later said. "I said I
don't care if they can't get along in Palestine and Jerusalem. We have to
show Palestine and Israel how it can happen. You can do this."

But the resentment was strong.

"I said, 'No! Come on people. We have to rise to the occasion.'"

Father Cronin is Irish-American, as are many of his parishioners. He tried
to talk with them about their own hurts in comparison with the Muslims.
He said Irish-Americans should be able to relate to the injustices against
Palestinians.

"Why don't you understand these people?" he said of his questioning of the parishioners. "They're the same people. You feel hurt. You were done in. You got screwed by the British. The potato famine. You were shamed."

Father Cronin shook his head. "All these things. And we don't grow up. We just don't grow up."

He knew tolerance was not enough. They should be proactive. So Father Cronin began working on a welcoming committee, to greet Muslims when they came.

᠁

I'D LONG BEEN fascinated with the race issue in Chicago.

In 1984, Michael and I visited Bridgeport, the infamous 11th Ward south of downtown that was home to old Mayor Richard J. Daley. We found a struggling black writer working in an ice cream shop in a nearby black neighborhood. He never crossed an invisible line into the white 11th Ward. Once a black friend of his did, and a mob attacked his car with baseball bats and rocks.

"It still surprises me, the racism here," the man said. "I lived in South Carolina, and it wasn't like this." He'd also lived in New York City and said that while such a thing might happen on an isolated street, he never ran into whole neighborhoods that were off limits to blacks. We then interviewed whites who bragged how they'd attacked blacks who drove into the 11th Ward.

During that period, we were spending a lot of time in the South, and we never heard of such incidents occurring there. That isn't to say the South doesn't have racism. But as we walked near Daley's old house—strangers in the Honkie Hood—we were glared at by whites peering through parted curtains. I felt uncomfortable in a way I never did in Alabama and Mississippi.

While doing that story and another a few years later, I came to learn why. Old Mayor Daley was brilliant at using race as a wedge to get elected, pitting one group against another. The city lives with the ghosts of his hate. The presence of so many whites originally from Eastern Europe, where my own roots partly lie, and where there's a history of racism, was another component. What kind of white you are matters. These factors have led to the racism in Chicago being especially virulent.

This white/white division, on top of the white/black division, was the backdrop when numerous Arab immigrants began arriving in the 1980s, joining the small Arab-American community that had long existed in Chicago. I was familiar with the old racial dynamic to which these immigrants, many from Palestine, entered. But the hatred they encountered wasn't merely an extension of that conflict. I asked myself: What was different?

For one, the Arabs came just in time for the Wal-Mart economy. These were not like immigrants from Taiwan or Hong Kong, elites with money. The prospects for Jalal and his friends were indeed bleak. They were competing for the same lower-end jobs as whites, guaranteeing conflict. This was akin to the old pattern of each immigrant wave becoming a new group for the preceding group to hate, as has always happened in America.

Yet there was more going on. It wasn't that Muslims were simply the new American "niggers," the most hated and feared of minorities, for fear of blacks has (save perhaps for the era of the Black Panthers) most often been individualized for non-blacks, as captured by the Willie Horton stereotype of the black man who will rape or rob a single white person—not of a group of black men who would fly planes into towers.

The closest historical model that I could think of for the reaction to the Arab immigrants in Chicago was the fear-driven hatred of foreigners that led to the 1927 execution of Nicola Sacco and Bartolomeo Vanzetti, the anarchists who were convicted of murder on no evidence. Then, as now, a climate of fear produced scapegoats. Our fear is not specific; if it were, Americans would be terrified of Saudi Arabians specifically—since most of the 9/11 actors were Saudi.

Through the decades, Arabs have always been portrayed in movies and literature as a suspect group. It has never been popularly cool to be Arab. A lot of Arabs came to the U.S. a long time ago but didn't keep their names. They were the invisible immigrants. For example, who knows Muzyad Yakhoob? That was the name of the actor Danny Thomas, star of the popular television show that incorporated his name, which ran from 1953 to 1964. His parents had immigrated from Lebanon.

Was it like World War II, when 120,000 West Coast Japanese-Americans were put in camps?

The headlines tell how fast this happened:

Japanese Aliens Roundup Starts / F.B.I. Hunting Down 300 Subversives and Plans to Hold 3000 Today.
—*Los Angeles Times*, December 8, 1941

The Japanese-American Reaction: "We Are Loyal Americans— We Must Prove It to All of You."
—*San Francisco Chronicle*, December 8, 1941

In 2001, the United States did not commit such a full-scale breach of individual rights. In World War II, we were fighting an axis of nation-states. No one knew when the war would end, but that it would end was clearly understood. Today, with terrorism from Al Qaeda and myriad other Islamic fundamentalist groups, one cannot imagine a sudden turn in two or three years that will ensure victory. There is no endgame. Thus, there is no imaginable end to the racism experienced by people such as Ray Hanania or Jalal, or any others among the one to three million (depending on whose figures one believes) Arab-Americans. Today, we grill 130,000 Middle Eastern men and lock up some 1,200 of them. It's unlikely we'd repeat a larger imprisonment, but who knows? If a nuclear device were to detonate in an American city, anything would be possible. Even an incident less horrifying could have devastating consequences for Arab-Americans.

No historical models or speculations defined what I was seeing in Palos Heights. There had been great tension in the southwest Chicago suburbs before 9/11; the terror attacks alone did not explain things. I spent a lot of time with Muslims and Arab-Americans, but with each trip, I left Chicago frustrated. I realized this while sorting through my notes in those early months. I began to fear I was working on two books: one about neo-McCarthyism, and another about race. It took a long time for me to see that the topics were connected, and to understand the part about race may not really be about race at all.

It was God. It went way back in time—to the Crusades. There were eight major Crusades by Christians against Muslims (and other "heretical" people) between A.D. 1096 and 1270, and the brand of nationalism I was now witnessing was literally an extension, albeit long-drawn, of these passions. The Crusades seemed to be coded in the genetic makeup of some white Christians. There had long been a suspicion in America of any religion different from Christianity. (Consider the persistence of anti-Semitism, even though Jews and Christians are inseparably linked by a common religious tradition.) But Muslim Arabs were a people, as one white man in Chicago told me with derision, "who bang their heads on the floor" during services.

The situation in Palos Heights was an extension of the Crusades on American soil, a sort of "son of the Crusades," minus the killing. It revealed invidious attitudes that went into overdrive after 9/11. Early on, when George W. Bush called the American response a "crusade," it likely was merely a slip from a man who didn't study history in college and who didn't know how loaded that word was. But the actions and words of those in and around the administration would soon confirm the stirring of an ancient religious conflict, even if no one ever again used the C word.

Things came to a boil in late 2003, after military affairs analyst William M. Arkin, who writes for the *Los Angeles Times*, published a piece about Lt. Gen. William G. "Jerry" Boykin, the three-star general who is the Bush administration's top anti-terrorism official as deputy undersecretary of defense for intelligence, an office overseen by Donald Rumsfeld. This office is charged with finding Osama bin Laden and other leading "targets."

Arkin documented how Boykin had been traveling the United States, speaking from the pulpits of churches while dressed in full military uniform, tying the war on terrorism to religion.

In Oklahoma, Boykin said: "Ladies and gentlemen, this is your enemy. It is not Osama bin Laden, it is the principalities of darkness. It is a spiritual enemy that will only be defeated if we come against them in the name of Jesus and pray for this nation and for our leaders."

At the Good Shepherd Community Church in Sandy, Oregon, he stood in the pulpit and said: "I want to impress upon you that the battle that we're in is a spiritual battle. Satan wants to destroy this nation . . . and he wants to destroy us as a Christian army."

And he once told the story of Osman Atto, a Muslim being hunted in Mogadishu.

"He went on CNN and he laughed at us, and he said, 'They'll never get me because Allah will protect me,'" Boykin said. "Well, you know what? I knew that my God was bigger than his. I knew that my God was a real God and his was an idol."

Like John Ashcroft, Boykin was born into a Pentecostal family. His wife of twenty-five years left him because, in Boykin's own words, she told him, "you're a religious fanatic."

It is not simply Boykin's fundamentalist rhetoric—as virulent as it is and as high up as he is—that exposes the administration's Crusade-like mindset. What is more revealing is the reaction of Boykin's superiors following the exposure of his pulpit pronouncements. As controversy grew over Boykin, George Bush remained silent. Rumsfeld defended him. Boykin was not removed from his position. Further, some religious Republicans in Congress sent around a letter calling for Boykin to be left alone, that any action taken against him would "intimidate the free religious exercise of his faith."

The administration should have been extra sensitive, given that the United States was allegedly trying to win the "hearts and minds" of the Muslim World and show that this was not a repeat of the Crusades. Instead it was clear that we were fighting a battle of our fundamentalists versus their fundamentalists. We were engaged in a form of evangelical nationalism. Followers find justification for their actions in the Holy Bible, believing, as Rev.

Franklin Graham (son of Billy, presider at Bush's 2001 inauguration) said, that Islam is "an evil religion."

In his book *War Is a Force That Gives Us Meaning*, Chris Hedges wrote how Dr. James Luther Adams, his ethics professor at Harvard Divinity School, said they'd end their careers fighting an "ascendant fundamentalist movement," what he termed "the Christian fascists."

Further insight into America's fundamentalists comes from a look at the case of Eric Rudolph, who was sought on a host of crimes: the 1996 bombing at the Atlanta Olympics that killed one woman and injured one hundred others; attacks on abortion clinics that left people dead and maimed; the bombing of a gay night club. For five years, Rudolph evaded capture in North Carolina. A former airborne soldier, he was a survivalist, but had a lot of help from locals who fed and harbored him, including white supremacists and the Christian Identity movement.

Reporters who interviewed residents found many who were openly supportive. Then, after Rudolph's arrest in 2003, one restaurant in Peachtree, North Carolina, put PRAY FOR ERIC RUDOLPH on its marquee. "Bless his heart," the owner told *New York Times* reporter Jeffrey Gettleman. The owner was starting a fund to pay Rudolph's legal fees, and customers were eager to donate.

The thought of a significant number of Americans willing to support such homegrown terrorism is equally as frightening as the terrorism coming from overseas—perhaps more so.

None of this is to say that the residents of Palos Heights, Illinois, are anything like the fundamentalists who aided Rudolph, or even in league with General Boykin. But their actions in the year 2000 offered a lot of insight into the unleashing of this ancient hatred, and the attitudes of post-9/11 Homeland America.

≈

WORD HAD SPREAD around Palos Heights about the terminal cancer suffered by Donald Koldenhoven, the son of Dean and Ruth. Donald died on Monday, July 10, 2000. In the days leading up to Donald's death, Alderman Jim Murphy had been meeting with Rouhy Shalabi, the mosque foundation's attorney, trying to cut a deal. There was talk, briefly, of upping the payment to $300,000. On Thursday, the day that the Koldenhovens buried Donald, Shalabi signed off on the deal. They'd take the $200,000 and walk.

A special council meeting was hastily called for the next day. Mayor Dean heard about it. He thought: *They are calling the meeting figuring I won't come the day after I buried my son.* Alderman Murphy later publicly said that this was not true, that he called the meeting because Shalabi was going out of town.

Whatever. Mayor Dean strode in. As soon as they were seated, Mayor Dean asked why the meeting had been called. The anti-mosque aldermen stated the deal had been cut the previous night, and now they wanted to form a committee to seek funding from a bank.

Mayor Dean asked why this business couldn't have waited until the regularly scheduled meeting on Tuesday, just four days away. The aldermen made a motion to form the committee. Mayor Dean ruled the meeting illegal, and adjourned it.

The official meeting lasted seconds. But people lingered and the public comments went on for two hours. Some aldermen chose to speak as citizens if they could not legally have a meeting. It was bitter. Aldermen and citizens blamed Mayor Dean.

"He's the one who says, 'You are bigots,'" Alderman Frank Passarelli yelled when he took a turn. "He's to blame."

Alderwoman Corsi refused to call Mayor Dean "mayor," instead using his last name. She said he had betrayed the community, and spoken badly about it in public. Thus he did not deserve the title. Only a few residents defended Mayor Dean.

Still, Mayor Dean did not tip his hand as to whether or not he would veto the buyout offer. That would have to wait four days. Mayor Dean was confronted when he went out in public.

"What do you think of your Muslims now, Mr. Mayor!" one man shouted at him, holding the paper with a picture of a Muslim during the Pledge of Allegiance. "Look at them. They aren't doing the pledge!"

"Isn't that wonderful," Mayor Dean said. "Look at that picture. We have the freedom not to do the Pledge of Allegiance. What a great country."

Mayor Dean walked into the Tuesday council meeting with these points on his mind: he had to protect the First Amendment. And that Jesus said, "Love thy neighbor."

"It was these two things that told me I gotta do what I gotta do," he later recalled. "They want you to think you thought long and hard about this. It was a no-brainer."

At the start of the meeting, he vetoed the buyout. He called it "fiscally irresponsible," as well as an insult to Muslims. Six votes were needed to override the veto—the aldermen who supported the buyout did not have them. Thus, the veto stood.

In the public comments period, several residents called for Mayor Dean to resign, saying he'd made the town look like it was full of bigots. But Ray

Hanania thanked Mayor Dean for his courageous stand. Father Ed Cronin spoke on behalf of his and six other churches in the city. He encouraged city leaders to begin a dialogue with the goal of healing the community.

But healing would prove to be a tough proposition. An election was coming the following year, in April, 2001. The mayor's office was on the ballot.

"Are you going to run?" asked the Palos Heights city attorney, an American Indian who was sympathetic.

"I'm going to lose," Dean said. "But I have to run."

Hanging over the election would be a continuation of the mosque controversy. The Al Salam Mosque Foundation filed a lawsuit. It backed out of buying the church. Shalabi said he worried about violence if the foundation bought the building. But he said the city legally owed the foundation the payoff.

॒

THAT SAME APRIL election would be important for Ray Hanania. He became involved as a consultant in an effort to finally elect some Arab-Americans to office in the southwest suburbs where he lived. If some Arab-Americans could be elected, it would be the start of increased visibility and credibility—they could see themselves in the mirror. The mosque controversy had been his inspiration. A record eight Arab-American candidates were running, most seeking a spot on the board of School District 230, which takes in a huge swath of towns in the southwest Chicago suburbs. There are 6,600 students in the district, 10 percent of them Arab-American.

In 1994, Ray and others had gone to the District 230 school board asking why, if Arabs were only 10 percent of the student body, did they comprise 90 percent of the student expulsions? The answer was that the Arab kids were in gangs.

"Wait a minute," Ray recalled saying. "Now I know why they're being expelled. It's really a racial attitude. You're cutting breaks for non-Arab kids. When it's an Arab kid, you believe he's a street-gang member, so this is an opportunity for you to get rid of him."

Ray felt the Arab-American community had to have some impact on policy. He and others saw 2001 as a pivotal election.

Among the eight candidates who came forward or were recruited to run was Nareman Taha, a twenty-five-year-old mother in the town of Burbank, to the northeast of Palos Heights and Bridgeview. Nareman, a school counselor who had recently graduated with a master's degree from the University of Illinois at Chicago, ran for the Burbank School District. In the end, Nareman got 831 votes—which is about the number of registered Arab-Americans in Burbank—placing fifth. All seven other Arab-American candidates lost.

In Palos Heights, Mayor Dean did worse than the Arab-Americans. He got 599 votes out of 4,647 cast, 12.8 percent.

Not long after, Mayor Dean traveled to Arizona to climb a mountain he'd once ascended with Donald, on a vacation when the boy was six years old.

"If I die, will I go to heaven?" Donald had asked when they got to the summit, said Dean, recalling that long-ago day. He had said that he would.

"Then I want to go holding your feet."

Mayor Dean went now to contemplate that request. He was alone. He climbed the peak and stood on an outcropping of rock. He was illuminated, Rembrandt-like, by a low sun angling from beneath a dark-clouded sky. He asked a stranger who'd also made the climb to take his picture. Mayor Dean looks at peace in the photograph.

A year later, in the days following 9/11, people would come up to Mayor Dean in public places and accost him.

"I don't like Muslims or anyone from the Middle East!"

"Jesus was from the Middle East," Mayor Dean would respond.

He watched the papers with growing concern about the Crusade-like character of the war on terrorism, and the evangelical push to condemn Islam.

"It was extremists that took the planes and crashed them into the towers and the Pentagon. The reason I say that is they did not wear uniforms, they were not from one military, or any one country. They were criminals on their own, grouped together to do this dastardly act. We also have extremist Christian people. They're called televangelists. [Pat] Robertson, you know, down the line, [Jimmy] Swaggart, [Jerry] Falwell, all of them. Mr. Falwell can get on TV and say, 'Mohammed was a terrorist.'"

And then later there came Rev. Jerry Vines, who called the prophet Mohammed "a demon-possessed pedophile." Vines was the former president of the Southern Baptist Convention, a collection of 42,000 churches with 16 million members.

Mayor Dean wondered how he would react if someone got on television and called Jesus a terrorist. He made a fist, said he'd punch them.

"You don't say that about my religion. You can murder people with words just as much as murdering with a sword. These televangelists are guilty of murdering people with their words. Don't call the founder of their religion a terrorist. You're going to get a lot of people pretty well peeved at you. There's no doubt about it."

Mayor Dean retreated from public life. Then, in early 2002, he received a call from Caroline Kennedy. She told him that he'd been named co-winner of the John F. Kennedy Profile in Courage Award by the Kennedy Library Foundation in Boston. Winning with him was United Nations

Secretary-General Kofi Annan. The award is named after *Profiles in Courage*, the 1957 Pulitzer Prize-winning book by President Kennedy, which told the stories of eight U.S. Senators who risked their political careers to fight for their beliefs.

To commemorate the award, Annan and Koldenhoven each received a Tiffany-designed replica of an old ship lamp that JFK had liked. Just before it was presented to Mayor Dean, Senator Ted Kennedy quipped that it wasn't often that he got to introduce a Republican.

Etched on the award are JFK's words:

"In whatever arena of life, one may meet the challenge of courage, whatever may be the sacrifice he faces, if he follows his conscience . . . each man must decide for himself the course he will follow."

NEWS DIARY II

WAR & TAXES

IN WORLD WAR II, taxes were raised to pay for the war. At the time of Korea, taxes were raised to pay for the war.

And then came World War Forever.

> Nothing is more important in the face of a war than cutting taxes.
> —House Majority Whip Tom DeLay

Facing a terrible economy following a huge decline in stock prices, the president pushed Congress to cut taxes for the rich, saying they would invest their windfall and prosperity would follow, with the creation of jobs. Congress went along, even though the tax cuts would increase the deficit.

The president was Herbert Hoover and the year was 1930. It was the dawn of the Great Depression, and the worst was yet to hit—food lines, farm riots, despair.

After George W. Bush's 2001 $1.3 trillion tax cut, which he promised would increase jobs, the country lost two million jobs. Then came Bush's 2003 tax cut for the rich, which he promised would increase jobs.[1] Even if each promised job came true, the government, by Bush's own figures, would spend $550,000 in lost revenue per new job. Bush was the first president since Great Depression-era President Hoover to have a net loss of jobs while in office—by the time of the 2003 tax cut, 2.3 million fewer Americans were working.

When there was an uptick in jobs late in 2003—126,000 in October—pundits rejoiced and proclaimed that Bush's tax cuts were kicking in. But ignored in most American newspaper and television reports was the fact that half those jobs were of the Wal-Mart variety, or in low-paid food services—junk jobs. Continuing a thirty-nine-month trend, highly paid manufacturing jobs fell, by another 24,000 that same month.

FOLLOW THE MONEY

NEWS ITEM, January, 2003: the Federal Reserve Board released a report on the change in family finances, based on data collected between 1998 and 2001.

Change in Median Family Net Worth
(Difference between net assets and liabilities)

	Top 10 Percent	Middle 40–60 Percent	Bottom 20 Percent
1998	$492,400	$58,100	$6,300
2001	$833,600	$62,500	$7,900
	(+69 percent)	(+8 percent)	(+25 percent)

Some of them would like to turn this into class warfare.
—George W. Bush, defending his $800 billion tax cut plan.

Same month, January, 2003, and the president was in St. Louis, pitching the tax cuts. Some local wealthy elites were invited for the photo op. They showed up wearing ties, but the White House staff asked the men to remove them so they would appear more like ordinary Americans. Behind Bush was a canvas printed with the words "Strengthening America's Economy." The fake backdrop showed printed images of cartons of manufactured goods that said:

MADE IN AMERICA

In the foreground were stacks of real boxes that filled the warehouse. Brown tape covered certain lettering. When reporters peeled the tape off these boxes, there were the words:

MADE IN CHINA

Later, as the Iraq War wound down, the president became assertive at home in the face of high approval ratings. White House advisers said they were now on a "war footing" with Congress as they sought the most aggressive tax cut possible.

The rich got their relief.

Ask not what your country can do for you . . .

And the newspaper read:

—SCHOOL LUNCH PROGRAM FOR POOR KIDS TO BE CUT

—ELDERLY TO PAY MORE FOR HEALTH CARE

—STATES GOING BROKE

. . . Ask what you can do for your country.

—A forgotten leader

Robert Reich
said we are not just an economy
but a society
no one listened

Mr. Greenspan

EMPIRICAL ECONOMICS was dead. It was now a science with algebraic modeling.

And along came Alan Greenspan, who as a young man had seated himself at the feet of Ayn Rand after having read her prepublication manuscript for *Atlas Shrugged*. Inspired by Rand, in 1963 Mr. Greenspan wrote about the perils of regulation. Unleash the regulations. Let the market be free.

Breathless pundits extolled the ever-rising market. The Dow would hit 36,000. Making things no longer mattered. It was all ideas now, all intellectual property.

And Americans should shop till they drop.

Fukuyama called it the "end of history." America had won the Cold War. To the victor went the markets.

Atlas didn't shrug
Atlas kicked ass
and when Atlas spoke
everyone listened

APRIL 14, 2003: REPORT SAYS INTERNAL REVENUE SERVICE GOES AFTER ORDINARY AMERICANS. Syracuse University study finds "big fish" get away; IRS ignores auditing of "prominent Americans"; Bush administration not serious about corporate tax cheating.

> Now observe the results of a society built on the principles of individualism. This, our country. The noblest country in the history of men. The country of greatest achievement, greatest prosperity, greatest freedom. This country was not based on selfless service, sacrifice, renunciation or any precept of altruism. It was based on a man's right to the pursuit of happiness. His own happiness. Not anyone else's. A private, personal, selfish motive. Look at the results.
>
> —Ayn Rand, *The Fountainhead*

Where Is the Love?

> THIS COUNTRY, it is the best, the worst. Where is the love? Here you have things. But what about family? I worry about my children. Nothing has changed since 9/11. For a little bit, people were different. But they are back to what they were. They think money will make you happy. Where is the love? Where is the love?
>
> —Tina, a maid in a building on West 119th Street in New York City, who immigrated from Barbados and is raising her children, ages five and twelve, January 28, 2003

Apologies to Anatole France

THE MARKET
in its majestic equality
allows both the rich and poor man
to trade in world currency

SELLING WAR was good for radio business. McVay Media, a radio station consulting firm in Cleveland, Ohio, advised stations on what to put on the air during the Iraq War:

- Patriotic music that makes you cry, salute, get cold chills. Go for the emotion!

- Encourage listeners to write: sixty-second poems, and patriotic messages to produce and air throughout the day.
- From your music archives, resurrect Byron MacGregor's "The Americans," and Red Skelton's "Pledge of Allegiance."
- Air the National Anthem at a specified time each day as long as the USA is at War.

IN MARCH 2003, WRVA, a Clear Channel station in Glen Allen, Virginia, held a "Rally for America" to support the Iraq war. Glenn Beck, who hosts a conservative talk show broadcast to one hundred stations, spoke. Clear Channel stations supported rallies in favor of the war in thirteen other cities, including Atlanta, Cleveland, Richmond, Sacramento, and San Antonio.

The Clear Channel website listed these rallies, until there was a furor; they were then deposed. The network has a reputation for centralized power at its San Antonio headquarters.

John Hogan, president and CEO of Clear Channel Radio, insisted local managers made their own decisions about the rallies. He called anyone who questioned this "shameless and irresponsible" in a statement.

CHRISTMAS SEASON, 2001. Ohio's Mahoning Valley. Morning radio, public service announcement. The station manager urges me to go out and shop. That's how we can be patriotic.

Buy Buy Buy.

Want that computer? Go out and charge it. Show the terrorists they can't win. Buy Buy Buy.

Show the world we are strong.

> Get back to normal.
> —President George W. Bush

Rationing Limits in World War II

A SIXTEEN-OUNCE bottle of catsup = 20 points.

A Porterhouse steak = eleven points per pound / Limit: twenty-eight ounces of meat per week.

Sugar = seventeen points per pound / Limit: five pounds every two and a half months.

Coffee = one pound every five weeks, or one cup per day.

> Use it up, wear it out, make it do, or do without.
> —A popular slogan in World War II

The hottest-selling SUV in 2002 was the Hummer 2. It weighs 6,400 pounds, twice that of a Ford Taurus. Its Vortec 6000 V8 316 horsepower engine gets eleven miles to the gallon, as little as nine in the city.

The H2 is the second generation incarnation of the Humvee, the civilian version patterned after the military vehicle used in the Gulf War and the Iraq War. Actor Arnold Schwarzenegger bought the first civilian version to come off the assembly line in 1992.

The original Humvee cost $100,000, and included amenities such as helicopter lift hooks. At $50,000, the H2 looks the same, albeit sans lift hooks. Both models have more in common with a tank or a Brink's armored vehicle than a car. General Motors was requiring dealerships to build new showrooms resembling military barracks, using exposed bolts and brushed steel.

The sales brochure is glossy and bold, a glory of metallic triumph, like a printed version of a Leni Riefenstahl film. Out front, a headlight fills the frame, staring at you like an eyeball. Steely and angular images are on heavy paper stock. On one page are the words,

A NEW MISSION
THE H2

Turn the page: a view from below, of a Hummer coming at you, dust flying.

> Hard, strong lines in the nearly vertical windshield, rectangular windows, level roof and upright rear gate, carve a familiar Hummer silhouette . . . Muscles still ripple under the skin, but the H2 doesn't intimidate.

Dr. Clotaire Rapaille, founder of Archetype Discoveries, a consulting firm used by the big automakers, explained to a *New York Times* reporter that when his company interviewed people about the H2, they "told me I can protect my family. If someone bumps into me, they're dead. People love this feeling . . . the reality is you want to show strength." He noted that after the 9/11 attacks, "we feel we are at war and people feel the need to be protected."

By October 2002, the H2 was outselling all other SUVs. In six months, General Motors sold more H2s than it did the original Hummer in ten years of sales since 1992. Dealers were expanding and could not keep up with demand.

Later during the Iraq War, other SUVs showed slowing sales, but not the Hummer. It was selling at a rate of three thousand per month.

"When I turn on the TV, I see wall-to-wall Humvees, and I'm proud," Sam Bernstein, a Hummer owner, told the *New York Times* as the bombs were falling on Baghdad. Another driver, Travis Patterson, told the paper "it oozes patriotism. You put some flags on the Hummer and drive down the road and everyone is honking and waving at you."

> From a marketing point of view, you don't introduce new products in August.
> —Andrew Card, George W. Bush's Chief of Staff, speaking about why the President withheld until September 2002 his hard push to build support for a war against Iraq President Saddam Hussein.

NOT THE TIME TO MARKET THESE PRODUCTS

ON SEPTEMBER 10, 2001, industry insiders went to see Michael Caine in the premier of his new movie, *The Quiet American*, based on Graham Greene's novel about a naive American who goes to Vietnam trying to help in 1952. His performance was applauded. Critics said it was his best role. But the next day changed everything.

Harvey Weinstein, cochairman of Miramax, told the *New York Times*, "You can't release this film now; it's unpatriotic. America has to be cohesive and band together. We were worried that nobody had the stomach for a movie about bad Americans anymore."

The director was Phillip Noyce, who made *Patriot Games* and *Clear and Present Danger*, based on two patriotic Tom Clancy war novels.

In late 2002, Caine lobbied Weinstein to release the film so he would be eligible for an Oscar for best actor. He had to throw a lot of weight around to get Weinstein to budge. He told interviewers, "I wouldn't make an anti-American movie—I'm one of the most pro-American foreigners I know. I love America and Americans." It didn't have to be widely distributed. It only need play in a few theaters for one week in Los Angeles and New York. After much pressure, Weinstein reluctantly agreed. The film was released in four theaters.

Caine got a nom. That meant good box office potential, millions of dollars. Suddenly, *The Quiet American* went into wider release. But Caine didn't win.

Then they were making the Denzel Washington film, *John Q*, about a blue-collar worker who takes over a hospital at gunpoint because the HMO won't approve a heart transplant for his son. Director Nick Cassavetes asked Steve Earle to write a song. Earle told David Corn of *The Nation* that knowing Hollywood, he wrote a father-son song. Cassavetes wanted something more political. So Earle ramped it up, a song that included a blast at HMOs, the war on drugs, and gated communities. Cassavetes approved—the song would go over the closing credits.

"But September 11 happened, and they stopped returning my phone calls," Earle told Corn. "Finally they said . . . that in this climate it could be seen as too critical of the Bush Administration and everything."

Earle was again in the news not long after for "John Walker's Blues," a song about John Walker Lindh, the twenty-one-year-old American sentenced to twenty years in prison for fighting on the side of the Taliban. Country radio stations erupted, and one commentator accused him of being the "Jane Fonda of the war on terrorism."

When Madonna gave a concert in Los Angeles just before the Afghan bombing, she asked for a moment of silence for the 9/11 dead, but also urged restraint. The audience screamed, "USA! USA!" She did not repeat a call for restraint the next night.

American Freedom

FLAGS SNAPPING. From poles. Antennas.

USA.

Freedom.

You can choose between any of one newspaper in most cities. You can choose between any two bookstores. Any of three office supply outlets. Any Wal-Mart. Home Depot. Or Lowes. A Big Mac. Whopper. Fries.

Freedom. Just another word for nothing left to choose.

Flags were for sale everywhere. In the weeks after 9/11, they were simple flags in the form of peel-off decals and cloth. Sales were brisk. But by that December, truck stops across the country uniformly reported to me that sales had fallen.

Within a year, manufacturers got creative. At a Sheetz gas station in Breezewood, Pennsylvania, we found a box of flag motif window-stick decals at $2.99 each. They were the size of an open hand, with rubber suction cups used to affix them to auto and truck glass. These were exactly like the BABY ON BOARD decals one saw in car windows during the 1980s:

—DON'T MESS WITH THE U.S., with a fighter jet in the middle
—Peace fingers, the Churchillian *V* for victory, in red, white, and blue
—GOD BLESS AMERICA
—THESE COLORS DON'T RUN
—NO NUKES, in the center of a circle with a slash through it
—JUSTICE WILL PREVAIL
—AMERICA STANDS TALL
—LET'S ROLL
—PROUD TO BE AMERICAN

The manufacturer hedged bets—a little. The results of the "decal poll": of the sixteen decals in the box, three were "liberal," in the form of two NO NUKES and one "peace fingers."

USA. Land of the Free. Pee in a bottle if you want the job. Cameras watch. From bridges. In rest areas. Malls. At work.
    "For your protection."
    We must truly be free. If they watch over us so carefully.

WILL CAMERAS STOP TERRORISM?

We can look at London for guidance. A camera system initiated to combat IRA terrorism has sprouted into a network with an estimated 2.5 million cameras. The average Londoner is caught on film about three hundred times per day . . . no terrorists have been caught by their use.
—Rep. Constance A. Morella, a Republican, in a House committee hearing on March 22, 2002

BOOK THREE

BYRD PLEADS TO AMERICAN PEOPLE
—*Charleston Gazette* headline, October 11, 2002

It is the leaders of a country who determine the policy. It is always a simple matter to drag the people along whether it is a democracy or a fascist dictatorship, a parliament, or a communist dictatorship, voice or no voice, the people can always be brought to the bidding of the leaders . . . All you have to do is tell them they are being attacked and denounce the pacifists for a lack of patriotism and exposing the country to danger. It works the same in every country.
—Senator Robert C. Byrd of West Virginia, in a speech on the floor of the U.S. Senate about invading Iraq, repeating words spoken a little over half a century earlier by Herman Goering, founder of the German Nazi Gestapo and president of the Reichstag

1

IT'S JUNE 2000, a little over a year before Katie Sierra will walk into Sissonville High School wearing her shirt. Michael Williamson and I are in Tennessee at the Crow's Nest Restaurant, where breakfast for three costs twelve bucks and change, dining with the slate-gray-haired woman who runs the social services program for Clay County. The woman is telling us stunning statistics that defy what visitors see when they drive into the wooded and rolling county on their way to cast for largemouth bass in Dale Hollow Lake, a slackwater reservoir like others on what once had been the mighty Tennessee and Cumberland rivers. Franklin Roosevelt's New Deal Tennessee Valley Authority and its dams brought this region out of poverty, luring factories with the promise of cheap electricity and a hungry labor force.

There are 7,236 residents in Clay County, but only 629 are employed here in the early summer of 2000. Once there were many more jobs. The biggest employer had been Oshkosh B'Gosh, the Wisconsin jeans manufacturer that located a plant in the main town of Celina in 1953. This "new economy" of a half century ago changed Clay County. Oshkosh had twelve hundred workers in Celina at the peak in the 1960s and 1970s. People bought nice homes. Kids went to college. Things went well for nearly fifty years as the local economy expanded. Then the North American Free Trade Agreement (NAFTA) was signed by President Bill Clinton. The Celina plant was downsized after NAFTA; all sewing operations moved south of the border, to Mexico and Honduras. Just two hundred workers remained, those who prewashed and stonewashed and acidwashed children's clothes.[1]

The slate-haired woman—whose name I'm not using because her boss would later call in a rage, saying she was not authorized to speak officially—tells us that unemployment was 28 percent after main operations ceased. The rate was now officially 8 percent. This is the image the boss wants to project, the face that the casual visitor driving through can see, that everything is back to normal in Clay County, that everything is okay.

But it's not okay, the woman tells us. A tad over 1,700 former Oshkosh workers and others now drive out of the county each day so they can work. Many go to the city of Lafayette, forty-five miles distant, spending two hours a day in their aging cars traveling winding roads to earn half the $12 to $13 dollars an hour they made at Oshkosh. One single mother supporting three children has two jobs, paying $5.90 an hour each. That woman and her children sometimes go hungry. The county food bank has less food than it had the previous year. It was very personal to the slate-haired woman, for she runs the food bank and has to look such hungry working people in the eye and tell them she's out of food.

We leave the slate-haired woman and cruise Clay County.

It's the height of the newest "new economy," with all talk centered on technology and the NASDAQ index. The previous fall, Al Gore was speaking about it. "I'm proud of what we've achieved," he said of the economic policies of Clinton and Gore. "We now have nearly 19 million new jobs."

Among the 629 people employed in Clay County is Elizabeth Boles. She landed one of these new economy jobs—at a just-opened Rite Aid drugstore. Her salary on piecework in the old manufacturing economy: as much as $14 an hour. In the service economy: $5.15. She chose this job so she wouldn't have to commute to the distant town for two hours each day.

Elizabeth is a single mother with one son, Dusty, twelve. She's lucky to have the house, which she bought on her old salary. It's a fine little home, set in a wooded lot. A passerby would never suspect her hard times.

"You make $10 or more an hour, then you drop to $5.15," she says, trying to explain. She trails off. Her demeanor is one of defeat.

"People in Washington look at the papers and see you're working," Elizabeth finally says. "On paper, you're working. I don't have stock. Or a bank account. I'm just surviving. People aren't starving. But they are going to bed without all they should be eating. Dusty and I are not big eaters."

Her 1992 Honda Accord has 120,000 miles on it. She lives in fear of it dying. A car payment would mean disaster. "Dusty wants a computer. That's $1,500 I don't have." She even has trouble buying school clothes. I ask why she doesn't seek help, such as getting food stamps. She wrinkles her nose. No way.

"Too proud, I guess."

Before leaving this small Cumberland River town, we meet another former Oshkosh worker now in a service economy job. She now makes five and a half bucks an hour. Throughout the interview, she kneads a fold in her pants.

"I haven't talked about this," she says in apology for being nervous.

She often made two times the daily production quota. "I worked fifty-four to sixty hours a week. I missed a lot with my daughters. I was made to feel I had to be there." The bosses discouraged vacation. "They didn't want the good workers out. I was late for work one time in fourteen years. It snowed, a big snow."

One daughter has great grades. She's college-bound. But the other one who is younger "works hard to just get Cs and Ds. What happens to the kids not bright enough to go to college? She's slow."

With Oshkosh gone, this latter daughter seems doomed to a low-wage job. "I wonder if I'll be able to take care of her." She's on the verge of tears. She apologizes. She stares at her hand gripping the pant leg.

She and her husband use credit cards to maintain their former lifestyle—they're now $40,000 in debt. This seems not so smart, but they made the decision for the kids. Their choice is to get their daughters up and out into the world, pay the consequences later—either by working till they die, or suffering bankruptcy.

As we drive out of the county, en route to Texas, I turn to Michael and predict that in November, Al Gore will lose Tennessee to George W. Bush.

✍

MANY WERE stunned when Gore did lose his home state.

There were a multitude of reasons, but anger over job loss loomed large—the U.S. Department of Labor estimated that NAFTA cost Tennessee 11,000 jobs while Gore was vice president. A lot of people we talked with were bitter about NAFTA in a most profound way.

We were in Tennessee because of an assignment from the now-defunct *George* magazine. Its editor, Frank Lalli, wanted a piece on child poverty in the backyards of the major candidates. Frank had called because of our history—Michael and I had produced a trilogy of books on American workers and poverty, as well as a body of journalism on American social conditions.

For our first book, *Journey to Nowhere*, Michael and I spent three years, beginning in 1982, crisscrossing America—often in boxcars—following the new homeless, many of whom had been displaced by closed factories and steel mills. It takes several years of descent for a person to be transformed from a middle-class American into a hobo, and we documented this process. Our necropolis was Youngstown, Ohio, which lost 40,000 high-paying steel-related jobs after 1977. In our second book, *And Their Children After Them*, we looked at the fate of the nine million Depression-era cotton sharecroppers in the South. The final book, *The Last Great American Hobo*, was about one octogenarian hobo's life, and the other hobos who shared his camp.

Between these books, we produced an array of news stories for the *Sacramento Bee* on American life. We saw the wealthy side, from Hollywood to Silicon Valley. We lived on the California farm of a Republican, the Iowa farm of a Democrat, rode on duty for a week straight with a Miami police sergeant, hung out in the *colonias* of Texas and the *barrios* of Los Angeles, insinuated ourselves into the lives of Hell's Angels, drug dealers, politicians, steelworkers, suburbanites. In different presidential election years, we drove the nation, two twelve-thousand-mile stints for a thrice-weekly feature in which we explored the lives of average people.

We could sit at a morning campfire with hobos, then later that same day fit in at a millionaire's home.

I mention all this to say we knew quite a bit about a wide range of people in the United States by the year 2000. America, in essence, was our beat.

Some things had become clear after nearly three decades of documenting the moving picture of America, and talking with thousands of people caught up in the dramatic transformation of the country. The change could be statistically charted. But Michael and I had been tracking it emotionally, watching as angst grew, especially in a swath down the center of the United States, a region roughly five to seven hundred miles wide. For this territory, there was a depression on. If this American movie had a soundtrack, it would have been the steadily rising bluesman's wail.

Few heard it. We didn't exactly have to fight off a crowd of other writers and photographers. You didn't read much about the places we traveled to and wrote about and photographed, the ruined towns that once produced steel, textiles, grew food. These were occupations that had provided real jobs and a way of life—gone.

Writers such as William Greider have hammered home the impact of globalization. In his book, *One World, Ready or Not,* Greider writes: "Shipping high-wage jobs to low-wage economies has obvious, immediate economic benefits. But, roughly speaking, it also replaces high-wage consumers with low-wage ones. That exchange is debilitating to the entire system." America is kept rocking by consumer spending, which fuels two-thirds of the economy. Kill the consumer, and the whole thing crumbles.

To much of the public, the industrial decline was a natural course of events. That's just the way it goes, times change, and so on. It appeared in the press that the world economy, via American capitalism, was a natural force without manipulation or malice, and anyone, such as Greider, who questioned it was a Luddite or worse. The "free market" was something that just occurred organically.

But if one studies what really happened, the crisis was as dramatic as a Dust Bowl, only this was a human-made disaster.

In his book *Blowback: The Costs and Consequences of American Empire*, Chalmers Johnson outlines how U.S. policy in the last half of the twentieth century furthered its empire, largely by basing soldiers all over the globe.[2] Johnson, a former CIA consultant, a one-time Vietnam hawk, and an emeritus professor at the University of California, San Diego, argues that the United States is just like the Roman empire—far-reaching, powerful, and doomed by its own hubris. The ultimate blowback. He predicted terrorist attacks like 9/11, which came a year after his book was published, long before President George W. Bush declared a doctrine of "preventative war."

Johnson also looked at economic blowback. "The hollowing out of American industry . . . is a form of blowback—an unintended negative consequence of American policy—even though it is seldom recognized as such," Johnson wrote. One source of economic blowback was the government's assistance of the manufacturing sectors of Cold War allies, in the form of technology giveaways and skewed trade arrangements.

Another source of blowback described by Johnson was President Richard Nixon's dismantling of the Bretton Woods international monetary agreement, in the face of economic pressures stemming from the Vietnam War. The original agreement was reached at a meeting of the Allies in the New Hampshire town of Bretton Woods in the summer of 1944. The idea was to avoid the collapse of world financial markets as had occurred in the 1930s, in a crisis that strained the underpinnings of German society and sped the rise of Nazism as well as Italian fascism. Bretton Woods set fixed exchange rates for the world's currencies, tying all currencies to the U.S. dollar. The United States promised to convert those dollars into gold on demand. Bretton Woods also created the International Monetary Fund (IMF) and the World Bank.

This system worked well until the Vietnam War. Nixon chose to withdraw from Bretton Woods in 1971 because the war was so incredibly costly; the dollar had to be released from the stricture of tight exchange rates to head off domestic economic crisis. As Johnson says, a better answer would have been to end the war, balance the budget, and keep this important monetary tool. Instead, under Nixon, different national currencies would be allowed to "float," or be valued by the market.

This sent the world economy back to the nineteenth century, in a way. Profit was now made by trading currencies, not by making real goods. And with the advent of speedy computers, money was thrust in and out of countries irrespective of underlying value. "Vulture capitalism" was the result. For example, argues Johnson, speculation in the early to mid-1990s artificially inflated the so-called Asian tiger economies of South Korea, Singapore, Indonesia, and others, and then enabled the wild flight of capital that led to their collapse in late 1997. The IMF stepped in and imposed drastic measures—the IMF basically being an arm of American capital—which led to a devaluation of those Asian economies. Then American firms went in and bought companies for pennies on the dollar. For some, this was a highly remunerative exercise; Asian leaders, on the other hand, could not help but sense they'd been taken for a ride.

Now even more American jobs were being shipped to these former Asian tigers—everything from the manufacture of semiconductors and computer equipment to service jobs such as telephone call centers. This blowback to both Asian companies and American workers might never have happened if the United States hadn't worried about domino theories and foolishly squandered its wealth in the Vietnam War.

I remember listening to MIT economist Lester Thurow back in 1988, when he explained that most Americans don't know that the United States emerged from World War II with a 75 percent share of the world's economy. This, he noted, was an unnatural state of affairs that existed because we had the only unbombed manufacturing infrastructure among the world's major industrial powers. Some leaders disliked the Marshall Plan and they desired to destroy the industrial capacity of Japan and Germany for good, turning them into nations of "goat herders," as Thurow put it. Agrarian revenge didn't triumph because of two major non-altruistic arguments in favor of the Marshall Plan. One: robust economies among our former enemies would provide markets for American-made goods. Two: the recovery of Germany and Japan both militarily and economically would place them as strong allies on the front lines for the United States in its Cold War against the Soviets.

As Thurow spoke in 1988, Japan and Germany had regained a significant share of the world economy. He said that the natural order of things (a return to the pre-bombing World War II equilibrium) would leave the United States with less than 20 percent. A return to this parity, he said, would mean that the U.S. economy would have to shrink to a size far smaller than its recent low point during the 1982 recession—if this contraction were to come all at once, it would mean a recession five times as bad as 1982. Essentially a mini-depression. I was with a group of other journalists when Thurow told us this, and I remember our incredulous reaction. How could this come to pass without political fallout, without another Great Depression, without, in effect, the fall of the American Empire?

I wondered: Would this eventually lead to trouble? How and when?

⟨⟩

IN 1995, Michael and I were back in Youngstown, where we had begun *Journey to Nowhere*. In the early 1980s, we had watched as houses burned at the rate of two a day—some fires set by owners for insurance, others mysteriously—as people fled the city. We interviewed unemployed workers who would later commit suicide or die young of heart attacks. We followed some of them as they hit a desperate road, seeking work.

Our main source was John Russo, a labor studies professor at Youngstown State University, later the head of the school's Center for Working Class studies. He'd spent years going to funerals of suicide and heart attack victims—his friends. Upon our return in 1995, there was just one steel mill left in the Mahoning Valley, to the north in the city of Warren. The plant had just gone through a violent strike over a plan to sell it to a venture capitalist, which would have incurred heavy debt and likely have led to its shutdown. The workers had had other mills shut on them, and they vowed to fight this time. Homemade bombs were thrown, windows smashed in a fury that was ignored by the national press. John took us to the union hall, where we listened to the angry workers who'd won their walkout because the owner realized after fifty-four days that not settling was ultimately too costly. Word was that the workers would have dynamited the blast furnace had they lost, effectively killing the mill.

"Blowing it up would be better than going through that again," a worker told me, referring to the other shutdowns. As if to emphasize their resolve, someone slipped us one of their homemade grenade bombs made for the strike.

We left the hall, and John took us to the site of the vast Youngstown Sheet & Tube's Campbell Works.[3] Michael had photographed the rusting ruins in 1983, but now nothing was left—just a few miles of meadow returning to forest. As Michael lined up an "after" shot, I noticed John off to the side, crying. We were just two miles from his house on the north side of town, but he hadn't visited this part of the city in years.

John despaired about the outfall of the economic destruction. In the 1996 reissue of *Journey to Nowhere*, I wrote,

"There's a lot of anger in working people," John says. "It's not unlike the anger in prewar Germany and prewar Italy. In the 1930s, America could have gone either direction," he says, meaning either toward Franklin Roosevelt or extreme nationalism. During the Depression, Father Charles Coughlin and his radio hate ministry thrived and had some ten million listeners; a number of Americans supported Adolf Hitler. John points out that both communists and capitalists despised Roosevelt. But capitalists allowed themselves to be saved by FDR, because communism was then a credible threat. "There had been the Bolshevik revolution fifteen years earlier," John notes. Now there's no threat from the left. Capitalism has nothing to worry about.

"That is why history does not replay itself. The current debate is narrow, because the possibilities have been reduced." John fears the anger will be channeled into right-wing hate. "There is the old famous line by the CP: the worse it gets, the better it gets," John says of the Communist Party's belief that bad times recruited members. "Now the reality is the worse it gets, the worse it gets."

When we first documented disenfranchised workers, Michael and I believed we were on the front end of a 1930s-style growing awareness. We'd be part of enlightening Americans. In turn, something would be done to help. After all, our parents and grandparents had lived through those times, and the lesson had been that society ultimately worked to fix what was broken.

And it didn't just make egalitarian sense. How could society economically allow a massive segment of the middle class to fall into poverty?

Naïveté is too mild a description for our optimism. The American working middle class would continue to be ignored, to understate it. There was a blinding focus on money in the 1980s and 1990s. Later, I began to think of this as the "Brazilianization" of America—a growing Third World amid the First World.

Back in 1982, when we jumped aboard a freight train with new hobos who were former factory workers, we also thought that at least their anger would morph into a political force. When it didn't, I turned to history for answers. I kept gravitating in my reading back to the 1930s.

The 1930s was, of course, a time of incredible political extremes. Many Americans flirted with fascism amid economic chaos, just as others flirted with socialism and communism. Essentially, America was divided into thirds:

the right, the middle, and the left. We may have two major parties, but American politics was and is really apportioned into these thirds, with both ends battling for the middle third's soul. For a time in the early 1930s, the hard right and left pulled a significant portion of the middle to either end of the political spectrum. Then Roosevelt came along, and pulled it back to the center, or, in his oft-repeated phrase, "slightly to the left of center."

Yet in the Great Depression, the right was ascendant. Fascist groups were formed, such as the Silver Shirts. In 1935, novelist Sinclair Lewis published the ironically titled *It Can't Happen Here*, in which a popular fascist leader is elected president and establishes a totalitarian United States. Some wealthy people purchased "riot and civil commotion insurance." A substantial number of Americans admired Adolf Hitler, including Charles Lindbergh and Henry Ford, who were both given medals by the dictator. Others looked to Benito Mussolini for inspiration.

When war started, even Roosevelt recognized this political reality. Jewish leaders begged him to decry that Jews were being exterminated in death camps, but Roosevelt was loathe to do so, fearing a backlash from extreme right-wing members of Congress. And some wonder why the Allies, once they controlled the skies over Germany, didn't ever bomb the bridges the trains used to take prisoners to the death camps. When one reminds Americans of our fascination with fascism, one encounters rolled eyes, or discomfort, or denial. And yet the historical record is chilling.

Even though in hindsight it seems there could have been no other course of history than the New Deal and America escaping fascism, people forget what John Russo knows to be true, that America could have descended into extreme nationalism in the 1930s. The existence of the Bolsheviks in Russia gave Roosevelt a bogeyman. The American business elite truly feared the same thing happening here as occurred in Russia—violent revolution. Roosevelt was smart enough to know that this would never come to pass. It was clear, both then and now, that American workers will never stage a revolution. But this fear was enough to allow Roosevelt to leverage the conservative elite for some social change. The nation was lucky a Roosevelt came along. But the right lived for revenge.

Payday for that revenge began with Barry Goldwater in 1964, and the rise of the right in the decades that followed. By 1995, hate radio was growing, and Ronald Reagan had chipped away at the New Deal. Reagan called his ascendance the "end of malaise and hopelessness," and "morning again in America."

Yet nothing was triggering an early 1930s-style ascendancy of the extreme rabid right. I quoted John Russo in our book, but John seemed to me to be exaggerating the 1920s and early 1930s comparison with Germany and Italy. Even though I'd lived through years of witnessing anger and despair among the American working class, I couldn't imagine an event that would unleash a sinister genie that would put us over the edge into a battle between the good of tolerance and the force of dark nationalism.

It seemed we'd just muddle along, with millions of Americans living in despair, struggling to survive or just barely making it from paycheck to paycheck.

Six years after we stood with John, in the meadow that had once been a mill, came the morning that changed things.

2

"HOMELAND" rapidly became a commonly used synonym for the United States among the Bush set. It was a word "so redolent of the German *heimat*," as noted by the writer and editor Tom Engelhardt, a reference that was probably lost entirely on the people who coined the Department of Homeland Security and the Homeland Security Act.

Heimat is an ancient word. Centuries ago it meant "farmhouse," or "farm property," but it evolved to have many meanings, none literally translatable into English. The word connotes "identity" and "culture," and even "utopia." *Heimat* is "a place longed or yearned for . . . a real, imagined, or even mythical place of security," according to *Constructing* Heimat *in Postwar Germany: Longing and Belonging*, by Christopher J. Wickham.

For us, the word "homeland" took on an altogether new meaning after the September 11 attacks. But in reality, the evolution had been underway for three decades as a result of profound changes in the economic and cultural landscape that had left a large number of Americans confused, angry, and fearful.

The recurring war imagery so prevalent in what was now freely called the Homeland in 2001, 2002, and 2003 kept me thinking of what John Russo had told us back in 1995, and what I knew of interwar history and the stresses on German society in the 1920s and '30s. Then I had a phone conversation with a woman of Indian descent who had grown up in Germany and now lived in New York City.

"It's Weimar!" she said.

The Weimar to which she referred is the German Weimar Republic, the period from the Treaty of Versailles at the end of World War I through 1933, when Hitler came to power. In this interval, Hitler's ascendancy was fueled by the anger of the citizenry because Germany was economically crippled. During the Weimar Republic, *heimat* took on a dark tone, used by Teutonic nationalists to evoke a past of economic well-being and military prowess.

To the woman on the phone, who had only lived in the United States for a few years, the manifestation of Weimar was the incredible demonstration of flags. To her, the blaze of red, white, and blue was a nationalistic display that would be unthinkable in today's Germany. It harkened too much to the rise of Nazism and its reliance on the overdrawn symbolism of flags as the Weimar Republic fell.

Perhaps this woman was stretching things. After all, not everyone who flew a flag after 9/11 was a nationalist. Plenty of liberals and middle-of-the-roaders I knew displayed flags, and they didn't intend to convey this kind of a message.

It was something else that so terrified this woman. Because she was South Asian and had an accent, she too felt compelled to put a flag in her window, out of fear, to show she was not "other." She'd conformed to the will of the masses. To her, that is what most made it Weimar. She was living in her own personal Weimar.

Comparing the United States to the Weimar Republic will invite instant howls of protest in some circles, for what comes to mind are thousands of leftist websites equating George W. Bush to Hitler. These are as erroneous as those who claimed Saddam Hussein was Hitler. The Hitler comparison is a tired cliché that has been overused by both the left and right.

Yet it's eerie that it crops up so often these days. An early mention came not from the left, but from Karl Rove, Bush's chief advisor, who, not long after 9/11, watched a World Series crowd "erupt" when Bush threw out the first pitch. The President flashed a thumbs-up—and thousands returned it. "It's like being at a Nazi rally," said Rove, as paraphrased by Bob Woodward in his book, *Bush at War*.

I unearthed no public reaction from the White House. Another Nazi comparison a year later, however, caused a furor. German Justice Minister Herta Daeubler-Gmelin was quoted in the paper *Schwaebisches Tagblatt*, saying that with war on Iraq, Bush "wants to divert attention from his domestic problems. It's a classic tactic. It's one that Hitler used." She was forced to resign soon after making the statement.

Then there's the case of executive producer Ed Gernon, who had long wanted to make a movie on Hitler. The production company Alliance

Atlantis sold it to CBS. The four-hour project, *Hitler: The Rise of Evil*, neared airing as Baghdad fell. Gernon was interviewed by *TV Guide*.

"It basically boils down to an entire nation gripped by fear, who ultimately chose to give up their civil rights and plunged the whole world into war. I can't think of a better time to examine this history than now."

Gernon pointed out that fear drove Bush's preemptive war policy and the approval of it by many Americans. In 1930s Germany, Gernon said, a parallel fear gripped Germans.

"When an entire country becomes afraid for their sovereignty, for their safety, they will embrace ideas and strategies and positions that they might not embrace otherwise," Gernon said.

An advance copy of *TV Guide* was leaked to the New York *Post*.

"The scraping sound you hear next month will be Hollywood's anti-Americanism hitting bottom with the CBS movie, *Hitler: The Rise of Evil*," said one *Post* column. "An act of slander against the president of the United States—and by extension, toward the United States itself," another *Post* writer noted.

People often scream the loudest at the truth and truth-tellers. Gernon was immediately fired by Alliance Atlantis.

When the filmmaker said his movie was a cautionary tale, he was not invoking post-Hitler Germany, but *pre*-Hitler Germany. This is a critical distinction. Gernon was describing how a country has to travel down a road to end up as Germany did, consumed by anger and fear. This may take years; the United States is at the beginning of that road.

That America may be at the start of a Weimaresque journey is not anti-American name-calling. The 1919–1933 Weimar period culminated with Hitler, but it was about a whole lot more than Hitler. Let's take Hitler out of the main picture and look at the history.

☙

A NEW Germany was born with the election of January 19, 1919, when 435 members of the National Assembly were chosen. It was a centrist vote, with 76.2 percent casting ballots for moderate parties, the largest being the Social Democrats. The right won just under 15 percent, the socialists, 8 percent. The communists boycotted the election. The following month, the freshman assembly met in the city of Weimar, home of Goethe. Berlin was not picked for the new capital because of its association with imperial Germany. It was the first time Germany had any form of democratic government.

For most of the nation's history, there had not been a single strong German state. In the Middle Ages, there were some three hundred separate states in what is now Germany. Both Britain and France emerged in the seventeenth and eighteenth centuries as powerful and united nations, and there was a flowering of democracy. But Germany remained mired in an era of rival princes.

All that changed when the Prussian Otto von Bismarck, through brute force, "blood and iron," united Germany between 1866 and 1871. Thus was born, William L. Shirer wrote in *The Rise and Fall of the Third Reich*, "the problem child of Europe and the world for nearly a century, a nation of gifted, vigorous people . . . inculcating a lust for power and domination, a passion for unbridled militarism, a contempt for democracy and individual freedom and a longing for authority, for authoritarianism."[1]

Bismarck's goal was to overthrow liberalism, boost the power of conservatism. After defeating the French in 1871, Germany's only great power rival was England.

World War I, of course, changed all that. After their defeat of November 1918, the Germans were stripped of much of their wealth and power at the Treaty of Versailles, which parceled out German territory to France, and gave lands back to Denmark and Poland that had been taken in previous conquests. Most important, it mandated reparations to be paid for the war—not only in gold, but in timber and minerals. The army was substantially weakened, with armaments and manpower limitations to ensure that Germany would not again threaten Europe.

The Germans were in great denial about their loss of power. The new Weimar government delayed ratification of the treaty until nineteen minutes before the deadline. The conservative minority was instantly vocal, in the first meeting leaping to the defense of how Kaiser Wilhelm II, along with his generals, had conducted the war. Their loss of power rankled deeply.

The bill for reparations was not clearly spelled out until 1921, when the Allies tallied up the total: 132 billion gold marks, or $3.5 billion in U.S. currency. This was a stunning figure. At the same time, the United States pressured Europe to repay war loans, which put the heat on the Allies to get money from Germany.

The mark began to slip. In 1921, it hit 75 to the dollar. In 1922, 400 to the dollar. In early 1923 the mark was 7,000 to the dollar and by the end of that year was valued at 4 billion to the dollar.

History books show pictures of Germans carting baskets and wheelbarrows of money to buy bread. The average German from the middle and working class howled. Bank accounts became worthless, and with economic deprivation came growing anger.

What did the government do? Instead of raising taxes on the rich who could afford to pay, it lowered them. The terrible conditions were actually good for the industrialists and landlords. They wanted the mark to tumble, because they profited: the industrialists were able to erase debts by paying them off with worthless marks. The government paid attention to the rich at the expense of the masses.

The Weimar Republic was blamed for all that was wrong. It was attacked from its inception by Bolsheviks on the left, and later by Nazis on the right.

Amid this, a curious pattern emerged. Liberals were charged with treason and given long prison terms when they pointed out German violations of the Treaty of Versailles. But rightists, even those who tried to overthrow the government with guns, received far lighter sentences.

Hitler was among the many rightists treated with leniency, even after he attempted a coup in the famous "beer hall putsch." It started on the night of November 8, 1923, at the Buergerbraukeller, a large beer hall in Munich. The next day, the anniversary of the German republic, Hitler led some 3,000 storm troopers toward downtown Munich. They had machine guns, and Hitler carried a revolver. Police challenged the mob. Gunfire erupted, leaving sixteen Nazis and three policemen dead, with many wounded. Hitler was sentenced to five years in prison. He served nine months and was released.

Following Hitler's imprisonment, conditions in Germany improved, reducing Hitler's appeal. A boom economy emerged in the 1920s. Inflation was curtailed. The American Dawes Plan softened the hardship of reparations. The concept of the "world economy" might seem of recent vintage, but Americans were investing abroad in the 1920s. American financiers poured $7 billion into Germany between 1924 and 1930. Unemployment fell, the economy grew.

By the 1928 election, the Nazis were marginalized. They captured just 810,000 votes out of 31 million; the party had only a dozen seats out of 491 in the Reichstag.

The dawn of the U.S. Great Depression turned events around again. "No longer could the nation [Germany] support itself by foreign borrowing," wrote historian William K. Klingaman in his book, *1929: The Year of the Great Crash*. "In the wake of the crash and the subsequent worldwide credit stringency, hard-pressed foreign investors anxiously withdrew the short-term loans that had kept the German economy afloat for the past six years . . . the Berlin stock market crashed; exports dried up . . . factories shut down and unemployment mounted to dangerous heights." In the 1930 election, the Nazis garnered 6.4 million votes, and 107 seats in the Reichstag.

"Democracy and liberalism were wrong," Hitler said. Though not a majority, the Nazis wielded a lot of power. The moderates could not maintain a working majority in a parliamentary form of government. There were too many parties working at cross-purposes.

In the 1932 election, Hitler ran for president on a platform that pointed an accusing finger at the weaknesses of the Weimar Republic and the terrible conditions Germans faced. Field Marshall Paul von Hindenberg got 49.6 percent of the vote; Hitler was the next highest, with 30.1 percent.

Because no one got an absolute majority, there was a runoff. Hitler changed tactics. He focused on a bright future—jobs and better business conditions. Still, he was only able to get 36.8 percent, to Hindenberg's 53 percent.

It seemed to be a decisive rejection of extreme conservatism. Most votes were cast in favor of the republic. But there was violence in the streets; fighting broke out between the Bolsheviks and Nazi S.A. troops, the brownshirts and the communists attacking each other with fists or guns.

Meanwhile, the National Socialist German Worker's Party, the Nazis, continued to press for political power. In the 1932 election, the party overall got just 37 percent of the Reichstag vote. It was their crest. The other 63 percent was fractious, however. The major party, the Social Democrats, were worn out—according to Shirer, "dominated by old, well-meaning but mostly mediocre men." Shirer termed them "too timid" to take the risks necessary to stop the extreme right.

As for the communists, the party's leaders subscribed to the theory that the worse it gets, the better it gets. They figured that they would allow the Nazis to take over, which would lead to the collapse of capitalism, affording thee communists an avenue to seize power later. What they did not count on was Hitler's rise to chancellor under President Hindenberg.

Yet it would require an act of terror for Hitler to take his quest for power to the next level.

On the night of February 27, 1933, the Reichstag caught fire. Hitler and his henchmen instantly blamed the communists, though one lone crazed man was arrested. Some historians say it was likely an arson set on the orders of Herman Goering and Propaganda Minister Paul Joseph Goebbels. Regardless of the cause, the act of terror was used as the rationale for a mandate. As the ashes smoldered, Hitler pushed Hindenberg to grant him dictatorial powers, cutting back on civil liberties, such as the necessity of warrants for searching houses and freedom of the press. Hitler called it a "defensive measure against communist acts of violence endangering the state."

He was granted the powers. In the next election, for the first time, Hitler had control of all the benefits of incumbency—air time, money, and position. There was an orgy of swastika flags, billboards, massive rallies. Yet he got just 44 percent of the vote. It was the last democratic election held while Hitler was alive.

Days later, on March 23, 1933, the new Reichstag gathered to pass the Enabling Act, the "Law for Removing the Distress of People and Reich." It granted Chancellor Hitler the right to "deviate from the constitution," and weakened Parliament. This act became the legal foundation for Hitler's power grab. From then on there were rigged elections, purges in which opponents were shot, and all the trappings of dictatorship. Germany's Weimar period had ended. "Raise high the flags!" went the line from the Horst Wessel song, which became one of the two national anthems under the Nazis as they began their march to apocalypse.

⁄⁊

AS HISTORY shows, everything about the Weimar era was steroid-packed with extremes—violence by thugs that no modern democratic society would tolerate, bizarre currency fluctuations, a Great Depression. In the recent war, the nations of Europe had lost millions of citizens. There was stunning bitterness across the continent.

It may seem inconceivable to us that a new Hitler could emerge in modern times, trying to force armed revolt, suspending elections, dragging a country into a world war. The latter could only happen under a weak parliamentary form of government. The American two-party system may be flawed, but it's far harder for a fringe group to gain power.

As for race, the norms of contemporary society would not allow open racial hatred.

⁄⁊

BACK IN 1983, I stood amid the ruins of U.S. Steel's Ohio Works in Youngstown, watching Joe Marshall and his son, Joe Jr. The elder Marshall had landed at Normandy on D-Day in 1944, and was one of only four survivors from his unit. He'd returned home to the mill, and his son had followed him into the plant. It had shut its doors on them three years earlier, throwing thousands out of jobs. The blast furnaces had just been dynamited, the three towers tumbling in unison in a cloud of dust, as if hit by a Tomahawk missile.

"What Hitler couldn't do, they did it for him," Joe Sr. uttered that late winter afternoon, as he surveyed the destruction.

I wrote this in my notepad, put it in *Journey to Nowhere*. Years later this line caught the attention of Bruce Springsteen, who after reading our book one night, was inspired to use a variation of what Joe said in a song he would call "Youngstown," about "Jenny," a blast furnace and a man doomed by industrial decline. Bruce sang: "Those big boys did what Hitler couldn't do."

Joe Marshall Sr. saw it coming before any of us.

In January 1996, Bruce performed his song at Stambaugh Auditorium in Youngstown. Bruce met the Marshalls and John Russo after the show. Joe Jr. had never recovered from the shutdown. He was then working three jobs—as a part-time sheriff's deputy, a guard at a hospital, and a freelance guard for hire at weddings and events. He was divorced and living at home. Between the jobs, he was only able to get three hours of sleep per night, not including catnaps. The three jobs combined paid far less than what he'd earned in the steel mill. He'd traveled looking for work, and tried to learn new skills. After years of effort, he'd done all he could do. Three part time jobs was now his fate.

By the time Joe Jr. met Bruce, he had shadows beneath his eyes from sleep deprivation. The down-turned lines of sadness at the outside corners of his eyes and mouth, seemingly temporary back in 1983, were now permanent, though he wasn't mean or angry. Far from it. He looks like the nice guy that he is. He once confided to us that he'd never be able to shoot at someone who was stealing to eat. And when he talked of the four prisons that were the new industry in Youngstown, he knew they hired former steelworkers and their children to guard former steelworkers and their children.

While traveling and doing research for this book, I kept thinking of Joe Marshall Jr. I kept seeing his face in those of others who were far angrier. Germans had the ravages of a war and its economic aftermath to amp up the populace in the Weimar period. The people I was interviewing in America had the impact of a virtual three-decades-long war waged against the working class. As with the Germans in the Weimar period, many Americans long for a nation that is powerful—at least in economic terms. Americans may not be lugging bushel baskets of money to buy bread, but they're trying to live on Wal-Mart wages, paying Silicon Valley-level prices for mortgages and rents in the hinterlands. These Americans want back the America they remember. But they are unable to do anything to restore that bygone era, or even to see their point of view expressed.

The parallels to the German Weimar are many: the falling towers are the equivalent of the Reichstag fire. The USA PATRIOT Act (the acronym stands for "Uniting and Strengthening America by Providing Appropriate

Tools Required to Intercept and Obstruct Terrorism") parallels the Enabling Act. Like the German Social Democrats, the American Democratic leadership proved itself to be timid, old, and worn out in the face of mounting conservative power. The United States is not a parliamentary form of government, but Democrats have long been splintered. As the late House Speaker Tip O'Neil once noted, it is really five or six parties under the umbrella of one. Factionalism has in recent years rendered the party internally Weimar-like. Meanwhile, over the past two decades, the extreme right has taken over the Republican Party, which is strong and speaks with one voice. Congressional moderates can at best be counted on two hands, as Republicans have shot to the radical right. And most important, there exists anger that has been years in the making.

Talk radio is one expression of the anger and frustration. In 1980, there were just seventy-five stations in the nation that were all talk. There weren't that many conservative hosts. Now, there are 1,300 all-talk stations, and conservatives rule these airwaves. Talk radio—and its cable television cousin—rose to popularity as anger and fear deepened in American society. These shows were not a cause, but a free market response.

Anytime I listen to talk radio, it strikes me as a virtual beer hall. Hitler and Goering (who organized and energized the brownshirts) and other conservatives spoke in crowded beer halls for hours at a time, to incite the citizenry. One recalls the frenzy from newsreel images of Hitler, fist shaking, spittle flying, hair wildly flopping.

Conservative radio and television hosts today include Neal Boortz, Glenn Beck, Sean Hannity, G. Gordon Liddy, Rush Limbaugh, Oliver North, Bill O'Reilly (the most-watched actor on cable news), Michael Reagan, and Michael Savage.

The bigs on radio are Limbaugh, with 14.5 million listeners, Hannity with ten million, and Savage with six million, according to *Talkers Magazine*. While these numbers are impressive, there's likely a large overlap in listenership. And the vociferous conservative commentators have a profile out of proportion with their actual influence; a high decibel level is its own force.

In Weimar Germany, the beer halls were where the conservatives found recruits to become storm troopers. In Homeland America, few have crossed the line into violence. But some listeners have crept toward that line, said U.S. Senator Tom Daschle, D-South Dakota, in a news conference in late 2002.

"What happens when Rush Limbaugh attacks those of us in public life is that people aren't satisfied just to listen. They want to act because they get emotionally invested. And so, you know, the threats to those of us in public life go up dramatically," Daschle said, adding that there had also been threats of violence against his family.

Today, no one is locking up liberals on treason charges, or shooting them, as might have happened in 1920s Germany. But in another Weimar echo, conservatives are treated much more leniently for the same offenses. One imagines what would have happened if Bill Clinton were in office and had lied about the reasons for war; he was impeached for less significant matters.

When Columbia University held a "teach in" on the Iraq war, thirty professors spoke to some three thousand students. Professor Nicholas De Genova, in his fifteen minutes, called for the "fragging" of U.S. soldiers. And he wished for "a million Mogadishus." This statement set talk radio on a jihad against him. Seventy-eight New York state legislators signed a letter condemning De Genova's statements. Republican Governor George Pataki questioned his fitness as a professor. Then 104 Republican members of Congress sent a letter to Columbia President Lee C. Bollinger, asking that De Genova be dismissed.

One might find De Genova a fine target for censure. His comments were certainly irresponsible. But compare them to the words of the well-known conservative commentator Ann Coulter.

In an interview with George Gurley of the *New York Observer*: "My only regret with Timothy McVeigh is he did not go to the *New York Times* building."

About President Bill Clinton: he was "white trash," and "like a serial killer." He was also "creepier and slimier than Kennedy . . . He's behaving like some sort of sultan or tin-pot dictator . . . We're now at the point that it's beyond whether or not this guy is a horny hick. I really think it's a question of his mental stability . . . I think it is a rational question for Americans to ask whether their president is insane."

A database search found no state-legislature censure of Coulter. No lawmakers signed letters or passed resolutions. Imagine what would happen in Weimar America if a liberal on a national talk show said that George Bush was insane and a serial killer, or that the *Weekly Standard* be bombed.

And then there was the controversy over the Dixie Chicks, whose lead singer Natalie Maines ever-so-gently questioned Bush and the Iraq War. "Just so you know, we're ashamed the president of the United States is from Texas," said Maines to a London audience. Maines grew up in Lubbock, Texas.

Country stations boycotted the group's music. Maines issued a groveling apology. No matter. The boycott continued. The South Carolina legislature was moved to pass a resolution asking the group to apologize directly to the state, and to play a free concert for soldiers. Country singer Toby Keith flashed doctored pictures depicting Maines with Saddam Hussein (as lovers) on large screens at his concerts. Keith was heralded as a hero for this. When Maines went on a counteroffensive and attended a country music awards ceremony wearing a tee shirt with "f.u.t.k." imprinted on it (a Chicks publicist said the letters stood for "freedom understanding tolerance knowledge," but fans and foes took the shirt to mean something far less benevolent toward Toby Keith), the attacks against her increased in fury. She received death threats. In Bossier City, Louisiana, KRMD 101.1-FM radio organized a "Dixie Chicks Destruction Day" attended by a few hundred protesters, where a 33,000 pound monster tractor was used to crush Dixie Chicks CDs.

Meanwhile, the mainstream press was largely uncritical or silent for the two years after 9/11. It embraced collective conformity, a Weimaresque submission without question. No Goebbels was required. Few newspapers did their jobs. Even when Democrats began raising their heads and finally criticized Bush, the press was cautious.

On television during the Iraq campaign, Americans saw few images of actual war, with the focus instead on homespun stories of troops. Fairness and Accuracy in Reporting found 76 percent of all sources were officials past or present, and that on the four major networks monitored, just three out of 393 sources were against the war. Some anchors wore American flag pins.

During George W. Bush's press conference on the eve of the Iraq War, for the first time reporters were chosen in advance, and not allowed to raise their hands. And for the first time in the half century that she has sat in the front row since John F. Kennedy was president, not only was Helen Thomas not allowed to ask the first question, she was shunned. The White House feared a hard question from the eighty-two-year-old former United Press International writer.

The press conference was staged. Even Bush seemed to acknowledge this when, looking down at the list of chosen reporters, he said, "This is a scripted . . ." before he caught himself. Tom Rosensteil, of the Project for Excellence in Journalism, said the press looked like "lapdogs." Everyone was polite, before and after. A Canadian writer described it as a "well-choreographed ballet of sleepwalkers."

One compares this press conference to what happened in Spain after Jose Couso, a Spanish television cameraman, was killed in Iraq at the Palestine Hotel by a U.S. tank shell. Dozens of those who cover the Spanish Senate dumped cameras, tape recorders, and notepads into a pile. They stood in silent protest when Prime Minister José Aznar showed up. And hundreds of journalists blockaded the road outside the U.S. Embassy in Madrid. Television cameramen and still photographers covered their lenses to protest what they said was the U.S. government's intent to stop independent coverage of the war.

The American press fell down on other fronts. For two years, the drive to take back civil liberties in the name of Homeland Security was an underreported story, as the government pushed to become the postmodern *Schutzstaffel*, or SS, with supreme powers.

Five weeks after 9/11, the USA PATRIOT Act was passed. At the same time what was then called Total Information Awareness (TIA) was being developed by DARPA (see News Diary I). TIA would collect stunning data through a program called "LifeLog": student grades, medical history, travel, each credit card purchase, and so on. It would be a "virtual centralized, grand database."

"The embryonic LifeLog program would dump everything an individual does into a giant database: every e-mail sent or received, every picture taken, every Web page surfed, every phone call made, every TV show watched, every magazine read," wrote Noah Shachtman in *Wired Magazine*. Though Congress banned its use on citizens, DARPA went ahead to develop it for use on foreign nationals.[2]

And then on January 9, 2003, an eighty-six page draft of a new and "improved" USA PATRIOT Act, known as "The Domestic Security Enhancement Act of 2003," was leaked by a staffer in John Ashcroft's office and posted on the Center for Public Integrity's website. The bill had one hundred provisions. Among them, any American could have his or her citizenship revoked if found to have provided "material support" to terrorist organizations. "Material support" was left undefined, just as the list of terrorist organizations is a secret.[3]

Also in the proposed bill, the government would build a huge database of DNA samples from citizens. No court order would be required to collect samples—simply the suspicion of a cop would be sufficient. Businesses that erringly fink to the feds on their customers' supposed terror activities would be immune from lawsuits. And police would also be exempt from lawsuits if they conducted illegal searches, so long as they were following orders.[4]

The police state mentality among those in power nationally filtered down to the tiniest of police departments. In Barre, Vermont, for example, Tom Treece was teaching public issues at Spaulding High School. He had students do artwork for the course unit on Iraq. Students were expected to debate whether the U.S. should invade and were to create a poster expressing their views. One showed George Bush with his mouth covered by duct tape, and it said "My fellow Americans, put your duct tape to good use: Shut me up!"

Officer John Mott from nearby Barre Town (an unincorporated settlement near Barre) heard about this, drove to the school in uniform at 1:30 AM, and talked a custodian into unlocking the door, according to published reports. Mott went to the classroom and photographed the artwork. He told the Barre *Times Argus* that "I wanted everybody else to see what was in that room," and that he was "insulted."

The outraged Barre city council sent a letter to Barre Town officials saying Mott was out of his jurisdiction and was trespassing. Barre Town officials said they handled the situation as a "private personnel matter." Rush Limbaugh praised Mott on his show. The pictures were also posted on Limbaugh's web page.

Supreme Court Justice Antonin Scalia said on March 18, 2003, in a talk at John Carroll University in Cleveland, "Most of the rights you enjoy go way beyond what the Constitution requires. The Constitution just sets minimums." In wartime, he added, "the protections will be ratcheted right down to the constitutional minimum." Scalia didn't expand any further on what he meant, and we are left to ask ourselves whether, given that the war on terrorism will go on for many, many years, we want to live in a society with minimal constitutional rights?

✍

IN THE FALL of 2000, with the presidential campaign in full swing, a report was released by the Project for the New American Century, an extreme-right think tank, entitled "Rebuilding America's Defenses: Strategy, Forces and Resources for a New Century."

The report called for Pax Americana, for the U.S. to "secure and expand zones of democratic peace; deter rise of new great-power competitor; defend key regions; exploit transformation of war." It called for a massive expansion of military power and presence, to "fight and decisively win multiple, simultaneous major theater wars."

Global hegemony is vital, according to the report, which named China as a foe. But the biggest enemies were seen as Iran, Iraq, Libya, Syria, and North Korea. Iran was named as potentially as dire a threat as Iraq. Most mentioned were Iraq, Iran, and North Korea. "We cannot allow North Korea, Iran, Iraq or similar states to undermine American leadership, intimidate American allies or threaten the American homeland itself," the report said. Even Europe was viewed as a threat.

The report asked for "demanding American political leadership rather than that of the United Nations." It hinted that the U.S. should develop biological weaponry. It insisted the new administration act within six months for a new security plan to control the world.

Militarizing space would be key, as would establishing a "Space Command." The report asked for "safer" nuclear weapons to be used commonly in war. It called for pulling out of the Comprehensive Test Ban Treaty, and sneered at the 1972 Anti-Ballistic Missile treaty.

The report essentially mandated preventive war, saying "American military preeminence will continue to rest in significant part on the ability to maintain sufficient land forces to achieve political goals such as removing dangerous and hostile regimes when necessary."

The list of "project participants" included Donald Kagan, William Kristol (the editor of the *Weekly Standard*), and Paul Wolfowitz. James Woolsey, the former CIA head, was also involved with the Project for the New American Century.

Were these men eager for something catastrophic to happen that would bring them power? They wrote, "Further, the process of transformation, even if it brings revolutionary change, is likely to be a long one, absent some catastrophic and catalyzing event—like a new Pearl Harbor."

This group of men had labored in obscurity through the Clinton years, waiting for their day. Under Clinton, they were powerless.

Wolfowitz and the cadre of Strangelovian hawks would take key positions of power only after a new man was installed as president by the U.S. Supreme Court. In the Bush White House, Wolfowitz would become Deputy Defense Secretary. Kristol would have a role as a booster. Another crony of this think tank was Richard Perle, who ended up on the Defense Policy Board, which advises the Pentagon.

From their perspective, it was a most remarkable confluence—a man at the helm who would take their ranting seriously, and their own Pearl Harbor in the form of 9/11.

Their excitement was profound. The cover of the *Weekly Standard* on October 15, 2001, read: "The Case for American Empire." Inside, Max Boot, the *Wall Street Journal* editorial features editor, wrote that "Afghanistan and other troubled lands today cry out for the sort of enlightened foreign administration once provided by self-confident Englishmen in jodhpurs and pith helmets."

In 2002, Bush would embrace everything about the Project for a New American Century report. It became the "Bush Doctrine," which called for preventive war. It included his infamous "Axis of Evil" speech in which he recklessly equated Iraq, Iran, and Korea.

"Steadfast in our purpose, we now press on," Bush said. "We have known freedom's price. We have shown freedom's power. And in this great conflict, my fellow Americans, we will see freedom's victory."

Richard Wagner, the composer exalted by German rightists, hoped Germans would "become not rulers, but ennoblers of the world." The United States was now the Wagnerian ennobler.

A week before Baghdad was taken, Woolsey described the Iraq War to students at the University of California, Los Angeles, as the start of the "Fourth World War." The third, to him, was the Cold War. "This Fourth World War, I think, will last considerably longer than either World Wars I or II did for us."

The U.S. faces three enemies, Woolsey told the students: Iran, the "fascists" of Iraq and Syria, and Islamic fundamentalists.

"As we move toward a new Middle East, over the years and, I think, over the decades to come . . . we will make a lot of people very nervous. Our response should be, 'Good! We want you nervous. We want you to realize now that for the fourth time in one hundred years, this country and its allies are on the march.'"

Richard Perle wrote, "What will die is the fantasy of the UN as the foundation of a new world order. As we sift [through] the debris, it will be important to preserve, the better to understand, the intellectual wreckage of the liberal conceit of safety through international law administered by international institutions."

John Bolton, a director of the New American Century project, now the assistant secretary of state for disarmament affairs, told Ariel Sharon that the U.S. would next deal with his neighbor Syria and nearby Iran.

Then, after Defense Secretary Donald Rumsfeld warned Iran and Syria about "hostile acts," a close aide to Bush went to the Oval Office to inform the president that Rumsfeld "raised the specter of a broader confrontation," according to *New York Times* reporter David Sanger.

Bush's response?

"Good."

≈

THE UNITED STATES was now openly saying it would engage in eternal war against nations that had not attacked it. Like the Germans, we would "march." And like the anti-Weimarist Germans, there were elements in power bent on destroying what they viewed as an old liberal order. Many were eager for glory.

Across the Homeland, the voices of opposition were marginalized. (They were millions strong and yelling loudly—only no one in the media listened or noticed.) As in the Weimar Republic, the opposition party was cowed, with a few notable exceptions.

Commenting on the ascendancy of the cadre of hawks in *The Nation* on April 21, 2003, former Senator George McGovern wrote,

> Appearing to enjoy his role as Commander in Chief of the Armed forces above all other functions of his office, and unchecked by a seemingly timid Congress, a compliant Supreme Court, a largely subservient press and a corrupt corporate plutocracy, George W. Bush has set the nation on a course for one-man rule.

Senator Robert C. Byrd, displaying a rare sense of history and of the gravity of Bush's actions, spoke on the Senate floor:

> Yet, this Chamber is, for the part, silent—ominously, dreadfully silent. There is no debate, no discussion, no attempt to lay out for the nation the pros and cons of this particular war. There is nothing.
>
> We stand passively mute in the United States Senate, paralyzed by our own uncertainty, seeming stunned by the sheer turmoil of events . . . And this is no small conflagration we contemplate. This is no simple attempt to defang a villain. No. This coming battle . . . represents a turning point in U.S. foreign policy and possibly a turning point in the history of the world. The nation is about to embark upon the first test of a revolutionary doctrine applied in an extraordinary way at an unfortunate time. The doctrine of preemption—the idea that the United States or any other nation can legitimately attack a nation that is not imminently threatening but may be threatening in the future—is a radical new twist on the traditional idea of self-defense. It appears to be in contravention of international law and the UN Charter. . . .
>
> There are huge cracks emerging in our time-honored alliances, and U.S. intentions are suddenly subject to damaging worldwide speculation . . . This administration, now in power for a little over two years, must be judged on its record. I believe that record is dismal. In that scant two years, this administration has squandered a large projected surplus of some $5.6 trillion over the next decade and taken us to projected deficits as far as the eye can see. This administration's domestic policy has put many of our states in dire financial condition, underfunding

scores of essential programs for our people. This administration has fostered policies which have slowed economic growth. This administration has ignored urgent matters such as the crisis in health care for our elderly.

This administration has called into question the traditional worldwide perception of the United States as well-intentioned peacekeeper. This administration has turned the patient art of diplomacy into threats, labeling, and name calling of the sort that reflects quite poorly on the intelligence and sensitivity of our leaders, and which will have consequences for years to come. Calling heads of state pygmies, labeling whole countries as evil, denigrating powerful European allies as irrelevant— these types of crude insensitivities can do our great nation no good. We may have massive military might, but we cannot fight a global war on terrorism alone.

In only the space of two short years this reckless and arrogant administration has initiated policies which may reap disastrous consequences for years . . . We are truly "sleepwalking through history." In my heart of hearts I pray that this great nation and its good and trusting citizens are not in for a rudest of awakenings.

※

AFTER IRAQ was taken and there was strong and continuing resistance to the occupation, Americans suddenly appeared bad players at the game of empire. The pith helmets and jodhpurs just didn't fit the force of "liberators." And the natives were showing themselves unimpressed by the modern-day avatars of the white man's burden.

Even if the Bush Administration crumbles like a house of rice paper and the Democrats rally, we still will be left with a lot of anger and fear: fear of terrorism, and the economic anger that has been so long in building. The impact of three decades of virtual war on working-class Americans will not vanish with the next presidential election cycle.

Americans are now sullen, afraid, helpless, in denial. *Boston Globe* columnist James Carroll calls it "a communal self-blinding." For many, the default chant of "USA! USA!" is a way of drowning out the realities we don't want to face. Americans don't want to admit there's been any change—in their economic status, in their level of safety.

Stoking these fears—the easy and nationalistic way out—has been a tactic of the Bush administration. Terror threats always seem to go up when a new policy is pushed. As writer Eliot Weinberger has said, the administration in tandem with the media creates "a kind of techno-rave of the disturbing and the frightening, with each new artificial panic blending into the next and erasing the memory of the previous one."

Fueling fear is easy. Dealing with the underlying issues, difficult to address in sound bites, is not.

There are two ways for a society to collapse. One is from external forces. The other is from self-inflicted wounds, a Pogo-like consumption of having met the enemy, and seen that the enemy is us. The definition for the word "homeland" continues to evolve. Homeland is now our *heimat*. We will collectively write the next chapter of what it means.

We are a terribly divided country, and may grow farther apart as more Americans fall into economic ruin due to the stunning amounts of money it will cost to keep up with the extremist conservatives' plan for Pax Americana. As Chalmers Johnson noted, Richard Nixon, instead of withdrawing from Bretton Woods, could have spared the nation crippling debt by ending the Vietnam War. That debt came back to haunt America in the 1980s in the form of high interest rates that, along with blowback from disastrous Cold War industrial policy, grievously harmed workers.[5] Proponents of military adventuring never stop to factor in costs. War is their emotional outlet. Working-class proponents of war are the ones who, ironically, will suffer most the economic cost that comes later.

What kind of America do we want to live in, for ourselves, for our children and our grandchildren?

3

MY FATHER'S cremated remains lay beneath an American flag held by four soldiers at Arlington National Cemetery, a year after 9/11. Seven other soldiers each fired rifles three times. Steve Maharidge gets twenty-one shots and a hole in the ground here because they gave him a Purple Heart after he was wounded in the bloody South Pacific island fighting. He got a piece of Japanese steel in his back that they never could get out, and it was there somewhere amongst the ashes.

Dad never talked much about the war. After he died, I sought out and found guys from his unit, L Company, 3rd Battalion, 22nd Marine Regiment, 6th Marine Division. George Popovich told me about the night on Guam, July 25, 1944, when he and Dad were in a trench on the Orote Peninsula battling the Japanese just feet away. A mortar round or a grenade blew behind my father, killing the two men on either side of him, spraying shrapnel into his back. Come morning, there were fifteen dead Americans in the trench, two alive—Dad, wounded, and George.

The injury was no ticket home. They patched Dad up and on April 1, 1945, he and 239 other men hit the Okinawa beach. The unit was among those that took Naha, the first and only Japanese city captured in the war before the atom bombs were dropped. According to information from the government, only thirty-one of the 240 came off the island alive.

It was near the end of the "good war." In the Okinawa campaign, the northern portion of the island was quickly taken—the prize being the Yontan Airfield, to use in launching attacks against Japan. There was political pressure to crush the Japanese, and so my father and thousands of other U.S.

soldiers were ordered to march south. Among the many critics of this campaign was General Douglas MacArthur. He argued that the Japanese 32nd Army, dug in on the southern third of the island above the city of Naha, could not meaningfully threaten U.S. troops. MacArthur said a frontal attack would be "sacrificing thousands of American solders."

He advocated starving the Japanese out, rather than press a head-on assault against the formidable Shuri Line, culminating at Sugar Loaf Hill. With ship and air support cut off, the Japanese would weaken as the weeks wore on. MacArthur was ignored, and the bloodiest days of the Pacific war were to come as the Americans taught the Japanese a lesson.

In the end, 12,281 Americans were killed in the entire campaign, and well over 200,000 Japanese and Okinawans.

I once asked Dad about attending veterans' events—why didn't he go to parades and so forth?

"Fuck that!" he said. "There are no heroes. Just survivors." A pause, a vacant look, not at me or anything in the room. Then looking me right in the eye, quietly: "You just survive."

Dad never owned an American flag. Never flew one.

Weeks after burying Dad, I spent Thanksgiving in Chicago, at the home of Dick and Nancy Cusack. Dick had also been in the war, and had landed on Okinawa at the end of the campaign. We talked about it, how that war affected his generation. Some guys were like my Dad, who came home and stayed drunk for four years. Dad coped in a Hemingwayesque manner—in an eternal quest to forget. Others were like Philip Berrigan, Dick's roommate when they were at College of the Holy Cross, and who that fall of 2002 lay on his deathbed halfway across the country.

Dick recalled how World War II affected Phil. Phil and my dad may both have been sickened by combat. But Phil was no Hemingway. He became a Roman Catholic priest, a pacifist, who grew increasingly active against what he saw as "the American empire." Dick talked about the time during the Vietnam War when the FBI went after him and Nancy, accusing them of helping Berrigan and his brother, Dan, who were then fugitives from the FBI after the brothers broke into draft offices and destroyed records, sometimes by pouring blood on them.

Conversation turned to the present. I'd been told by my mother and others that during World War II, one didn't see American flags flying all over the place as one does today. Dick confirmed this. One saw service stars in the windows of homes of men who were in the war, he said. There were flags, but not the flagfest one now witnessed. For sure, there was plenty of patriotism and nationalism, as well as racism (against Japanese Americans) in World War II. But something was different now.

I asked why there were not as many flags in a war in which we lost some four hundred thousand servicemen, the combined death total from combat and other causes.

"Because it's fake," Dick rapidly replied, speaking of the supposed unity the flags represent in Homeland America. Dick died early in the summer of 2003. With the loss of my Dad, Dick, and others, the living memory of the "good war" was rapidly becoming extinct. Their experiences add up to the truth missing from the whitewashed myth of the "greatest generation."

✍

IN 2002, Americans purchased 100 million U.S. flags, compared with 40 million in 2000, according to the National Flag Foundation. There were no sales figures specific to September through December of 2001, a spokesman told me. Anecdotally, however, many stores were sold out of flags in those months.

That winter, I carefully watched the flags, trying to discern all they might mean, looking for regional patterns. I preferred back roads. A heavy flag belt stretched on into Chicago. But once I left there and traveled the two-lane roads of downstate Illinois and beyond, there was a noticeable drop. Miles of travel, no flags.

These were white areas. Then, in western Oklahoma, suddenly there were many flags in two small towns. It was puzzling. Then I sighted Mexican restaurants and stores. Probably there was a meatpacking plant nearby. The flags may have been flown by Mexicans, for immigrants are often superpatriots. But most flags were on large homes, unlikely to be owned by newcomers. Were they flown by fearful whites living among a large immigrant population, eager to show that this is America, in the face of the only outsiders they could see?

Passing through Oklahoma City, I stopped at the site of the Alfred P. Murrah Federal Building, blown up in 1995. American flags were everywhere around the memorial to the dead. The same flag Timothy McVeigh thought he was fighting for, in the Gulf War, and later at home, when he drove the explosives-filled Ryder truck to the site.

Many raise the flag to show support for military action and America on the march. To others, the flag represents our community sense, America banding together. In Chicago, I saw Muslims wearing flag buttons, flying flags on their businesses. In the Chicago Ridge Mall, a Muslim man wore a flag shirt, with the letters USA! shouting down the arm. Perhaps for this man, walking with a woman in a hijab, a flag shirt was the only defense against being attacked.

The German flag was deified by rightists in Weimar Germany. One reason is that it exhibited unity to a country that was really very young and not yet fully formed—the unification of Germany had only happened five decades before the start of Weimar. While we are over four times the age, in the scheme of world history, the United States is also still very young— in some ways younger than the Germany that followed the Treaty of Versailles. We are a teenager, as societies go. With the arrival of each new immigrant wave, we're a nation constantly being redefined.

Some have long wanted to deify the U.S. flag. For years Republicans, including John Ashcroft when he was a U.S. Senator, have tried to amend the constitution to make desecrating a flag illegal. Oddly, at the same time the flag is idolized, I find it imprinted on my plastic garbage bag, or in the newspaper that I am expected to discard. I've seen politicians wiping their mouths with flag-embossed paper napkins. On October 4, 1968, Abbie Hoffman appeared before the House Un-American Activities Committee wearing a flag shirt. Capitol police arrested him for "mutilating the flag" and proceeded to publicly rip that shirt off his back. He quipped, "I regret that I have only one shirt to give my country." But now we have flag shirts, hats, pants, and even underwear worn by "patriots." I've seen flag condoms for sale in the men's rooms of redneck bars.

As 2002 progressed, the flag increasingly was used as a statement of peace against blind patriotism. This sometimes invited stompings by citizens who had differing views on patriotism, at other times the threat of arrest by police.

One of these incidents occurred on September 26, 2002, when two police officers went to the dormitory occupied by students John Bohman and Juan Diaz at Grinnell College in Iowa. They had a U.S. flag hanging upside down in their window. The students had used the international distress signal to signify their protest of U.S. foreign policy. The officers ordered them to remove the flag, or face arrest. They complied, but later went to the Iowa Civil Liberties Union.

In December, a First Amendment lawsuit was filed by the ICLU on behalf of the men. The suit asked the federal court to nullify Iowa's flag law, which declares it illegal to "publicly mutilate, deface, defile or defy, trample upon, cast contempt upon, satirize, deride or burlesque" a U.S. flag.

"A lot of people on the campus wanted to do a big huge demonstration," John told me when we talked. "It was a lot of the anarchists." He was not keen on this. "I had a feeling it would be more a piss-on-America day, rather than a debate."

John, nineteen, was a soft-spoken and deep-thinking young man. A lot of reporters wanted to make him out as radical. This bothered him. He felt his had been a rather minimalist statement.

"It was a pretty dire situation at that time. The vote on Iraq was coming up. You had to do something. I was hoping people would stop and ask why we would do such a thing. I felt the very values the flag stood for were in distress. It's really interesting how it's become a symbol of conservatism."

This answer came fast. Then a long silence.

"There's a growing sense that it's us against the world," he finally said. He feared the concept of "preventive war."

"We are making something really horrible legitimate with our own actions. I was talking with a friend about Rome the other day. There are a lot of similarities. An overreaching empire. A focus on the coliseum—sports. Maybe we are making the same mistake. When people get riled up with nationalism, they have blind faith. That's really scary."

"Nationalism" kept echoing in comments similar to John's as I traveled the country.

✍

IN THE PAST century and a half, U.S. nationalism has crested over a half dozen times: the 1848 Mexican-American War, in which the United States annexed Texas and California and much of the rest of the West; the Spanish-American War; both World Wars I and II; the McCarthy period; the Vietnam War; and now the post-9/11 era. The Spanish-American War was most pivotal. It was America's first real projection as a nation with ambitions beyond the North American continent, and it influenced later periods of war and nationalism, including post-9/11 America. According to former diplomat Warren Zimmermann in his book *The First Great Triumph,* five men were responsible for pushing us into war with Spain: Assistant Navy Secretary Theodore Roosevelt, U.S. Senator Henry Cabot Lodge, Secretary of State John Hay, U.S. Naval officer Alfred T. Mahan, and colonial administrator Elihu Root. Zimmermann wrote that these men "can fairly be called the fathers of modern American imperialism and the men who set the United States on the road to becoming a great power."

There had been a policy of not being expansionist since the administration of Ulysses Grant. The majority opinion favored "continentalism," that the U.S. not expand beyond North America. The notion of Manifest Destiny had existed since the 1840s, but on the eve of the war with Spain, it had merged with the natural selection theories of Charles Darwin. Some academics and theologians twisted Darwin to fit their desires to see the United States become an imperial power, because the country was "naturally fit" to do so.

American evangelicalsbelonging to the U.S. Evangelical Alliance saw themselves naturally selected to spread faith and dominate brown people. In 1885, the group's leader, Josiah Strong, published *Our Country*, a best-selling book that sold 185,000 copies. This book posited that the white man was "divinely commissioned to be, in a peculiar sense, his brother's keeper." America was destined to rule the world, and Strong saw the country moving "down upon Mexico . . . out upon the islands of the sea, over upon Africa and beyond."[1]

Others had mercantile desires—money could be made through empire. For Theodore Roosevelt and Lodge, however, the motive was not religion or markets, but simple expansion. They were among those who had watched European powers moving into the Middle East and Africa. Roosevelt had his eye on Hawaii, which he feared Japan would seize. Zimmermann wrote that "Roosevelt went further than most imperialists in exalting war as an end in itself."

A little less than a year before the war with Spain, Roosevelt (a Harvard graduate who had then never seen combat) gave a speech at the Naval War College, in which he said, "All the great masterful races have been fighting races . . . cowardice in a race, as in an individual, is the unpardonable sin."

The Spanish had been awful in their administration of Cuba, and a civil war had erupted there in 1895. Some Americans immediately wanted to get involved. But most businessmen were not part of the push, for they feared that the recovery from the 1894 Depression, in full swing by 1897, would be cut short by war. It was the Darwin-minded expansionist elites, led by Roosevelt, who wanted war, and they were aided by the yellow press.

Roosevelt worked feverishly behind the scenes in the William McKinley administration to push the war with Spain. McKinley, who had vivid memories of the horrors of the Civil War, was opposed. But then an act of supposed terrorism—the sinking of the battleship Maine in Havana Harbor—gave interventionists an excuse, for they called it an act of war by Spain. It later proved to be an accident caused by an exploding boiler, due to a coal-bunker fire.

There was outspoken dissent by the likes of Carl Schurz and Mark Twain. Republican Senator George F. Hoar asked how Americans could "strut about in the cast-off clothing of pinchbeck emperors and pewter kings?" Less noble in tone was William James, who said the quest for power caused the country to "puke up its ancient soul."

But after the Maine, there was no stopping war. Victory would net for the United States the colonies of Cuba, Puerto Rico, and the Philippines. Business leaders saw the Philippines as vital to trade in Asia, and believed that other adventuring could open more markets.

"The Philippines are ours forever," said U.S. Senator Albert Beveridge of Indiana. "And just beyond the Philippines are China's illimitable markets. We will not retreat from either . . . the power that rules the Pacific is the power that rules the world. That power will forever be the American Republic."

Even McKinley signed on after victory. Of the Filipinos, McKinley said it was the Americans' duty to "uplift and civilize and Christianize them, and, by God's grace, do the very best we could by them, as our fellow men for whom Christ also died."

America had crossed a threshold. By the eve of World War I, the nation was a player on the world stage. But some Americans of German and Irish descent were against fighting on the side of the Allies. And pacifists viewed it as a European problem, one of international bankers and the Old World aristocracy. In the face of this, President Woodrow Wilson romanticized the war to sell it to the public, calling it a "crusade."

Because many immigrants were opposed to the war and immigration was at an all-time high, many longtime Americans feared the newcomers as war approached. But it wasn't just a natural-forming hate that arose: Wilson stoked it. In private, Wilson admitted his fears of riling nationalism, but felt it was necessary to get men to submit to the draft, and to get the nation behind the war in other ways. He was cynical. "Lead this people into war," Wilson said, "and they'll forget there even was such a thing as tolerance."[2]

The Committee on Public Information, a propaganda agency run by journalist George Creel, was created by Wilson one week after the declaration of war. The CPI's job was to convince the public that America was fighting for freedom. It promulgated these notions: all Germans were evil "Huns," there were spies among immigrants, anyone asking questions was secretly helping the enemy, pacifists admired the "Huns," and unionizing was treason.

In 1917, Wilson signed the Espionage Act, which assigned severe penalties for anyone interfering with the war, including those accused of fomenting disloyalty. The Sedition Act of 1918 went further, outlawing anything "disloyal, profane, scurrilous, or abusive" about the United States, the flag, the Constitution, or even the military uniform.

These acts led to more than one thousand convictions. Few of the convicted were actual traitors. Most were union organizers and pacifists. For example, some one hundred members of the Industrial Workers of the

World in Chicago were found guilty of being against the war, when they were simply unionizers. For being in favor of resisting the draft, Eugene V. Debs was sentenced to twenty years. Socialist Congressman Victor Berger also got twenty years, for writing editorials against capitalism in the Milwaukee *Leader.*

With the CPI's encouragement, American super patriots watched "enemy aliens." In some places, roving bands of patriotic thugs made immigrants sign liberty bond pledges, or harassed immigrants who didn't fly flags, in some cases forcing people to kneel and kiss the flag. Germanic names were erased from everyday terms. Restaurants changed the name of sauerkraut to "liberty cabbage," hamburger to Salisbury steak, frankfurters to hot dogs. Dachshunds became "liberty pups."

There were parallels eight decades later, in 2002, when the Pentagon proposed the Office of Strategic Influence, which would in part disseminate disinformation to the overseas press, or pay foreign journalists for favorable coverage. It was shot down, then reappeared in 2003. After French opposition to Bush's War in Iraq—in an echo of the "liberty cabbage" era—French fries were renamed "freedom fries" by Neal Rowland, the owner of the franchise restaurant Cubbies in Beaufort, North Carolina. French dressing became . . . well, you know. Freedom fries were served with a tiny American flag. For a time, sales soared. Ohio Republican Bob Ney, on the committee responsible for House operations, ordered the word "French" stricken from all menus in the Capitol Building. Now America's leaders ate freedom fries and freedom toast.

And Republicans were scripted to respond to any criticism from Senator (later presidential candidate) John Kerry, D-Mass, by saying, "He looks French."

This nationalism on the eve of the Iraq War followed long-standing historical patterns. It happened in Germany on the eve of World War II, and it happened in Argentina and the Balkans decades later—dissenters were scorned, pilloried, and marginalized as their nations spiraled down shadowy trails to self-destructive wars. Except now, we had entered a period the world had never seen before. The United States of America was the sole superpower, with an array of high-tech weapons that gave it an ability to wage war unchecked. In 1898, there were other powers to challenge America in a head-on military battle, and that continued until the fall of the Soviet Union.

While I would hear ordinary Americans sometimes using the word "nationalism," it was not a word that appeared in print or in public utterances in any mainstream setting. Yet print and broadcast news would freely use it to refer to the actions of other nations, such as China wanting to control its currency, to European nations wanting to keep out genetically modified crops. Everyone was nationalistic—except us. We were simply patriotic.

⟡

IMMEDIATELY FOLLOWING September 11, 2001, world sympathy was with the U.S.; all eyes were on the site of the World Trade Center, and to a lesser degree, the Pentagon. Most everyone I knew in New York City—journalism students and friends who were writers and photographers—got to so-called Ground Zero within hours or days, despite concentric rings of police whose job it was to keep them out.

A student, Matt, showed up dusty and bedraggled in my office that day, with a charred trade center paper he'd found in the street down there. A former student now working in television news ran from jury duty near City Hall and was standing next to the first tower when it came down—Lisa was blown by the tremendous wind generated by the pancaking floors, certain she was going to die. She made it out, barely. Michael Williamson made it in that first day. Another friend rode a bicycle there, crossing each police barricade by saying she lived just on the other side. One photographer faked credentials. Another writer buddy befriended a trucker, reaching the Trade Center site carrying a notebook in his pocket and a bag of ice under his arm. He took the ice to the bar where cops and firemen hung out, turning himself into a hero's hero.

It was the biggest story of our lives. I listened to their tales of stepping over shoes with feet still in them, and of other such grisly sights. Still I had not gone. Nor would I go.

Throughout early October 2001, I watched the smoky plume rising over lower Manhattan from a distance of no closer than ten or fifteen blocks, and usually from a hundred. The story I desired was not amid the ruin. I tell my students to practice "Star Trek journalism," that is, go where no one else is going. Not only is it a waste to be one of the pack; what is happening off to the side is often the best story.

I felt compelled to wander the city, watching and listening. Outside the Village Theater on Bleecker Street, I overheard two women talking. One said triumphantly, "Now Americans know what Jews in Israel have been dealing with." I understood her to be calling for the toughest kind of American militarism.

I was soon drawn to peace protests against the bombing of civilians in Afghanistan. Most were organized by the International ANSWER Coalition—the acronym meant "Act Now To Stop War and End Racism." ANSWER had been formed three days after 9/11. It was an amalgam of groups, including the Workers World Party, a radical socialist group. They gathered in Union Square, Times Square, or at Rockefeller Center. There were people in solidarity with the people of El Salvador. Lesbian activists. The ubiquitous supporters of Mumia Abu-Jamal, a death-row inmate found guilty of killing a cop, but whose trial was deeply flawed. The flag of Angola. The music of 1960s folk singer Phil Ochs. It was people standing at microphones, talking about the past—everything except anything to do with Afghanistan or the attacks.

I quickly found myself ignoring ANSWER, and instead watching and listening to the citizens of the city as they passed these protests. The body politic was very much afraid, vengeful, and angry. I saw raw wrath from people of every race, gender, and age.

Typical was the ANSWER event on October 27, 2001. There was a litany of speakers, then a march of some one-thousand people from Times Square toward Eighteenth Street. During the speeches, numerous hecklers wanted to punch the protesters. It was a blur of images, a cacophony of invective. One white guy walking by said, as a Palestinian woman spoke on the stage, "Someone ought to shoot her."

A black woman bystander shouted, "Pray for war!"

"Go back to Afghanistan, motherfuckers!"

"Fuck Allah!"

"Fuck 'n nuke 'em all!"

And so on. Fingers were flipped, screams were so numerous as to be unremarkable. When the march began, citizens spat on some of the marchers. I moved with the crowd, down Broadway, when in the thirties a Latino bystander started yelling at a Latino marcher.

"Fucking bomb 'em!" screamed David Brell, twenty-one-years old and of Puerto Rican heritage.

"Lower-class Hispanics are going to war, brother!" responded the sign-carrying marcher, Giovanni Harran, of Colombian heritage. He implored Brell to consider what this meant.

Brell thought a second. Then he said, "I think we should blow the motherfuckers up!"

"The real ones, we need to blow up!" said Harran.

Brell was puzzled. He turned and walked with Harran for a bit.

"Who's that?"

"We've been oppressed for so long, brother," Harran explained. "Why do you think Hispanics are poor? The capitalist system! It's been used against us. That's what we need to blow up."

Harran, who was a college student, went on with a lesson in multinational capitalism. Brell listened. Then Brell had to leave. Harran bid him a friendly farewell.

I ran after Brell, caught up with him across the street.

"I guess they got their reasons," said Brell, shaking his head about the marchers. But he told me he didn't understand a thing Harran had said.

I ran back to the march, catching up with Harran.

"Yeah, he understands," Harran said when I asked if Brell grasped the lesson in capitalism. Just then, a middle-aged black vendor screamed at Harran, gave the finger.

"You went to Vietnam, brother, I know! You should understand!" Harran yelled back.

Getting back to my question as we walked, Harran said, "This, my Hispanic brother doesn't understand—that is the broader perspective." Harran said Brell knows he's been oppressed, but not how it ties into the present situation. What is the present situation? Low-paying jobs that keep minorities in poverty—and turns them into roadside bomb fodder.

"He'll understand that soon enough. That it's all about the 5 percent against the 95 percent."

I pointed out that I'd not seen any working class marchers. I asked how they will reach the working class.

"What we will do is engage them in dialogue."

But how?

"Like we're doing now."

I certainly had no answers. What did anyone really know? In that fall and winter of 2001, all I could do was watch and talk and absorb the anger and confusion, and try to make sense of the nationalism I was seeing in the angry citizens.

The rally with the rawest display of nationalism happened just a week before Christmas 2001, on West Forty-ninth Street across from the Christmas tree at Rockefeller Center. It was a Saturday, the streets jammed with tourists who'd come to watch the skaters on the ice rink, to drink hot toddies—not to see several hundred ANSWER people and others penned in by a ring of cops.

The mood was ugly. As a hostile bystander argued with a protestor, calling him a traitor, another man began screaming from the other side of the barricade.

"Get the fuck out of the country! Get out!" Josh bellowed to the gathering protestors. He was red-faced, sputtering. I asked Josh why he was here.

"I was down at Ground Zero. I've seen a lot of fucking friends die."

Josh is a paramedic. He told me and my friend, photographer John Trotter, about how he waited to help survivors at a base medical center set up at Liberty Plaza for casualties that never came. In the weeks that followed, he spiraled into a depression. He rolled up his left pant leg, showed a tattoo: 9-11-01, in blue, two-inch numbers.

"Take a fucking picture of that," he said. John did. "Day of infamy. And people out here protesting. The cops that died. The firefighters. People who cleaned shit for a living, making $300 a week. What happens? They're dead. There's still more to come. There are sleeper cells here."

The protest began. Josh resumed screaming at a series of speakers. A cop nudged Josh across Forty-ninth Street. American flags waved in the breeze above a Santa Claus ringing a bell. A speaker talked about justice, not war.

"Justice, not war!?" Josh sputtered. "What does that mean? It doesn't make any sense!"

The passersby rooted him on.

"You tell them!"

A speaker now said, "No to scapegoating of Arab-Americans."

"What planet is that guy on?" a passerby asked loudly to a companion.

Now someone sang a civil rights song about marching on Montgomery and Selma. Then a few people unfurled a Mumia Abu-Jamal banner on two poles. Suddenly, Mumia's face was grinning directly at Josh across the street.

"There's a cop killer right there! A CONVICTED cop killer!"

Josh positively gyrated.

"Don't you have a brain?!?"

A woman speaker talked about the 1960s.

"Different time, lady!" Josh hollered.

The message was locked in the past. There was little about the present. This went on for a long time. The reaction of the crowd was not simply dislike. It was seething.

"How can you allow them to do this!?" one woman screamed at a cop. The people in the crowd were ready to abandon the U.S. Constitution. The Bill of Rights. Give up everything America stands for. And this wasn't only happening in New York.

The previous evening, nearly three thousand miles away, Janis Besler Heaphy, the publisher of the *Sacramento Bee* newspaper, had been scheduled to deliver a mid-year graduation address for California State University, Sacramento, to some seventeen thousand people at an arena.

Heaphy talked about an awakened sense of patriotism, and upholding American values. But when she began talking about racial profiling and civil rights, the crowd began heckling, stamping feet, clapping. The president of the college tried to quiet the crowd. But when she resumed, she was again drowned out. She was never able to finish.

A significant portion of that crowd didn't want to hear about preserving civil liberties. And now, days before Christmas, ostensibly a season of love, I watched jingoism erupting a continent away. The crowd was angrier than it had been an hour earlier. A speaker talked about the Afghan bombing, asking, "Does it justify killing innocent children?"

"It does justify it!" a woman walking behind Josh barked.

These comments came not from rednecks, but geeks and little blue-haired ladies who suddenly sprouted Freddie Krueger voices.

But the biggest boos came not from the loudest speakers. When Michael Ratner, an attorney with the Center for Constitutional Rights took the microphone, he talked quietly about America's role in the world. He asked why we are hated, about how our policies are affecting impoverished people across the globe.

"We're creating terrorists," Ratner calmly said. "We have to look at why."

The crowd across Forty-ninth Street went ballistic, all the way back to the tree a half a block distant. The Santa stopped ringing her bell and waved a fist, shouting. It was mean and nasty.

"Boo! Boo! Boo!"

A spontaneous cheer went up.

"USA! USA! USA!"

It sounded like a football crowd.

Some cops now had billy clubs out. From my experience in other riotous situations, I kept an eye on escape routes. A year and a half later, Ratner would tell me he had expected to be attacked physically. But Ratner cut his presentation short, the other speakers were soon done, and there was a brief march that ended without major incident.

In 2003, Chris Hedges, a *New York Times* reporter, was invited to give the graduation speech at Rockford College near Chicago. Hedges had written *War Is a Force That Gives Us Meaning*. Wars are something Hedges knows well, having covered them most of his life—from Central America to the Middle East to the Balkans. Hedges had been shot at in Iraq, and imprisoned there; he has been jailed in the Sudan, beaten by the military in Saudi Arabia, strafed by Russian MiGs in Bosnia, and so on. Hedges's book exposes the myths fueling war in all societies, and it looks deeply at the moral and political underpinnings of nationalism.

When he took the stage at the outdoor graduation that day in May, he opened his talk with the words, "I want to speak to you today about war and empire." He invoked the theme of his book, challenging the crowd to face the issue of American nationalism, and what the ultimate cost of this nationalism might be.

Of Iraq, he said that "we are embarking on an occupation that, if history is any guide, will be as damaging to our souls as it will be to our prestige, power, and security. But this will come later, as our empire expands, and in all this we become pariahs, tyrants to others weaker than ourselves. Isolation always impairs judgment and we are very isolated now."

Hedges connected the United States to the violence of its allies, especially the leaders Ariel Sharon and Vladimir Putin. He talked about the rage of a world impoverished, half of it living on less than two dollars a day. "Terrorism will become a way of life, and when we are attacked we will, like our allies Putin and Sharon, lash out with greater fury. The circle of violence is a death spiral; no one escapes. We are spinning at a speed that we may not be able to hold."

The crowd grew angrier with each word. News accounts reported that students shouted, "God bless America!" Twice someone cut the microphone. Several people tried to clamber upon the stage. There were boos. Foghorns wailed.

Hedges soldiered on, not wanting to let the mob take over. At one point in the eighteen-minute talk, he said, "At a time of soaring deficits and financial scandals and the very deterioration of our domestic fabric, war is a fine diversion."

Fearing violence, campus officers rushed Hedges away from the event.

"I think what was so disturbing was that the crowd wasn't just angry, but there was that undercurrent or possibility of violence," Hedges later said on Amy Goodman's national radio show, *Democracy Now!* "People chanted the kinds of clichés and aphorisms and jingoes that are handed to you by the state. 'God bless America' . . . that kind of contagion leads ultimately to tyranny, it's very dangerous and it has to be stopped."

NEWS DIARY III

I AM IN Safer America, a street-level store on the corner of Ann and Nassau streets—blocks from where the towers stood—whose windows are filled in the manner of a high-end department store, only instead of Calvin or Prada it is full-body radiation suits. It's the eve of the Iraq War. People on the sidewalk stop and stare through the glass. Not stares of ridicule, but of longing.

For sale, a long row of gas masks. Parachutes. Radiation detectors for $149.

"We've sold out of all our food survival kits," the clerk says, adding that other business has been brisk. The White House through the Department of Homeland Security has been steadily beating the drum of fear, telling Americans that Saddam Hussein's minions or others were about to douse them with poisons.

At the back of the store, a large-screen video extols the Exe-u-chute, for jumping from tall buildings. A throbbing techno beat accompanies the video. It shows "executives" in suits and ties leaping off the top of a skyscraper. The wind is right, and it pulls them away from the building; the "executives" land on a patch of grass.

The video describes the parachute buckles as "military grade." One can purchase the H.O.P.E. chute for $1,145, the Evacuchute for $845.

A woman, around age sixty, with salt-and-pepper hair, enters the store. Carol looks upper class. She carries a small backpack from which she pulls a filter mask of the kind used by painters.

"Oh, that won't help you," the clerk informs her.

"What will?"

The throbbing techno music is the backdrop as the clerk shows her gas masks lining the store's Ann Street windows.

"These are military grade," explains the clerk, motioning to a black mask. The woman looks at the cost, similar to the flimsier-looking masks to the left, among them the MSA Response Escape Hood.

"These are the ones the police use," the clerk says of the disposables that go for $195. "When you look at an officer, you can see them hanging on their legs. They fold up small."

Pros of disposables: fast, easy, small. Cons: they don't last long. Carol has ten minute's worth of questions. The clerk is patient.

The MSA Advantage 1000, for $199, is reusable.

"That will last you years."

"Can I put it in the bottom of my pack and carry it with me?"

"You don't want to do that. It can get punctured. You want to keep it separate."

The filter must not be opened until it is to be used. They cost $39. The cheaper disposable mask's filter carries a rating that indicates it will last for forty minutes. The other, a little longer, but it depends on the load of atomic dust in the air, the clerk explains.

"Of course, this is just respiratory," the clerk says.

"What else do I need!?" Carol asks. "As silly as it sounds."

"It's not silly," the clerk assures her.

The clerk shows Carol full-body suits. There is the two-piece clear suit, but the full-body one-piece is better. The best buy, the clerk says, is a package deal, $265. This includes the MSA Advantage gas mask and filter, one Tyvek F full-body protection suit, potassium iodide, one pair of nitrile gloves and booties, one roll of duct tape, and one flashlight with two D batteries.

The clerk demonstrates how one has to duct-tape the gloves to the body suit, for full protection. The one-piece suit is very light. Carol palms it. She is interested in carrying the suit with her. Another customer enters, and the clerk leaves Carol to study the suits and masks. I talk with Carol.

"Red Alert, Orange Alert. I'm afraid," she says.

Last week, she explains, she went to buy a kayak at Paragon, the Union Square sporting goods store. She wants to be able to escape Manhattan when something happens. Carol does not use the word "if."

"But the clerk told me the currents in the Hudson are strong. He told me, you'd be swept out to sea. Or you'd drown."

The clerk talked Carol out of the kayak. I look at Carol, barely over a hundred pounds, and with no upper body strength. Wise was the clerk who let that sale go. But not having the kayak prompted Carol to come here. If she can't leave, she wants protection, at least until she can get out some other way.

"I don't know if they will let us off the island," Carol says in a whisper. "If there's something nuclear, they will force us to stay."

She's still thinking about escape routes.

"The best place to leave, if they won't let us cross bridges, is the Harlem River," adds Carol, speaking of the narrowest body of water separating Manhattan from the U.S. mainland, at the northern end of the island. The Bronx, of course, is the only non-island borough in New York City.

I am curious about Carol's politics. I ask about Iraq.

She winces.

"We're going to do terrible things. We're going to kill a lot of innocent people."

She expects terrorism will increase because of what the United States is doing now in the world.

"I'm afraid. But I don't know who I'm afraid of more—Al Qaeda, or my own government."

She is anything but a traditional "survivalist," like many of Safer America's customers. She works a dozen blocks from where the towers were, and knows the power of fear. I ask if she thinks she might be viewed as paranoid.

"I've already been through two terror attacks," Carol says of the 1993 bombing attempt on the towers, as well as 9/11. "There will be a third."

HITLER
HITLER
HITLER
HITLER
HITLER

hitlerhitlerhitlerhitler. If they said it enough times, maybe it would be true, that the little man in the Middle East was as big and bad as that other guy with the mustache.

Bush, the man without a mustache, leading the Empire, was on drugs or something. Languid, serene, as he wined and dined and extolled the great leaders of the world, big countries like Bulgaria, Spain, and one man in Britain.

In 1953, there was talk of preventive war against the Soviets.

"All of us have heard this term 'preventative war' since the earliest days of Hitler," said President Dwight Eisenhower. "I don't believe there is such a thing; and frankly, I wouldn't even listen to anyone seriously that came in and talked about such a thing."

Beware the military-industrial complex, the old general-turned-politician, Eisenhower, said.

Japan waged preventive war against the United States.

During the Cuban missile crisis, Arthur Schlesinger Jr. recalls JFK's brother, Robert, who was then attorney general, talking about JFK's rejection of the military's idea of a preemptive strike. RFK invoked General Hideki Tojo, who became Japan's prime minister in 1941, just as the Axis military leaders were planning for war against the United States. "My brother," RFK said, "is not going to be the Tojo of the 1960s."

PRESIDENT STICKS WITH TAX CUT PLAN FOR THE RICH

WE ARE FIGHTING FOR FREEDOM

SHOCK AND AWE COMING

code orange

TERRORISM IS IMMINENT, Tom Ridge tells the citizens of Empire

i am code blue

At Home Restaurant on Cornelia Street in early 2003, the lights go out. In the dark, stunning silence. Friends and lovers look at each other across tables.

"A terror attack?" asks a voice in the dark. When the lights come back up, everyone stares at everyone else.

AMERICANS SHOULD BE SCARED

STOCK UP ON SUPPLIES

TERROR IS COMING HERE

BLOOMBERG WARNS CITY NOT TO PANIC

MADELEINE PEREZ, a young journalism student, is at the counter of the police precinct in Brooklyn talking to officers Ramirez and Dominguez.[1]

The mayor that day urged residents not to panic about the upgraded terror alert. There were sixteen thousand trained officers to protect them.

Officer Ramirez says to Madeleine, "Until today, this was the quietest precinct in Brooklyn. Now, everyone is freaking out. They think everyone is in Al Qaeda."

All day, officers Ramirez and Dominguez have been taking calls from terrified residents. A ninety-year-old woman found anthrax. It was dust on an America Online disk. "These days, every Kentucky Fried Chicken box is a bomb."

In walks a man in tears. "A white bag on my steps! It might be a bomb!"

And the young journalist follows officers Ramirez and Dominguez to the porch, where they pick up the white bag filled with garbage.

The leader of Empire promised $3.5 billion for antiterrorism training and equipment. He stood for photo ops with officers and firemen. But officers Ramirez and Dominguez had no training, not even gas masks.

"We're just as scared as these people calling in," officer Dominguez says to Madeleine. "My mom calls every day to see if I'm okay. The reality is, I don't know what to do to stop an attack."

Times Square

THE TOURISTS walk past the Applebees and Olive Garden and the TGI Fridays and the Disney outlet. Having a real New York experience.

Through the falling snow, the news ticker around the Reuters building in Times Square announces,

> . . . Bush tells Saddam, "Game is over" . . .
> . . . State Department warns Americans to be on the alert for terror attacks . . .

And the words go around and around the building.

The Leader of Empire Warns of Gas Attacks

THE DEPARTMENT of Homeland Security tells us to buy duct tape and sheet plastic, and we will be saved.

Duct tape and plastic, stripped from shelves and racks, in stores in New York and Washington, parts of the interior. The leader of Empire warns the new man with the mustache could launch tiny drone planes, "unmanned aerial vehicles" from far out in the ocean, and that they could fly over the Homeland, spewing poisons. "A UAV launched from a vessel off the American coast could reach hundreds of miles inland," says the leader of Empire.

The journalists of Empire choose not to report upon the impossibility of this scenario.

> Amount of poison needed to kill a soldier in World War I:
>   One ton per death

> Estimated number of Kurds killed by Saddam Hussein in the chemical attack using unknown tonnage on the town of Halabja in 1988:
>   Five thousand

Dozens of fighter bombers were used, and it required numerous passes by the bombers over the town.

CITIZENS OF EMPIRE, creating sealed rooms that will be useless in protecting them from sarin and other agents, if the man with the mustache were able to bring over cargo planeloads of these chemicals. But the man with the mustache could not disperse chemicals in any meaningful quantities—no journalist asked how he would get a ship across the seas anywhere near America. And if a drone Cessna-sized aircraft did make it ashore and was not shot down, the tiny quantity of chemicals such a craft could release would be diluted by the wind. This would be true of even the most toxic substances.

After Iraq fell, the Americans found the drones: well, one of them. It was made from plywood and string.

> . . . Bush tells Saddam, "Game is over" . . .
> . . . State Department warns Americans to be on the alert for terror attacks . . .

MEANWHILE, AT THE FAR EDGE OF EMPIRE

AT THE COUNTER of a pharmacy in Carmichael, a suburb in California, a month before the leader of Empire warned his subjects they could become casualties in his crusade:

"Do you sell potassium iodide tablets?"

"I haven't seen those in years." A knowing smile from the old pharmacist who lived through the 1950s' duck-and-cover drills.

"I'm moving back to New York." The young woman helper in a white coat is confused, has no idea what potassium iodide is for or what these two men are talking about.

"Nothing is going to happen." A smile of condescension from the pharmacist who didn't inhale death for all those months and who is so certain of his safety at the western edge of Empire.

SAFER AMERICA

A SHELF FILLED with bottles of potassium iodide. Two hundred 65 milligram tabs for $22.95. On the label—"Radiation blocking tablets." A mushroom cloud. And a radiation symbol with a slash through it.

> USE AS DIRECTED BY PHYSICIAN. THE FDA RECOMMENDS TAKING POTASSIUM IODIDE IMMEDIATELY IF EXPOSURE TO RADIATION IS POSSIBLE (FOR EXAMPLE, IF DOWNWIND OF A NUCLEAR REACTOR DISASTER OR NUCLEAR EXPLOSION OR RADIATION HAZARD).

. . . Bush tells Saddam, "Game is over" . . .
. . . State Department warns Americans to be on the alert for terror attacks . . .

The hour [of the world's end] shall not occur until the Euphrates will disclose a mountain of gold over which people will fight.
—The Prophet Mohammed

THE CARP SPEAKS

IN THAT WINTER of war talk and terror alerts, at the New Square Fish Market in the town of New Square, New York, butcher Luis Nivelo was about to kill a twenty-pound carp to cut up into gefilte fish by clubbing it to death.

When Luis lifted the live carp from the box, it began speaking. At least that's what was reported in the newspaper of record in the big city thirty miles to the south, in its front page story on the eve of war.

"The fish is talking!" the frantic Luis cried. "It's the devil!"

Running for his boss, Zalmen Rosen, the fish monger for the seven thousand members of the Skver sect of Hasidim.

When Mr. Rosen came into the room, the carp spoke commands in Hebrew. *"Tzaruch shemirah"* (The end is near). *"Hasof bah"* (All people must account for themselves).

Mr. Rosen panicked, tried to hack at the fish with a machete. The fish resisted, jumping crazily. Mr. Rosen instead chopped his thumb and was taken by ambulance to the hospital.

Then they killed the carp.

WINTER WITHOUT END

THE HARLEM NIGHT twinkles, framed by the Morningside Heights window. In the cold of the goddamn long winter, endless winter, 125th Street, sirens, cop car lights, the Harlem YMCA, the tower with the office of the previous leader of Empire to the right, the G.W. Bridge to the left, the great expanse of Homeland sleeping in that dark west beyond the Jersey Palisades.

Somewhere in the Harlem night north of 125th Street, if he's out of prison, Gil Scott-Heron in his flat.

Writing, I hope, a song about spring.

Needin' Gil now, at 3 AM. Gil, they're televising their revolution on FOX, MSNBC, CNN. Help us get over this season which you called one of no more spring, summer, or fall, a season of frozen hopes, the season you called "Winter in America."

It's winter in America, June, July, December, March.

Needin' spring. Needin' your revolution. Not the one everyone thought you sang about, but the real revolution, the one you really meant, the one in which you don't need guns, bombs, or missiles, the one that begins in the heart and soul of every man and woman.

They say it's Code Orange. But it's just blue, Gil, in this damn winter that won't end.

THE CRUSADES

A GROUP named In Touch Ministries passed out a pamphlet called "A Christian's Duty" to thousands of U.S. Marines in Iraq. It asked them to pray for President George Bush, and included a tear-out sheet to be mailed to the White House to show the troops were praying for the leader. There was a pledge and a prayer for each day of the week.

THE PLEDGE: "I have committed to pray for you, your family, your staff and our troops during this time of uncertainty and tumult. May God's peace be your guide."

SUNDAY'S PRAYER: "Pray that the President and his advisers will seek God and his wisdom daily and not rely on their own understanding."

Each morning, Bush said he began his day reading "evangelical mini-sermons" before bringing his wife a cup of coffee.

NOT ALL CHRISTIANS ON BOARD

THE SOUTHERN BAPTIST CONVENTION, among others, endorsed the war, but numerous Christians did not.

Pope John Paul II in an address said, "No to war!" The World Council of Churches was opposed, and its general secretary, Rev. Konrad Raiser, called the war "immoral, illegal, and ill-advised." Also against the war were the U.S. and Canadian Catholic Bishops, the U.S. National Council of Churches, the Archbishop of Canterbury, and the National Baptist Convention USA, among others.

ON THE LINCOLN HIGHWAY

AS BOMBS FALL on the other side of the world, we are driving the Lincoln Highway, old U.S. Route 30, America's main street back in the days before the interstates, when they said one could not win a presidential election without winning the Route 30 states.

A Rust Belt newspaper in a town not far from Canton contains letters to the editor from Christians in favor of war. WAKE UP, AMERICA says the headline over one letter, in the prominent upper left corner of the editorial page.

> Can the war on terrorism be won while God's people sleep? A thousand times NO . . . After receiving the wake-up call from hell on Sept. 11, we felt the pinch and shook to action . . . Our president

cannot win this war, no matter how he tries, if the church sleeps. We must fight darkness with light through prayer . . . For we wrestle not against flesh and blood, but against principalities, against powers, against the rulers of darkness of this world, against spiritual wickedness in high places.

IN TOUCH MINISTRIES:
MONDAY'S PRAYER TO THE LEADER OF EMPIRE

Pray that the President and his advisers will be strong and courageous to do what is right regardless of the critics.

ON SEPTEMBER 28, 2002, antiwar demonstrations brought out hundreds of thousands of people in Europe. For two days, the *Washington Post* ignored the protests.

On October 26, 2002, one hundred thousand antiwar protestors showed up in the *Washington Post*'s hometown. There was a small photo at the bottom of page one, linked to a story about Bush's attempt to enlist South Korea and Japan in a war against Iraq. The article was in the Metro section.

The *New York Times* ran a 476-word article about the Washington march on page eight, talking about poor turnout.

At the *Minneapolis Star Tribune*, where ten thousand people showed up in adjacent St. Paul to protest the war on the same day, the paper ran the story on page twenty-two, beneath a headline that read, RALLIES REMEMBER WELLSTONE.

Much later, in the fall of 2003, after American troops were bogged down in Baghdad, President George W. Bush took back everything he had implied or said directly about Saddam Hussein being involved in the World Trade Center and Pentagon attacks when selling the Iraq War. Bush said that there was "no evidence that Hussein was involved with September 11th." Polls at that point showed 70 percent of Americans believed Hussein was responsible; this was largely due to the American press trumpeting Bush's previous remarks that implied this was this case, with little context or analysis.

Now that the record was set straight, Seth Porges of the newspaper trade publication *Editor & Publisher Online* noted that,

Of America's twelve highest-circulation daily papers, only the
L. A. Times, *Chicago Tribune*, and *Dallas Morning News* ran anything about it on the front page. In the *New York Times*, the story
was relegated to page 22. *USA Today*: page 16. The *Houston
Chronicle*: page 3. The *San Francisco Chronicle*: page 14. The *Washington Post*: page 18. *Newsday*: page 41. The *New York Daily News*:
page 14. The *New York Post* and the *Wall Street Journal* didn't mention it at all.

PUNISHING THE CRITICS

WHEN BUSINESSMAN Gerald Rudolph showed up to protest George W.
Bush's visit to an airport hanger in Columbia, South Carolina, in October
2002, Secret Service agents ordered him to a "free speech zone" a half
mile distant, out of sight. Bush supporters with signs were allowed to
remain.

In January 2003, eight-year-old Raphe Makarewicz showed up with his
mom and 150 other protesters in 19-degree weather in St. Louis, with a handmade sign that read, KIDS AGAINST WAR. Secret Service agents penned in
Raphe and the others many blocks from where Bush was presenting his tax
cut plan. One man refused to move, and was arrested for holding an anti-
Bush sign. He watched as a woman stepped in his place with a sign that read,
WE LOVE YOU MR. PRESIDENT. She was allowed to remain where Bush could
see her.

In Seattle, Seth Goldberg was flying to San Diego. Seth was picked out,
sent to the Transportation Security Administration's agent for special
screening. The agents found two NO IRAQ WAR signs in his bag. When Seth
arrived in San Diego and opened the bag, he found a note from a TSA agent
that said: "Don't appreciate your anti-American attitude."

At the Crossgates Mall in Albany, New York, Stephen Downs, sixty, a
lawyer who works for the state of New York, went with his son Roger,
thirty-one, to pick up custom-made T-shirts. They donned them and went
to the food court. Stephen's shirt said PEACE ON EARTH. Roger's said NO WAR
WITH IRAQ, and LET INSPECTIONS WORK.

While dining, security guards asked that the men remove the shirts.
Roger complied. Stephen did not. He cited his First Amendment rights. Mall
owners would later say someone complained and the shirts were disrupting customers.

Police were called. Stephen was arrested and charged with trespassing. "My conservative dad," Roger said to me a few days later. "He supported the Vietnam War."

Days later, 150 people wearing antiwar shirts came to the mall in support of Stephen Downs, who was not present. A passerby punched one of Stephen's supporters. He shouted, "Remember 9/11!"

No arrest was made in that case.

In Parsippany, New Jersey, people who called themselves patriots spotted green ribbons tied all over town. *This is anti-American! Endangering the troops!* The ribbons were torn down. Complaints were filed with city officials. The officials explained the ribbons were put up in recognition of National Organ Donor Awareness Month.

In Rochester, Minnesota, radio and TV commercials invited everyone to a rally to "support the troops." The Southeast Minnesota Alliance of Peacemakers had thirty members show up, one with a sign that said, SUPPORT THE TROOPS: BRING THEM HOME.

They were not admitted, told by police it was a private gathering. Alliance members wanted to stand in silent protest amid the three thousand prowar demonstrators. "You will be arrested," the cops warned. Alliance members were ordered by the cops to go across the street, where the patriots defending the homeland threatened them with death.

"I'm going to go home and get my gun!" one shouted.

The police of Rochester, Minnesota, standing right there, heard nothing, saw nothing.

Ben Cohen, the old ice cream guy from Ben & Jerry's, wanted to run an ad showing actual footage of war. The message was that America had two options: to disarm Iraq or inspect. One option, Ben said, "involves killing," and the other does not. But the ice cream man said, "linking death to war seems to be taboo." He discovered this when all the major networks refused to run the ad.

At Wheaton College, students hung an upside down American flag in a second floor window. A dead fish was tacked to their door. Rocks were thrown and there were bomb threats, screams in the night. Restaurants stopped serving Wheaton kids.

And the billboards announced,

UNITED WE STAND

THE FEDERAL COMMUNICATIONS COMMISSION in 2003 relaxed ownership rules for corporations, and companies like Clear Channel could now expand even further. FCC Chairman Michael Powell cut public comment short before the commission voted.

Clear Channel now reached 104.6 million U.S. households. Its profits were $724.8 million on $8.4 billion in revenue.

RED, WHITE, & SIX THOUSAND FOUR HUNDRED POUNDS

"THOSE WHO DEFACE a Hummer in words or deed, deface the American flag and what it stands for," said Richard Schmidt, founder of the International Hummer Owners' Group, in a *New York Times* interview.

News item: an American soldier climbs the statue of Saddam and plasters a U.S. flag over his face before they topple the man with the mustache.

Raise High the Flags!

The statue of Carl Schurz
Faces west.
In the winter of America
raindrops run down his cheeks.

Carl Schurz
MDCCCXXIX–MDCCCCVI
A Defender of Liberty
And a Friend of
Human Rights

A few days later, two teenage boys mill near the statue in the sun. They look up at Carl's face.
    "Who was he?"
    "He was like some land developer or something."

PROFITS TO ARMS SUPPLIERS

BECHTEL WINS IRAQ CONTRACTS

HALLIBURTON'S SUBSIDIARIES WIN OILFIELD CONTRACTS[2]

PRESIDENT PROPOSES

NATIONAL HEALTH CARE PLAN

FOR IRAQ

Black Hawk in the night sky over the Central Park reservoir.

Watching.

Forty-second Street station. The trains clatter from the tunnels uptown, downtown, crosstown, soldiers with automatic weapons, watching, across from the mime with the mask of shiny chrome, reflecting M-16s, motionless, watching back.

My future father off in some desert, with death, whose smell never will he escape.

BOOK FOUR

A sign in the window of T.K.'s Restaurant in
Chester, West Virginia, told passersby:

SUPPORT: DON'T PROTEST
LET THE POLICE
PROTECT
THE HOMELAND

Those who would give up essential liberty to purchase
a little temporary safety deserve neither liberty nor safety.
—Benjamin Franklin

Patriotism means being loyal to your country all the time
and to its government when it deserves it.
—Mark Twain

THE SIX-FOOT-THREE, rail-thin man came in from the cold, into the Coffee Pot at Forty-ninth Street and Ninth Avenue, an espresso hangout for Broadway musicians between matinees and evening shows. Eli Pariser looked nothing like the musicians, but with his close-trimmed jet-black beard and erudite manner, he also didn't resemble the computer geek he professes to be. Nor did he look like Karl Rove's worst nightmare, something he may well be. Eli is twenty-two years old.

When 9/11 happened, Eli was living in Boston, working for a non-profit as a Web designer. He feared violent revenge by the U.S. and didn't want to "see innocent people die. Bush's words were anything but comforting. He was going to go for military dominance."

So Eli e-mailed some friends, asking them to write politicians calling for restraint, and also to sign a petition. Those friends sent the e-mails on to others. On 9/12, Eli had three hundred e-mails in his in-box. Another man, David Pickering, was doing the same thing, and by 9/14, had one thousand signatures. Eli and David joined together and cofounded 9-11Peace.org. On 9/18, 120,000 names were on the petition.

Then the server crashed because "too many people were trying to access it." Within two weeks, they had a half million people involved. The Eli-David site merged into MoveOn.org, a Silicon Valley-based organization started by two people who opposed the impeachment of Bill Clinton. In mid-2002, MoveOn.org had 480,000 members in the United States, and 390,000 overseas. By the Iraq War in 2003, there were 650,000 U.S. members, with a worldwide total of 1.3 million.

MoveOn.org is credited with transforming the protest movement. Such Internet-based organizing accelerated antiwar coordination, doing in a few months what took four years to do in the Vietnam era. The U.S. historian Howard Zinn talks about how in the mid-1960s, in order to get even a handful of people to a meeting against the Vietnam War in Cambridge, Massachusetts, they would have to announce that the meeting was going to be about a half-dozen other foreign policy hot spots, in addition to the war in Vietnam.

The speed and amounts of money that MoveOn.org raises through its political action committee is stunning. When the late Senator Paul Wellstone voted against the Iraq War resolution, the MoveOn.org PAC raised $700,000 for him; then when Wellstone died in a plane crash, it raised $200,000 in two hours for Walter Mondale, who took Wellstone's place on the ballot.

By far the most visible event occurred after Eli put out a call to MoveOn.org members in early 2003; they wanted to buy newspaper advertising. The group had a challenge grant of $27,000, and Eli hoped to raised a matching amount.

Within two days, $400,000 had poured in. This helped fund a television spot patterned after Lyndon B. Johnson's 1964 "daisy" commercial, used against Barry Goldwater: a small girl plucks daisy petals, merging into battlefield images amid a countdown, and then a nuclear mushroom cloud.

When I met Eli at the Coffee Pot, MoveOn.org had just two paid staff members and three volunteers.

Eli did not punctuate his conversation with inflected progressive clichés. Rather, he was soft-spoken. Words like "cool" and "neat" often came up, as in, "there's all sorts of neat ways you can mess with people to do cool stuff."

People call, they volunteer.

"It's so rewarding to work with them. A lot of them say, 'I have never been politically involved,' or 'I'm not an activist, but I want to be involved.' The issue is this: engaging people in the political process. To give them hope."

We talked months before the Iraq War, but he knew it was inevitable. Eli might be young, but he knew well the failure of the 1960s movements: they could not sustain themselves beyond opposition to the war once the disco 1970s dawned. He does not want to repeat that history, and that means building something that will last.

He was thinking beyond Iraq. Way beyond.

"The name of the game at this point is connecting this political energy to longer-term energy." And then he said, "Regime change starts at home, and it starts now."

As an example of what is next, Eli explained that MoveOn.org would not simply poll its members as to whom the group would support to oppose George W. Bush or other politicians beyond the 2004 election; it would measure how many hours its members spend volunteering for each candidate.

"It will be the candidate our members put the most energy behind. It's cool."

I asked if he believed the Bush White House was carefully watching MoveOn.org. Eli laughed. He assumed so. "Karl Rove is a good strategist," Eli said.

Eli is unassuming, downplays his own ambitions, if there are any. He was working twelve-plus hour days, seven days a week. It's true grassroots. Everything about MoveOn.org's message was reasonable and simple. During the Iraq war, it was "Let the inspectors work."

I asked about ANSWER, overshadowed by MoveOn.org and others in those immediate months after 9/11. I spoke with disdain. But Eli was politic.

"ANSWER is our Earth First," Eli said, referring to how the Sierra Club views the more radical arm of the environmental movement; it simply makes MoveOn.org seem all that more rational. And besides, ANSWER gets "shoes out on the street."

As we parted, I thought of something an editor at *Mother Jones* magazine told me after she moved from Chicago to San Francisco to take the job. "In Chicago, we had organizers. Here, you have activists," she said. The latter spoke at microphones, but did not directly effect change.

As Eli hurried off to get back to his computer in the eight-by-ten-foot office that also serves as his bedroom, I was happy with the thought that even though Eli is using the Internet, he is simply an old-fashioned organizer, in the mold of the best of the 1930s left. The man I was watching walk out the door was perhaps one of the biggest hopes against the agenda of the extremist nationalists.

✍

HOPE LIVES in different ways. There is the work Eli is doing. And there is hope too in the story of Mayor Dean Koldenhoven. The last time I saw Dean, we met at one o'clock in the morning, in an all-night Palos Heights diner. Dean keeps late hours.

Our coffee got off to a somber start. Dean began talking about John Ashcroft, and I noticed a woman seated five tables away glaring at us. So did Dean, who often looked around. Like so many people I interviewed, he talked in low tones.

"You have to watch what you say and where you say it," Dean said, adding that because he talks with Muslim-Americans, he feels he's being watched by the government.

"I could not disagree with my president more than I have with this president, of all people," Dean said, referring to the fact that he voted for George Bush. "I thought I'd like the guy. It turns out he's a standard bearer for a bully government, that's the way I see it. And with John Ashcroft as attorney general, what he's doing is taking away our freedoms, one by one."

Dean was now trying to change the world, one child at a time. He was going all over the Chicago area, talking to grade-schoolers about the U.S. Constitution, using the Kennedy Profile in Courage award as his bully pulpit. Dean begins these talks by asking the kids if they know the first five amendments to the U.S. Constitution. One grammar school girl got four of them—the most of any youth he has talked with, even those in college.

Dean then goes on to explain them.

"I say I would appreciate you learning [the Bill of Rights], because you might have to be the generation that has to protect it, stand up for it, and bring it back alive. Our attorney general right now is taking it apart through the Patriot Act."

Dean explains to the children how the USA PATRIOT Act negates aspects of the First and Fourth Amendments, which deal with free speech and seizure and probable cause.

"I say to my wife, how can we can express this without being called kooks, or fanatics? 'Oh you don't know what you're talking about, the president knows what he's doing.' I'm hearing there must be something that he knows that he can't tell us. That's why we've got to trust him. And I say, you know what? I heard before it was all about Russia, how tough they were. They're so giant. And when the government broke down by itself, we found out that their military was so obsolete. They tended to have these rockets made out of plywood and when they did their march on parade day, there was a lot of fake stuff out there."

Our leaders knew, he said, but chose not to tell us.

"I don't believe them," Dean added about what he hears about the war on terrorism. "Don't give me that 'trust me' stuff. No. Uh-uh. I'm sorry. We've got a government still of the people. We've got to know. You've got to tell us. And if you don't want to tell us, I guess we've got to get somebody else in there. That's the only option we've got."

And so Dean works in his own small way. He encourages fifth- and sixth-graders to read newspapers. Dean wrote letters to the editor as a kid and saw them published; he pushes the kids to do the same, to become engaged members of society.

✍

I HAD DINNER on the Lower East Side with Amrik Chawla and his fiancé two years after Amrik had to run for his life at the base of the towers. His fiancé, a young Sikh woman from Chicago, comes from a family of men who do not wear the turban, and she was amazed by her husband's ability to weather dirty looks and shouts of "Osama."

One would think Americans would by now be aware of Sikhs, but that was not the case. Even non-turban-wearing Indians were sparking overreaction. In July 2002, a group of Indian actors that included the popular Samyuktha Verma were in a jetliner about to land in New York. The troupe was pointing to sights and marveling at the city, and this made passengers nervous—two F-16 fighters were called in to escort the jetliner down. It was among four hundred military interceptions up to that point following 9/11. Usually, it was Sikhs who caused the panic, and dozens were removed from planes. Random violent attacks on Sikhs continued.

Amrik was undaunted. He was a one-man racial awareness emissary. He'd recently purchased a place over in Hoboken, New Jersey. Right after he moved in, he went out to a nearby market, where a group of Latino teens made taunts as he passed.

"Hey, Osama!"

Amrik made his purchase and came out, walked directly up to the kids. But instead of verbally assaulting them, he began speaking in Spanish. He'd spent several years of his youth living in Spain. The kids were surprised, and some of them didn't understand.

"What's wrong with you?" he asked. "What kind of Latinos are you, you don't speak Spanish?"

A conversation ensued, and Amrik never had to yell at the kids. They hit it off, and they wound up walking back to his building with him. Now when they see him they wave. He views his role as educating one person at a time.

✍

WHEN JOHN TINKER wore his anti–Vietnam War armband in 1965, the high school seethed with hatred toward him. He recalled that year going to a peace march in Washington.

"It was a very empowering thing to realize you were not alone."

But in Des Moines, he was alone outside a small group of family and friends. The hatred of the community burned deep. But when he went back to his twenty-fifth reunion at Roosevelt High School, with no small amount of trepidation, he was in for a shock.

"They treated me like royalty," he said. Even enemies were nice. "Everyone congratulated me and thought I was a hero."

From this, he extracts a certain amount of hope that he applies to the current political climate. "I'm optimistic that people are capable of change. It just doesn't happen as quickly as you want. You have to plant that seed and water it."

So much had changed for John. Back in the 1960s, he held American citizens complicit with the policies of the U.S. government. His understanding evolved after a trip to revolutionary Nicaragua not long after the Sandinistas took control. He drove down a truckload of electronic parts to give to the people of Nicaragua.

"In Nicaragua, everybody would say, 'We don't dislike the American people, we dislike the policies of the government.' I always felt like saying, 'I think you should hold the people more responsible. They're paying all those tax dollars and not controlling what happens.'"

That trip began a process of inner growth. He now feels there's a difference between a people and their government. He believes the best way to change society is to work quietly and talk to people as he did with the ROTC instructor in Sissonville, West Virginia.

And a big part of changing the world is simply choosing how you live. John's an anarchist of sorts. His dream is Jeffersonian. Only instead of a nation of small farmers, he imagines a nation of people who salvage, who live independently from commercial culture.

"I do share a lot with the conservative point of view. The government shouldn't do that much. We have socialism for the rich, capitalism for the poor. The main problem is our society has been structured from the top down, by the industrialists, by the capitalists. We have to have more of a culture that is organized from the bottom up. That means us. Instead of turning to government and saying, 'That man should be doing this, doing that,' and being disappointed when government doesn't do [everything for us], we should be doing it [for] ourselves.

"I have an anarchist perspective. It's basically, you have less need for government when people take care of things on their own. I'd love to see a culture develop that would just diminish the political realm, and create a bigger cultural realm. But I don't think that anything will work until we incorporate real economy into our culture, until we are actually producing the things that we need. You can capitalize your own culture, or subculture, without stimulating your adversaries, the industrial system. Rather than buying your solution, salvage your solution."

Thus he seldom buys anything new, and he chainsaws fallen trees to heat the schoolhouse. And he salvages electronic parts for his work—the upstairs auditorium of the converted school looks like a set for the movie *Brazil*, the Orwellian-Huxleyan film that takes place in a dark future in which computers (held together by gaffer's tape) rule the lives of humankind. In this case, however, the parts enable John to live in a rural town.

🖎

ON THE EVE of the Iraq War in early 2003, I went to pick up a rental car in the 70s on the Upper West Side of Manhattan. As I walked down Broadway, I came upon a shouting man.

The man was running in a circle on the sidewalk. "Bomb Iraq!" he screamed. "Bomb Iraq!" He smashed his right foot down with each of the following utterances:

"Iran!

"Syria!

"North Korea!

"Fuck with us! We'll crush you!"

It was not a good start to a road trip in which I wanted to gain a sense of the American mood. I drove to Washington, picked up Michael, and we took U.S. 30 into the interior, to Iowa and back. Something was different from what I'd seen during the 1991 Gulf War. And compared to the period after 9/11, something was different now, too: there were noticeably fewer flags. There were signs posted supporting the troops, but few mentioned the president.

This was backed up by statistics kept by the National Flag Foundation. From 100 million flags sold in 2002, it was expected 60 million would be sold in 2003. Experts told reporters that the drop was attributed to the lack of support for the Iraq War.

We didn't see much display of jingoism in Indiana, Illinois, or Iowa—it was concentrated largely in the most economically ravaged areas of the Rust Belt: Ohio and West Virginia and Pennsylvania.

Yet in Duppstadts, a country store near Shanksville, Pennsylvania, 1.3 miles from where Flight 93 went down on 9/11—heavily stocked with flags and flag shirts and all manner of items for sale to those making pilgrimages to the site—we found people who voiced skepticism.

"There is a place for 'just' war," a Roman Catholic priest said, shaking his head about the war that would start a few days later. The priest, a local, was hanging out talking to the elderly clerk. "A just war is when you have exhausted all options. We aren't there." The woman behind the counter nodded.

For sure, we heard and saw pro-war support. But it clearly was a very divided country. I have to think that a majority of Americans do not want to be this century's Tojo, that they are against "patriot" laws that allow police to pull guns on patrons eating in ethnic restaurants, detaining them for hours, or to have the legal right to break into a home in secret and without a warrant.

✍

IN CHICAGO, the Center for New Community's Devin Burghart looks to history for hope. He compares the present period to the 1920s, when the left was beaten, following the extreme conservatism of 1915–1920 and the "Palmer Raids" of 1919 and 1920. Attorney General A. Mitchell Palmer conducted a red-scare witch hunt, arresting hundreds of communists or sympathizers, who often were neither, but simply workers trying to form unions.

After World War I, President Woodrow Wilson turned against labor. A heyday for the rich was dawning, championed by Andrew Mellon, the Pittsburgh banking mogul who became Secretary of the Treasury under Warren Harding and remained in that post until 1932 under Herbert Hoover. Mellon campaigned successfully to repeatedly lower estate and income taxes for the rich. He argued that the working class should pay the bulk of taxes so the rich could make investments. The booming stock market in the 1920s gave credibility to these policies. It left progressives wandering in the wilderness.

"The left hadn't kicked into gear yet," Devin said. "The Klan reached five million members. A lot of Klan members were in office, high and low. There was the National Origins Act passed in 1924." This act froze the ethnic makeup of America by setting quotas on who could immigrate on the basis of their numbers in the U.S. in 1890. Thus, Italian immigration shrank from 40,000 to 4,000 a year, and Japanese were virtually excluded.

Slowly, the left mobilized. Devin noted that by the early 1930s, the left had learned how to challenge the right through stronger organization and a stronger message. How will that happen today?

"The left and antiwar movement have got to stop this romanticizing of the 1960s and adapt to the present era," he said. "To so many on the left, they write off the middle of the country. To them, it's flyover country."

The United States is now comprised of three bodies of thought, and they are not divided along the lines of Democrat and Republican, liberal and conservative. On one side, there are those against empire and nationalism, and on the other, those in favor. And then there are those in the middle.

Progressives, Devin agrees, have to work on an appeal to the middle third of the body politic, just the same as in the 1930s. This is our generation's 1930s. With everything turned on its head, we are now as volatile a country as in that decade, and this middle third will make or break the American future.

Will it be the left or right that successfully tugs at them?

"It's all a matter of who gets to those folks first."

🥀

THE TERMS "liberal" and "conservative" have grown meaningless to describe today's struggle for America's future. Some nationalists are liberals-turned-warriors. Not all people on the right are nationalists. Many on the right oppose the USA PATRIOT Act and other repression.

By 2003, there was a merging of a diverse range of political interests when the American Civil Liberties Union joined forces with prominent conservative groups to oppose the so-called Patriot II. The ACLU sent a letter to House Speaker Dennis Hastert, signed by sixty-seven organizations, including liberal groups such as the National Lawyers Guild, Human Rights Watch, and Amnesty International. It was also signed by Americans for Tax Reform, the American Conservative Union, and the Eagle Forum.

"I'm not sure given the Republican control of the House and the Senate and the government that we can count on our left-of-center friends to look out for some of these issues," said Grover Norquist, head of Americans for Tax Reform, in an interview with *Salon*.

I've found some on the left who are opposed to working with the right, on any issue. But when I interviewed David Keene, president of the American Conservative Union, he said there has been no real opposition from his members to working with other organizations, left, right, or center.

"The left, they are coming at it with very little credibility," Keene said. "That's one of the reasons we are so high-profile now."

Broad-based opposition was evident across America. The Bill of Rights Defense Committee, a citizen's group in Massachusetts, said that by the end of 2002, seventeen cities had approved resolutions against the USA PATRIOT Act. A year later, the group reported that the number had risen to 210 cities and three states, including Hawaii and Alaska.

In Arcata, California, which is one of the cities that passed an anti-Patriot Act resolution, David Meserve ran and won a seat on the city council with the campaign slogan: "The Federal Government Has Gone Stark, Raving Mad."

❧

OUR ULTIMATE escape from the nationalism of the American Weimar means taking care of the interests of a broad range of workers—not just the elites. That means a return of well-paying manufacturing jobs. One solution that has been proposed is simply to withdraw from all trade agreements with other nations, and throw up barriers that would protect American products and workers. This is simplistic and unrealistic.

The answer for the hemorrhaging of American jobs is not simply high tariffs, say both Chalmers Johnson and William Greider. The writers offer similar solutions for the creation of a level playing field. Says Johnson: the "United States should establish minimum-wage levels for overseas workers exporting to America," and there should be "some version of labor rights on a global scale." Wages cannot be equal in all countries, but there should be more fairness.

The flaws of the world economy require world solutions, Greider maintains. Countries, for example, could demand that the World Trade Organization define child labor or the abusing of workers as "unfair trade." No workers in an advanced country can ever compete fairly with slave labor. Additionally, countries shouldn't be able to abuse the environment, making their products cheaper than nations with strong clean-air-and-water laws.

Another change is the attitude of Americans toward wealth and its distribution. One reason Germans desire a regulated society with a large social safety net is the cautionary tale of their Weimar period. They've seen firsthand what economic ruin leads to, and they don't want to repeat their Weimar experience. They know it's not good to have many bitter and angry citizens. This is a major reason Germans have not jumped on the free market bandwagon, and their CEOs make on average only forty times the lowest paid worker. Americans have ridiculed Germans for spending too much on their safety net, not getting with the program of American-style greed and ruthlessness.

The Germans know something we do not, something it seems we'll learn the hard way—unless we take steps to contain the festering anger that feeds into dangerous nationalism.[1] It would be best if we emulated modern Germany, not the other way around. But a U.S. social safety net akin to Germany's may be a fantasy. A more realistic solution, one that fits in with American-style capitalism, was proposed in 2003 by a consortium of ten labor unions.

The Apollo Alliance, through a plan named the Apollo Project, calls for a ten-year, $300 billion investment in energy independence—the creation of hydrogen-powered cars, energy-efficient appliances, high-speed rail, fuel cells, solar and wind power. As many as 3.5 million new well-paid manufacturing jobs would be created.

"Like President John F. Kennedy's Apollo Project, which put a man on the moon in under a decade, a New Apollo Project will bring together the country to create a safer world and a stronger economy," said a statement from the group, comprised of the United Steel Workers of America, the United Auto Workers, the Service Employees International Union, the International Associate of Machinists, and the International Brotherhood of Electrical Workers, among others.

"For just a fraction of President Bush's $790 billion in tax cuts, we can drastically cut our reliance on oil imports, increase the use of clean renewable energy, retrofit our homes and factories to use less energy, and rebuild the infrastructure of our cities so we can be more productive. In the process we can turn the Rust Belt into the Hydrogen & Hybrid Hub. Put mass transit on the fast track. Capture the markets of the future for U.S. products."

An Alliance poll showed the plan had a 73 percent approval among all voters in Pennsylvania, and 81 percent among blue collar men with no college education. The latter are the so-called Reagan Democrats "burned by the current economy," Apollo Alliance President Bracken Hendricks wrote in *The Nation*, "and they respond to a message of hope for good jobs and reinvestment."

Republican leaders have been silent about the plan, but many top Democrats are enthusiastic. The Sierra Club praised it, and it was endorsed by Greenpeace and by the Republicans for Environmental Protection.

When I talked with Hendricks, he told me it was no accident that Pennsylvania was chosen for the poll, "because that region will decide the future of the country." He recognizes that it's the Rust Belt where there is the most anger—and potential for hope.

The plan harkens to the 1930s, when progressives focused on issues affecting a broad range of Americans, and on jobs in particular. The plan is an answer for a lot of the frustration I felt not only during those early New York City protests, but for what I'd been seeing in America the past three decades.

Hendricks, who worked on issues of sustainable development for Al Gore during Bill Clinton's presidency, said the Apollo Alliance connected issues of jobs and the environment in a positive way. Speaking of blue collar workers, he said, "Casting them as reactionaries is a dangerous thing for the progressive movement. Figuring out a way they can be at the table for issues concerning social justice—we need to make that happen."

LETTER FROM THE WOODS

SOMETHING CHANGED in me that New York morning. It's only now, a continent and more than two years away, that I can even admit to and comprehend that change as I write this at the edge of the Pacific Ocean in the night woods of northern California, where the black-shrouded image of Manhattan seems like a bad dream.

By that evening in 2001, I had fallen ill from a dreadful flu, developing a cough that grew progressively worse. In the coming months, like all New Yorkers, I breathed sub-microscopic death from the smoldering ruins—the toxic mix of exotic metals, dioxin, plastic, computer parts, bodies. By December, when the smoke stopped rising, I was coughing blood. I didn't associate this with the World Trade Center, as I lived one hundred blocks distant. Weakened by flu and stress, I assumed it was tuberculosis from years spent living amid the homeless. After a battery of tests, a doctor told me otherwise.

At the start, I was bedridden. One day, I hobbled weakly to the park and the statue of Carl Schurz, where I was surrounded by pigeons. As I watched smoke rising in the downtown sky, inhaled its putridity, the birds rushed around my feet. I realized I was shuffling like one of the old men I'd seen feeding them. I suddenly knew the meaning of being eighty. I had no food for the birds.

As I wrote it, this book became personal to me like no other. For nearly a year, my World Trade cough continued. There was a forest fire that first summer that brought smoke to my valley here in California, and again the hacking returned with a vengeance.

At the beginning, I worked in the same way I had when covering civil war and revolution in Central America and Asia—by denying the emotional. It's

217

the only way you can work sometimes. This creates a different kind of stress, like having a mouse constantly chewing on a corner of one's soul, all the while pretending the mouse does not exist. When I'd been reporting outside the country, I could escape the mouse by coming home, getting back to "normal." Now there was mayhem in my own country, and for two years, I was immersed in the lives of those most caught up in the fallout. There was no other home to come home to.

After 9/11, a long love relationship dissolved, and it was entirely my fault. I've since found it impossible even to contemplate another serious one. I also quit a longtime teaching job. It's as if I were shorn of present and future that morning I stared at the columns of smoke rising in lower Manhattan. Nothing quite matters any longer, other than this book.[1]

And then it became personal in a way I never could have predicted. This book was nearing completion and I was again living in New York City in 2003, when my friend going back to the first grade telephoned from the southern state where he lives.

"I know where you stand," he snapped. We hadn't talked in months, but he knew of this book. He proceeded to disparage liberals and Democrats for wanting to do nothing to protect the country. "Cowardly," he said. He was for war, against Iraq, then other countries to follow.

I shot back that I didn't want anyone questioning my patriotism. I was unprepared for this assault—I went on about all the reasons why going it alone like cowboys in a cheap Western was a recipe for self-destruction.

"They hate us anyway. Why not go at them?"

"We've whacked the beehive."

"There's spray. When the bees come back, spray 'em, exterminate 'em. That's what Arabs understand, power. You show them. And if that doesn't work, kill 'em. Kill 'em all. They're gonna hate us, no matter what we do."

My friend of forty years was a rabid nationalist, talking as crazily as that man on Manhattan's Upper West Side, stamping his feet on the sidewalk as if crushing Syria, Iran, and so on, like ants. My head reeled.

Before I relate where I took that conversation, let me explain a bit of the history of our friendship.

ℒ

WE MET IN 1962. It was in first grade at a Catholic elementary school in Ohio, south of Cleveland. In our First Communion photo, we are smiling, standing side by side, hair buzz-cut, ears sticking out.

We were bound by a love of the woods. By fourth grade, we talked about becoming mountain men. We'd read Jack London's "To Build a Fire," about a Klondike miner who dies after falling through river ice. We each had blocks of woods behind our houses, where we spent increasing amounts of time in our own personal Klondikes.

I began writing stories for my friend, about woodland adventures. He'd request additional stories, thus encouraging my interest in writing. He was my first audience.

By sixth grade, we were visiting each other's woods. His woods were larger and much cooler than mine, a forest that had healed from past abuse, thick with second-growth beech, hickory, and maple. There were raccoons and fox to track, tiny frogs called spring peepers to catch, and fossil bra-chiopods and extinct sea worms to be found in the outcroppings of Devonian epoch shales.

We trained in mountain-man skills, such as building fires with just one match in sleeting weather, and "silent walking." We'd stalk through the forest and the first to break a twig was the loser. We became so adept that we were once able to sneak unseen upon a den of red fox pups. As we grew older, fishing captured our interest. We rode bikes to ponds, not all of which were legal to go to—the best involved trespassing on land owned by a Girl Scout camp. We learned which days the camp was unused and to check the house of the caretaker, who also acted as private security guard. If his patrol car was in the drive and his personal car gone, we'd head over the fence, fishing and swimming, spitting water at the sun.

In the early grades, our town was in its last days as a dairy farm center, a twenty-one-square-mile village of 5,600 residents. There was one traffic light, one barber, a Western Auto store. Our parents, suburban pioneers, had come the year we were born, 1956. By the time we graduated from high school, the town had become a full-blown suburb of over 25,000 all-white people. It was later found that realtors had conspired to never show homes to non-whites, which meant blacks. If there had been Muslims, Asians, or Latinos around, they certainly would have been kept out, but they existed somewhere over a distant horizon. It was a community created by angry white flight.

When Richard Nixon used the race wedge issue in that code-language manner Republicans were then beginning to grasp, he was speaking the language understood in our town. I remember Nixon, '68. I stood on Route 82 when he swung south out of Parma, driving past without stopping, to cheering crowds. He was our man, right there, waving from the top of the sunroof in the presidential limousine. That was the year a development was going up next to our Catholic school. The sign out front said it was "exclusive." This distressed our nun.

"Do you know what that means?" she asked in class.

It meant no blacks. She was emotional. My friend and I were most concerned about the loss of woods. But after class, we talked about her foolishness. Disliking blacks was imprinted as part of our culture. At that point in life, we'd neither met nor talked with a black person.

My friend went off to college. I began working as a journalist; each of our racial outlooks rapidly evolved into ones of deeper understanding. I don't know exactly when my friend became a Republican, but he was never the race-baiting kind—in fact, I'd witness him argue with people who said racist things, putting them in their place.

We continued hiking and fishing. He moved to the South, I to the West. We each had a certain kind of volatility and drive. I put mine into writing. My friend put his into business and became quite successful, essentially retiring in his early forties. It was our energy as well as our continued love of nature that connected us. We often went backpacking in Utah. It was a friendship that transcended time and place, of such depth that when he got married the first time back in the early 1980s and took his wife on a honeymoon pack trip in the desert canyons, I went along.

There was one significant change: we'd each drifted away from our childhood Catholicism. I became something of an agnostic. My friend turned to Bible study, eschewing Catholicism for Bible-based fundamentalism. He'd purchased a second home in Montana, and when I visited in the late 1990s, he insisted I come with him to a Bible study session. No way. He was pushing me somewhere I didn't want to go, somewhere his living in the South had taken him. He talked about The Word, about how once someone has been exposed to the Holy Bible, they were bound to live by it, and he fervently rambled on with conservative interpretations. I blew it off as we went to day-hike in the Swan Range, south of Glacier National Park.

≈

AND SO NOW we were on the phone. It had been over forty years since we'd sat near each other in first grade. I was in New York, he in his house on the grounds of an antebellum plantation that had a slave cemetery. My friend invoked an incident from our past to explain his stand on Arabs.

It was eighth grade. We'd gone on our bikes to fish in a local lake. I was wearing new boots. I stood on a board nailed to pilings out over the water, casting. My friend, goofing around, tapped me in the back with the tip of his pole. I lost my balance and fell in, soaking my new shoes.

"You chased me, threw rocks," he said of my angry outburst. "And I ran like hell. I was wrestling then, was in shape. I could've kicked your ass. But

I ran, scared."

It's the same with the United States and the world, he went on—we have to keep "them" scared. Arabs would run as he did from me, from the crazed superpower, and America would thus be safe.

He thought I'd understand the reminiscence, but I was thinking about his careful telling of it. I realized he'd rehearsed the call. He went on to say that the show of power in Iraq had worked, that the killing of some 7,000 to 8,000 innocent Iraqi civilians in the initial attack, and anywhere from 13,000 to 45,000 Iraqi soldiers, was justified. Triumphantly, he said we have not had another terror attack because of it. My friend repeated what were already then proving to be lies given as the reasons for the Iraq War.

I reminded him that the average time between major Al Qaeda strikes was between two and four years, and that they could rest, because our president was doing everything they wanted—he was their number-one recruitment tool. I was sputtering, went on to say most of the hijackers were from Saudi Arabia, there were no ties to Iraq, and besides, how was attacking a nation going to stop a stateless band of terrorists? I said Japan had used the concept of "preventive war" against us in World War II, and now we were doing the same thing.

"They were a gnat attacking us. Now it's the other way around."

"And this makes it right!?"

"We gotta open a can of whoop-ass. That's what they understand."

This was country-music jingoism. Like dark nationalists all through history, he was blindly following clichés handed to him by the state and now a corporation through a country song. I didn't know where to take the conversation, so I switched to business, something he understood

"Forget all other argument. We're dooming ourselves economically by trying to reach all over the world militarily."

"It's worth it. We've had great depressions before. We'll get through it. It's worth it even if it bankrupts us."

He talked of *The Waltons*, a sentimental television show about a Depression-era family that ran from 1972 till 1981. His rural land in the southern state would be a Walton-like refuge, where he'd survive the ruin.

"It's all in the Bible . . ."

I was no longer hearing. He was as fundamentalist as the people he hated. He seemed excited about economic Armageddon. Maybe it was no accident that George Bush Jr. had said several times in the 2000 campaign, "America needs more families like the Waltons." Bush and my friend didn't see it as did comedian Jay Leno, who noted, "The trouble with America is we have too many families like the Waltons. They've got no jobs . . .

no health care." I'd like my friend to meet Elizabeth Boles and her son in Celina, Tennessee, who are living a Waltonesque existence. I detected that she found no romance in it. My friend has money to survive a depression. He can afford his Waltons fantasy.

I thought of the kid with whom I'd cast lures in stillwater ponds and found ancient Indian arrowheads. I thought of the entire course of four decades of friendship. How had he arrived at this point? He was now a stranger.

"We're going to pay for your attitude and those who share it with you for a hundred years," I said simply to this sudden stranger, wanting to end the call. "This is the real deal. You and I are on opposing sides and I really hope you don't win."

My somberness threw him. This was not like other lesser debates we'd had over the years. I could handle his being Republican, as I have other friends who fall that way, and I can live with political differences. That is the power and beauty of our system. But this was different—a line had been crossed.

"Left, right, the pendulum swings back and forth," he said.

He told me he liked this debate.

It's more than a debate, I responded. I refused to talk any further about Arabs. We made some mindless small talk, then ended the call.

For months, the conversation tore at me. The divide between me and my old friend brought home everything that I'd witnessed in Homeland America, and though he was a stark nationalist, I also knew liberals who had ended friendships with other liberals who had turned into hawks. I sunk into a depression. I hadn't said all that I had wanted to say. I decided to put my thoughts into a letter.

> Dear Old Friend:
>
> I write this with a heavy heart, with fondness for all that once was, and in agony. At age ten, I wrote stories for you, and once again the best way to reach you is by writing. Our conversation increased my awareness of how divided our country is, how deep the emotions run, and just how high the stakes are.
>
> Do we want to be the America of vengeance, war, and empire, or the America that embodies the ideals on which we were founded, and all the good of which we are capable?
>
> We must choose who to elect to lead this country next. Herman Goering was correct that "it is always a simple matter to drag the people along." We can continue the current course

as you desire, or we can elect someone on the model of Franklin Roosevelt.

Our generation cannot truly understand the despair of the country in that era. In LeMars, Iowa, farmers took a judge from his bench and tried to lynch him after he wouldn't stop foreclosure hearings, and martial law was declared in some Iowa counties. People were starving. The sense of defeat was such that as Herbert Hoover was leaving office, he uttered, "We are at the end of our rope. There is nothing more we can do." Walter Lippman wrote that the nation would have "followed almost any leader anywhere he chose to go."

Roosevelt could have stoked nationalism, a course taken by so many other inferior leaders in times of chaos. He could have leveraged the rage to pull the country away from its post-World War I isolationism, making Americans forget their misery by launching additional empire-building.

But FDR didn't take the easy path. He made us look inward. There was no jingoism in his 1933 inaugural address. He gave his famous line that "the only thing we have to fear is fear itself." He didn't speak ill of other nations or cultures. He'd grown up in a wealthy family, but he didn't coddle the elite. He admonished businessmen for leading the country into economic ruin.

Had Theodore Roosevelt been at the helm in 1933, God knows what would have happened. Consider what Teddy as president once wrote to Senator Henry Cabot Lodge: "If we ever come to nothing as a nation, it will be because of the treachery of Carl Schurz . . . and the futile sentimentalists of the international arbitration type bears its legitimate fruit in producing a flabby, timid type of character, which eats away the great fighting features of our race."[2]

When you, my friend, call people who question "cowards," you are engaging in this kind of talk and what it leads to.

George S. Boutwell, a former U.S. Republican Senator and President of the Anti-Imperialist League of which Schurz and Mark Twain were members during the Spanish-American War, correctly predicted that our actions would lead to a war with Japan. It took forty-three years for Japan to take up its preventive war against our projection into what Japan saw as its backyard. Japan was wrong, for sure, but it was in the grip of its own military nationalists, whose rise to power was fueled by our imperialism, a blowback loop of stunning power. That "gnat" that attacked Pearl Harbor came to cause the death of dozens of thousands of Americans and scarred my father's life, and the lives of hundreds of thousands of other men.

Your father didn't experience combat, didn't have the demons that possessed my father. I, in essence, grew up with a casualty of America's decision in 1898 to become an imperial world power. You did not. Perhaps this is one factor that colors my view differently from yours.

Another is that while I've covered only two wars, I know enough about war to tell you that you have no concept of what is meant by opening a can of "whoop-ass." It's not a football game. Nor is it the sanitized videogame you see on American television. You, my friend, are a chickenhawk, someone who has never seen war but pays kids to fight and die in them for your macho posturing.

As we push further into the terrible void that began on April 21, 1898, our own history confirms a lesson that there will be blowback. We have smart bombs and Tomahawks, and think we are omnipotent, but it's all an illusion.

In 1898, the nationalists were giddy with a victory that netted real estate as distant as the Philippines. They then ignored the bloody three-year guerilla war led by Emilio Aguinaldo in which we turned out to be just as brutal as the Spanish in subjugating our new vassals.

You can justify it because we "won," against Spain, against Japan. By the last century's end, we had either vanquished or worn down all superpowers and regional powers that could challenge us. Until nineteen men, most from Saudi Arabia, armed with five-dollar box cutters, were all that remained to launch a successful attack against us. It was enough to cause us to lash out with bombs and guns, and with snickering insults to nations such as France that dared murmur dissent.

You told me you don't care what the world thinks, that we do not need these other countries. We can go it alone. You should be reminded by history that when one nation has absolute power, the rest of the world gangs up on it. The top is often the worst place to be, especially when you're alone at the top.

When I talk with friends in Europe and read its press, fear is the operative word. Not the kind of fear you desire, but fear that they're witnessing the awakening of a variation of the old German war machine. As William Shirer wrote, "The Third Reich was indeed friendless in a hostile world." The situations are not exactly parallel, but the end result is the same. A BBC poll of eleven thousand people in eleven nations after the recent war in Iraq found a majority of respondents viewed the U.S. as a greater threat to the world than Russia, China, Syria, Iran, or North Korea.

We're vulnerable to this sort of opinion in ways most Americans are unaware. The days have long since passed when we were a creditor nation. Someone wrote that we've become a banana republic with cruise missiles for brains. William Greider notes that as trade deficits continue to balloon, we are very much like the British empire was—a debtor nation. The British empire ended during the Suez crisis of 1956, not in a military defeat, but when the U.S.—the creditor—turned off the money spigot.

"You can't sustain an empire from a debtor's weakening position—sooner or later the creditors pull the plug," Greider wrote in *The Nation* in late 2002. "Bush and team regularly dismiss the worldviews of these creditor nations and lecture them condescendingly on our superior qualities. Any profligate debtor who insults his banker is unwise, to put it mildly."

If the plug is pulled, an economic decline will follow, which would cause us to descend more deeply into our Weimar and the nationalism it spawns. You will get your Walton's wish. I sincerely hope you do not.

It's not too late. We're at the front end of our Weimar. Things don't have to get worse. Our choice is clear: do the right thing, or head toward the end stage of dark nationalism. We've made some serious mistakes at home in shouting down all dissent and taking away constitutional rights; and overseas in waging wars against nations when we should instead be doing police work. Police work is not cowardly. It's smart. I want to stop specific culprits, not occupy foreign lands. The attack on America, and the ones that are to come, are horrible acts by a small band of extremists, whom we must pursue and stop, but not through even more horrible acts by another band of extremists operating in the name of God, the Bible, or my government.

There will certainly be another terror attack. Let's keep focused on going after the few hundreds of people responsible. If we lash out with more nationalistic warmaking, expanding our empire, the fabric of our society will disintegrate. Imagine trying to occupy three Iraqs at once. We will lose, not only militarily abroad, but at home. We can end the lying and the blitzkrieg foreign policy before we do additional damage.

Many Americans aren't as divided as we are. Many are unaware. They are in the middle. Unlike Kafka's Gregor Samsa, who wakes up in the morning to discover he has turned into an insect, most Americans have not even yet come close to awakening, much less looking in the mirror.

What occurred in Iraq is but one tiny chapter in what American nationalism has meant and will come to mean, the driving force that is allowing us to be transformed into this century's Nazi beasts.

I have images in my head, from print stories and television footage:

A story by the *Washington Post*'s Anthony Shadid, about a U.S. raid on a Sunni town, where there was a boy who was shy and troubled, who was used to spending his days watching four canaries and a nightingale. Edgy U.S. soldiers came. The family found the boy dead the next morning with two bullet holes in his stomach. The invading U.S. troops then threw tins of food from trucks to townspeople as if they were "monkeys," as one man described. There was a *New York Times* interview with a sergeant, who said, "We had a great day. We killed a lot of people." The sergeant told the *Times* reporter of killing a civilian woman. "I'm sorry, but the chick was in the way." There were images of husbands and wives and kids fleeing in old Chevys, who'd been shot, blasted dead.

And so on. This is "muscular foreign policy." This is what it means not to be "cowardly."

You may not care about these "bees." But what about our soldiers? One of the great untold stories of the war was exposed in an essay by Chalmers Johnson, the author of *Blowback*. America, Johnson says, may be killing its own soldiers.

Johnson notes the toll taken by the "Gulf War Syndrome." There were 760 total casualties from all causes during the first Gulf War in 1991. Since then, the Veteran's Administrations lists

8,306 dead and 159,705 injured due to "exposures" sustained in the war. Thus, Johnson says, "the casualty rate for the first Gulf War is actually a staggering 29.3 percent." While blame has been put on chemicals used by Saddam Hussein, evidence points to "depleted uranium" (DU) weapons used by the United States. The Pentagon likes DU, because it has 1.7 times the density of lead. DU is a waste byproduct from power-plant uranium. It burns as it goes through the air and atomizes upon impact as it blasts with ease through tanks and other armor.

U.S. tank shells each have ten pounds of DU, Johnson says, and each is essentially a radioactive "dirty bomb." In 1991, the Pentagon says at least 320 metric tons of DU ended up on the battlefield. A lot more DU was used in the 2003 Iraq War. DU is believed responsible for birth defects in Iraq and Kosovo where it was previously used. In 1996, the United Nations outlawed DU, calling it a weapon of mass destruction. The Pentagon refuses to decommission it.

We are the ones using weapons of mass destruction. We are killing the innocent on their side, and the soldiers on our side, men and women who can't get work at home other than $7-per-hour jobs at Wal-Mart. If weeping for victims on all sides makes me a "coward" or a "liberal," I have no problem with these labels.

You and I have picked our sides. You have your Bible, which I read differently than you do. In the terms that you seem to understand, it is you who are on the side of evil. If you come to your senses, great. I won't try to reason with you. As far as I'm concerned, our friendship is a casualty of this war.

I'll close with a proverb, e-mailed to me by the writer and editor Tom Engelhardt not long after 9/11, about a Native-American grandfather and his grandson. The grandfather tells the boy he is troubled.

"I feel as if I have two wolves fighting in my heart," the grandfather says. "One wolf is the vengeful, angry, violent one. The other wolf is the loving, compassionate one."

"Which wolf will win the fight in your heart, Grandpa?"

"The one I feed."

—Dale Maharidge
Humboldt County, January 7, 2004

NOTES

BOOK ONE

1

1   At the request of Amy Sierra, I have changed the name of her husband.

In this section, many quotes and letters by students at Sissonville High School are taken from court documents in Katie Sierra's trial; wherever possible, I relied on two or more depositions or the testimony of multiple witnesses.

2

1   Details about Sean Miller's final moments come from a story by Jacob Messer, in the *Charleston Daily Mail*.

3

1   I was living on both coasts and was in Manhattan on 9/11 and in the months that followed because I'd taken leave from Stanford University for a visiting gig at Columbia University's Graduate School of Journalism.

4

1   There was, of course, much more testimony in the five-day trial than is contained here. I condensed the most important testimony, based on uncorrected court transcripts as well as notes I took on a laptop computer during the trial, mindful of consistency and accuracy as I abridged the events of those five days.

5

1   When I met Lorena in Fayette, Missouri, in 2002, I realized we'd previously met. In 1984, she was monitoring the elections in El Salvador. Michael Williamson and I were

there documenting the interdenominational underground railroad that was smug-
gling political refugees from the country; one night we had dinner with Lorena and
her roommate in San Salvador.

2   Bush and INTERNATIONAL TERRORIST were the exact image and slogan on a shirt
    that would later lead high school junior Bretton Barber to be suspended on Febru-
    ary 17, 2003, by school officials in Dearborn Heights, Michigan. Bretton, a budding
    civil liberties expert who knew every detail of the Tinker case, was called in by Prin-
    cipal Judith Coebly, who herself brought up Tinker, erroneously telling Bretton the
    Supreme Court decided the school had a right to limit speech. He didn't educate
    her—rather, he went to the ACLU and the papers. Unlike Katie's situation, by then,
    Bretton's story made the national print press, which now was occasionally report-
    ing on neo-McCarthyism.

News Diary I

1   The material in this section was reported or witnessed mostly during our travels in
    2000. A winter cross-country drive took me through Lusk, Wyoming, which Michael
    and I have repeatedly visited and documented since our first trip there in 1984. As for
    the descriptions of steelworkers and farmers and textile workers, these come from
    my reporting over the past three decades in the Steel Belt, the deep South, and
    Midwest.

2   In late 2003, the Newell Co., which bought Rubbermaid, announced it was closing
    the plant. This meant a loss of 850 manufacturing and warehouse jobs; at the time
    of purchase, the plant had employed 1,400 workers.

3   The white-collar elite are next to experience what has already happened to steel and
    textile workers. By 2015, 3.3 million of their jobs, worth $136 billion in wages, will go
    overseas, according to a 2002 study by Forrester Research. The tech industry will con-
    tinue to be the first hit, but others such as architecture and radiology will follow.

4   We met Kenneth when he was sweeping the sidewalk in front of Gentle Touch Min-
    istries in Newport, Tennessee, in the summer of 2000. Through interviews with Ken-
    neth, I have recreated the conversation with his wife in Cleveland, and their travels
    which led them to living on the bank of the river.

BOOK TWO

1

1   I've relied on Anna Mustafa's recollection of her day at the Chicago Airport, both
    because she was later found not guilty of any wrongdoing by Judge Mary Ellen Cogh-
    lan, and because so many others in positions of authority in the community who
    know Anna told me she is extremely reliable. There are countless numbers of Arab-
    Americans who had similar experiences or worse. Anna's was representative of
    those I discovered.

②

1   For obvious reasons due to their thuggery, I've changed the names of the Sullivan
    brothers and others of the young whites in their group whom I interviewed on Sep-
    tember 11, 2002.

2   The Farm Security Administration, as part of Franklin Roosevelt's New Deal, pro-
    vided health care to rural farmers and migrants in a popular program. Amid a
    growing call for national health care, the American Medical Association lobbied
    fiercely to stop it. In 1938, the AMA compromised by endorsing private third party
    health insurance—and guaranteed that health care never became part of an enti-
    tlement, as it is in Canada. And of course, Bill Clinton tried again in his first admin-
    istration, and failed.

③

1   But one of the signature salutations of the group is RAHOWA!, short for "racial holy
    war." In the summer of 2003, the leader of the World Church of the Creator,
    Matthew Hale, was being held in custody under security described in one story as
    "most often reserved for al-Qaeda terrorists." Hale was charged with seeking the
    murder of U.S. District Judge Joan Humphrey Lefkow after she ruled against him in
    a lawsuit over the name of his church. An Oregon religious organization had sued,
    saying it had the rights to the term "church of the creator." Hale's attorney said a
    mole, who was paid $50,000 by the FBI, had set Hale up on the charge after infil-
    trating the group for two years. Hale pled innocent. Meanwhile, the church changed
    its name to the Creativity Movement.

News Diary II

1   Bush became the first president in modern history to call for a tax cut in time of war.
    Under Bush's 2003 plan, which passed into law, a millionaire received $93,500 on aver-
    age. In contrast, a couple making $41,000 with two children received $323; if they
    earned $63,000, they received an additional $77 in relief. Some 74 million people, over
    half of all households, got less than $100; of this group, 50 million got nothing,
    according to the Urban Institute-Brookings Institution Tax Policy Center.

    Amid the tax-cutting fever, a moment of honesty came after an outcry was
    raised over the cost of "homeland security" to the states. Instead of the federal gov-
    ernment helping out, Republican Senator Ted Stevens offered a solution: police and
    firemen should work overtime without pay. It was the least they could do to help out.
    Stevens said outright what the ruling class had been telling middle class Americans
    for three decades: work for free.

    This ethos inspired George Bush to change labor rules in 2003, mandating that
    workers in "positions of responsibility" wouldn't get overtime pay. Democrats tried
    to stop the change in the House, where it was called the friendly-sounding "Family
    Time Flexibility Act." But Republicans carried the day for the wealthy in a 213-210 vote
    favoring Bush's plan.

    Corporations would now have the "flexibility" to stiff as many as eight million
    workers who would lose time-and-a-half for overtime work after forty hours,
    according to the Economic Policy Institute. These could include firemen and police,

dental hygienists, chefs, and paralegals. Overtime pay is what was keeping many families afloat. Writer Molly Ivins pointed out that the guy flipping hamburgers on the McDonald's night shift could suddenly be named an assistant manager, with no change in his job or pay, and fall under the new rules.

As if that weren't enough, when the Iraq War began, House Republicans gave repeated speeches praising the soldiers, passed a resolution supporting the troops— and then minutes later voted to cut benefits to veterans.

BOOK THREE

1

1   In 2003, Oshkosh eliminated all manufacturing at its plant in Celina, Tennessee, closing the washing operations. The plant was converted to a research and development facility with just a handful of jobs.

2   I have grossly condensed the argument of Chalmers Johnson here, and I highly recommend his book *Blowback: The Costs and Consequences of American Empire* (Metropolitan Books, 2000) for additional reading.

3   The Campbell Works are recognizable to moviegoers from Michael Cimino's film *The Deer Hunter*. The blast furnace scene at the start of the film was shot here.

2

1   I rely on a large number of books for the history of Weimar, but the most important is William L. Shirer's *The Rise and Fall of the Third Reich*. I recommend it highly. It's a book that holds up a half century later.

2   One wonders whether, after the next terror attack, DARPA will meet as much opposition. It's the same with Operation TIPS (Terrorism Information and Prevention System), proposed and later shot down. TIPS would have been a national spy network, recruiting millions of informers—meter readers, UPS drivers, mail carriers, and so on—to be the "extra eyes and ears for law enforcement." It, too, is there waiting to be resurrected.

3   Writing a book critical of the government could be included, it seems from Ashcroft's testimony to Congress, when he said, "To those who scare peace-loving people with phantoms of lost liberty, my message is this: Your tactics only aid terrorists, for they erode our national unity and diminish our resolve. They give ammunition to America's enemies, and pause to America's friends."

4   Another provision would make secret from citizens the harmful chemicals used by industry, overturning now-public information that helps communities monitor dangerous conditions at companies.

5   I wonder if contemporary tax policy is a form of postmodern reparations. During Vietnam, Lyndon B. Johnson faced a choice of how to pay for the war: raise taxes, or deficit spend. The former was political suicide, the latter would be foisted on some future president. If a nation wants to play global Cold War cop, someone has to pay for the police force, and the bill did not come due till long after the war. Like Lyndon Johnson, George W. Bush faced a choice in 2002—but instead of it being between deficit spending or a tax increase, Bush chose to deficit-spend and give a tax

cut to the rich, which parallels what occurred early in the Weimar Republic, when the wealthy were taken care of at the expense of the larger society.

1 Strong wrote this fourteen years before Rudyard Kipling penned "the white man's burden" in 1899.

2 George Tindall and David E. Shi, *America: A Narrative History*, fifth ed. (New York: W.W. Norton & Co., 1999), 1141.

News Diary III

1 The names of these officers were changed as a condition of the interview by Madeleine.

2 The Dallas-based Halliburton Company, an oil equipment firm, was awarded $1.7 billion in no-bid contracts in the Iraq War, and stood to make hundreds of millions more with other no-bid contracts to rebuild oilfields.

When Vice President Dick Cheney left the first Bush administration, he became chairman and CEO of Halliburton. For years, he maintained his company was not dealing with Iraq, but in the early summer of 2001, the *Washington Post* reported that while Cheney was in charge, Halliburton's subsidiaries signed over $73 million in contracts with Iraq for equipment to produce oil. Halliburton was among the companies that helped Iraq expand its oil exports from $4 billion in 1997, to almost $18 billion in 2000. When Cheney resigned to become George W. Bush's running mate, he received $8 million in stock options, and continued to be paid by the company while vice president. He was opposed to sanctions for selling oil supplies to countries such as Iraq. In early 2001, the Bush administration began campaigning to relax a United Nations embargo on selling Iraq civilian goods, including oil equipment.

BOOK FOUR

1

1 In the Great Depression, the reason Franklin Roosevelt enacted changes such as time-and-a-half for over forty hours was to push employers to hire more workers, rather than working fewer harder. It was a tool to spread the wealth. Taxes were made progressive not simply to fund bureaucracy, as some on the right saw, but to correct the 1920s concentration of wealth. Roosevelt knew he had to share the wealth to end the Depression.

Letter from the Woods

1 As I write these final words, I slip into a funk unlike when I finished my other books. There's always a period of depression that comes after you type "The End," but this is far different. This book became my means of either coping or hiding in the face of so much depressing news and societal tension. A Spanish friend visited recently—Luisa had lived in the United States for many years before leaving to go

back to Madrid a few years ago—and she was shocked by the weird anxiety she found upon her return as she traveled around, as if Americans were all on various doses of crack. It was interesting to get such confirmation of what I strongly sensed about the country. I had been hiding from the mouse by the continuation of this work, which, as one photographer noted long ago, is all one is left with in such situations. The work is survival. But now the work is gone and I must deal with the mouse.

2   One finds it heartening that in one of his first speeches after announcing his presidential candidacy in 2003, General Wesley Clark said, "We've got to have a new kind of patriotism that recognizes that in times of war or peace democracy requires dialogue, disagreement, and the courage to speak out. And those who do it should not be condemned, but be praised. . . . Patriotism doesn't consist of following the orders."

INDEX OF PERSONAL NAMES

ACKNOWLEDGMENTS

MANY THANKS to Dan Simon, for his passion and vision and faith, as well as his outstanding editing and guidance. Also thanks to Tom McCarthy and all the other Seven Storians at the smallest big publishing house in America.

I cannot extend enough appreciation for the steady stream of Homeland America-related articles e-mailed by writer and editor Tom Engelhardt. His was not a blog—I often felt that he was my own personal wire-service editor as I read disparate newspapers and other sources from around the world, beginning right after 9/11. It was a period of blackout in the American media, and these were perspectives I would never otherwise have seen. And thanks to Frank Lalli, the editor of the now-defunct *George* magazine, who had the vision to send me and Michael out to look at the other America during the 2000 presidential election, a research trip that proved vital to this book.

Numerous friends stood by through the difficult reporting and writing days, a dark time for so many of us, and their support was immeasurable. I mention only some of them: Annie Cusack, I-chun Che, Elizabeth Kadetsky, Julian Rubinstein, Blair Tindall, John Trotter. Also thanks to Vanessa Mobely for the support and enthusiasm and ideas.

Much gratitude goes out to former Dean Tom Goldstein and to Academic Dean David Klatell at Columbia University's Graduate School of Journalism for providing a wonderful working environment, and for being so flexible and understanding with regard to my teaching schedule as this book unfolded. Also, a debt is owed to both my 2001–2002 and 2002–2003

Columbia students, whose reportorial scouring of New York City's streets added in both oblique and direct ways to this book—in particular James Brown, Jessica Bruder, Ellen Fullerton, Charles Harris, Leela Landress, Madeleine Perez, Oliver Ryan, Rinku Sen, and Matthew Van Dusen. Also thanks to two students of mine at Stanford: Mike Nalepa and Valarie Brar.

But most of all, words cannot express the debt I owe to Michael Williamson, by my side in the trenches of Homeland America for the past few decades on this strange journey to somewhere. It's been a long road, bro', and it would have been a desolate one had you not been there to share the passage.

ABOUT THE AUTHORS

HOMELAND is the fourth book from writer/photographer team Dale Maharidge and Michael Williamson. For *Journey to Nowhere: The Saga of the New Underclass* (1985), the pair traveled the nation by freight train and in an old car, living with and documenting Rust Bowl refugees in search of work. Bruce Springsteen's album *The Ghost of Tom Joad* features two songs inspired by the book, "Youngstown" and "New Timer."

Maharidge and Williamson's second book, *And Their Children After Them*, won the 1990 Pulitzer Prize for nonfiction. The team returned to the land and families captured in James Agee and Walker Evans's inimitable masterwork *Let Us Now Praise Famous Men*, extending the project of conscience and chronicling the traumatic decline of King Cotton. The two also coauthored *The Last Great American Hobo* (1993), a biographical snapshot of the last Depression-era hobo in the final years of his life and times.

Williamson, a staff photographer at the *Washington Post*, won a second Pulitzer Prize in 2000 for his work in Kosovo. His numerous honors include the 1994 Kodak Crystal Eagle Award for Impact in Photojournalism, a lifetime achievement award for documenting homelessness, poverty, and hunger in America, given by the National Press Photographers Association (NPPA). In 1995, the NPPA chose Williamson as newspaper photographer of the year. He is now finishing a book on the Lincoln Highway.

Maharidge is currently at work on a book about a small Iowa town. He has taught at the Graduate School of Journalism at Columbia University and at Stanford University, and he was a 1988 Nieman Fellow at Harvard University. His other books include *The Coming White Minority: California, Multiculturalism, and America's Future* (1996).